Resurrecting Allegheny City

Resurrecting Allegheny City:

THE LAND, STRUCTURES & PEOPLE OF PITTSBURGH'S NORTH SIDE

By Lisa A. Miles

For information, contact:
lisamilesviolin@comcast.net
www.lisamilesviolin.com

ISBN 978-0-9798236-0-2
Library of Congress Catalog Number 2007932820

Printed in the United States of America

*This book is supported by a grant from the Pennsylvania
Historical and Museum Commission and the Buhl Foundation*

Cover Illustration: *"Fountain in Front of Carnegie Free Library"*
    Pittsburgh City Photographer Collection, Archives Service Center,
    University of Pittsburgh

Book Design: Pytlik Design Associates Inc., Pittsburgh, PA

Artist Photo: Michael Mangiafico

for Jan

FOREWORD

Having had a grandmother who saved virtually nothing, I have often read with envy of those people cleaning out attics and discovering the letters, diaries, receipts, and jottings of their ancestors. The stories always describe the person's dream-like trip to another time and place as they delve into their findings. However briefly, they are transported to another world with comforts, cares, and a culture that seem both strange and familiar. What is true of personal papers is equally true of those of a community, particularly one that grew from a settlement to a village to a borough to a city. The records of Allegheny can take us to that other time.

When the question of the disposition of the Allegheny City records arose, the quantity and type of the material posed both a problem and an opportunity for the State Archives. The problem was that this was a very large number of deteriorating records from a level of government we had not heretofore processed. As the repository for the state's historical records, we had occasionally found it necessary to house some county records, but we are most concerned with records of state-wide interest. The condition of the collection also meant a lengthy processing time to clean the records. The opportunity was that we could now hold a sizeable, if incomplete, collection of 19th century records that outlined the growth of a major city. This would provide material for serious research in a field almost devoid of records outside of Philadelphia.

While the memory of old Allegheny still lingers, sometimes quite vividly, along the banks of the river of that name, it has largely dimmed elsewhere. Yet, as the existence of these records became known, we began to receive many calls and emails from people wanting to know what was here and when it could be seen. The nature of the requests changed our processing plan as we became aware of what information was most in demand. Also, it gave us an incentive to learn more about this partly forgotten city, progressive in its era and the third largest city in Pennsylvania at the time of its demise. There are many famous names that have an Allegheny connection—Carnegie, Heinz, Foster, Rinehart. There are many points of civic pride as well—the observatory, the university, the commons. But, the records capture everyone who helped to build the city, from the dwellers in the shanty on Warren Street to the next listed in the tax book, the inhabitants of a two story house and shop on East Street.

Cleaning the records meant a slower than normal turning of pages and this inevitably led to more time to read what was there. Buried among the normal, dry business of government are stories and names that take one back to the past. The employees, job titles, and pay of the park employees are there. The market stall rental books list the vendors and their professions. The quantity and type of goods hauled through the weigh stations are recorded. The beginnings of gas lighting, railroads, and the telephone system are described. Popular entertainments of the time, such as elocution demonstrations, are recorded in the Carnegie Hall rentals. Even the police dockets bring to life the disputes and mutual support found in the neighborhoods. Visually interesting are the many letterheads of correspondence from companies seeking city business and showing machinery types few have ever seen. Particularly poignant is the resolution of the McClure Township supervisors eulogizing President Lincoln at the time of his assassination. Within two years this community would vote to join the growing city.

Like the papers in the attic, the records of Allegheny City are incomplete. But what is there will resurrect the images of a city that deserves to be remembered. With this book, Lisa Miles has opened the trunk and begun that trip to the past. Using these records and other available resources, she has shown why the children of Allegheny have kept the flame alive. This was brought home to me most firmly when a long time resident wrote to describe her joy at seeing the records saved and concluded, "When we secede I'll carry the flag across the bridge."

Jerry Ellis, Associate Archivist
PA State Archives, Pennsylvania Historical & Museum Commission

Resurrecting Allegheny City
CONTENTS

LIST OF ILLUSTRATIONS

ACKNOWLEDGMENTS

My thanks go first to George Ellis at the Pennsylvania Historical and Museum Commission. From when we first talked in August of 2004, he was supportive of my plans to consider a book based on the Allegheny City archives, housed at the Commission. A *Pittsburgh Post-Gazette* article brought to my attention his involvement in rescuing the records, and giving them a home at the state capitol in Harrisburg.

George encouraged me in my desire to apply for a Local History Grant through the Commission, and once awarded (but long before formalized), he helped me stay patient while I had to wait to begin my research. Throughout my visits to study there, he was always a calm, steady presence. Despite being interrupted, by page calls, from his normal duties, he came down to the reviewing area to talk over any questions I had or to guide me as needed. His devotion to the cause of attending to those old, decaying papers was inspiration for my writing about what *might* have been found within them. He should be declared honorary Alleghenian, for in tidying up the papers, he learned so much about the lost city.

To the grant administrators at the Pennsylvania Historical and Museum Commission, who liked my Proposal and credentials, I am grateful. This includes Kenneth Wolensky, Gregory Moski and also Stephanie Byrd, who fielded my questions.

Back here in Pittsburgh, John Canning of the Allegheny City Society (dedicated to educating the public about Allegheny City) deserves next mention. He was the second person that I went to for counsel on pursuing this subject matter, as he had authored five small publications on particular facets of Allegheny City. John mentored my work and offered, from early on, the Society's support of it and the grant process to obtain it. Along with John, thanks go to the Society's David Grinnell, who is also archivist at the Historical Society of Western Pennsylvania. David guided me through some of the major Pittsburgh archival holdings related to Allegheny City, housed at the Senator John Heinz Pittsburgh Regional History Center.

Thanks to Louise Sturgess and the Pittsburgh History & Landmarks Foundation, who adopted the project as a sponsoring organization. It was their organization back in the 1960s, under James D. Van Trump and Arthur P. Ziegler, Jr., that spearheaded the Pittsburgh preservation movement by advocating for preservation on the North Side.

A tremendous debt of gratitude is certainly owed Dr. Doreen E. Boyce, President of the Buhl Foundation, here in Pittsburgh. Under her recommendation, the Buhl Foundation provided needed matching funds early on for the project. The Foundation has always been a major supporter of efforts to bring proper attention to the North Side. Dr. Boyce readily believed in and supported my work without my having to divert extraneous time and attention away from the content matter at hand—so rare for a foundation to do, yet so necessary, in order for scholars and artists seeking funding not to feel discouraged by the time-consuming process of proving oneself again and again.

To everyone at the Archives in Harrisburg who helped me negotiate my way through the catalogs, including Jonathan Stayer, who especially helped with land records, thank you. The same goes for all those in Pittsburgh who provided information to help my research along and those in the community who encouraged me, including but not limited to the input of Lois Winslow of the Children's Museum of Pittsburgh.

Seeing the dedication and work, a few years ago, of Christina Schmidlapp of the Allegheny Commons Steering Committee also excited and inspired me to pursue this project. I do hope the book similarly inspires many, and especially forwards the progress of the numerous smaller North Side neighborhood advocacy organizations.

Special thanks go to new colleague and friend Doug Suisman of Suisman Urban Design. Doug and I helped each other—he with providing some image models for the book, and I with textual information to him— as we both have a passion to have our work do good in the North Side community. His is especially admirable, as he is based in Los Angeles but doing consulting with the Children's Museum of Pittsburgh.

Acknowledgements

Love and thanks to my partner Jan, who along with our many creatures, shares this Northside perch with me, and is actually my biggest promoter. He also likes to joke that I am always pointing out, as we make our way around the North Side, every locale where somebody's outhouse once stood, and where 'so-and-so' did 'such-and-such.'

I tip my hat to my brothers as well, who have always been a source of strength for me, especially in these difficult past two years when my father took seriously ill. Before then, my Dad would visit our Perry Hilltop home, stand on the back deck and stroke his chin, looking out at the city skyline, Ohio river, hills, and the stadium of his beloved Steelers, and down upon neighborhoods that were a part of his Pittsburgh, but that he was less familiar with. His interest in my North Side and old Allegheny, as well as his love for me and support of my work, was with me throughout the writing of this book, and I also dedicate it to his memory.

INTRODUCTION

December 9, 2007 marks one hundred years that the City of Pittsburgh annexed a very large land tract that already had an illustrious history as a city of its own. What became known from that day forward as the North Side of Pittsburgh was originally a place called Allegheny City. This book was written to commemorate that place, a century after a date that would never be forgotten in the history and memory of the land, its people, and their structures.

At the time of the annexation, or what was called formally *Consolidation* with the City of Pittsburgh, Allegheny City was flourishing, in all ways imaginable. In 1907, Philadelphia had the top ranking in the Commonwealth, or state, of Pennsylvania with regard to population, land size and sheer economic power. Number two and three in the state ranking, respectively, were Pittsburgh and Allegheny City.

Two sister cities, both with tremendous success and prosperity that belied their relative youth, sat at the joining of three majestic rivers in southwestern Pennsylvania—the Monongahela, the Allegheny and the Ohio. One city was not content to share top billing, the other had no desires beyond counting the blessings of its land.

Allegheny City went into the annexation unwillingly. Despite eventual acclimation and indeed further prosperity as part of Pittsburgh, not in ten, fifty or even one hundred years would the fact of the very consolidation be *celebrated*, despite a generation of people that had long grown and passed away, people who once lived in Allegheny City. For some reason, its identity, indelible, hangs around as a mist for descendants of original families, for the transplants that have called the North Side their home since that fateful changeover, for historians, for visitors, and for all those still to come to this northern bank of the rivers.

But the Consolidation can and should, certainly and ceremoniously, be marked, as it is actually an emblem representing something else far more significant. The occasion of looking back a century to that date ironically points out not so much the merger, but more distinctly the land's unique origin and pervading identity. The unbelievable reflection also provides an unmistakable opportunity, unforgivable if lost, to resurrect Allegheny City as the North Side is moving towards its future.

Something else makes the centennial noteworthy. Archives of Allegheny

City, covering a time period from as early as the 1820s to the Consolidation, were uncovered and recently cataloged. A fuller picture than before of this area's history now awaits any visitor to the Pennsylvania Historical and Museum Commission in Harrisburg, which houses the vast collection of materials.

The Archives of Allegheny City are essentially municipal records, meticulous detailings of business transactions with the city, housing surveys, social institutions, infrastructure, discourse of the day, cultural developments and graphics detailing a land that was transformed from forest to common pastures to estate holdings to residential developments. They take the form of bound manuscripts, maps, loose letters, and everything in between. So extensive in size is the collection that it had to be relegated to a loading dock area at a University of Pittsburgh library prior to going to Harrisburg.

The records were shuffled about after the Consolidation in 1907. Surely in the very beginning they stayed in what had been Allegheny's City Hall. Perhaps decades later, still north of the rivers, they were housed at Allegheny's Carnegie Library and with others involved in preserving the area's history. At some point later in the century, they were gathered up from these various places and made their way over to the University of Pittsburgh in the city's Oakland neighborhood. They would be overlooked and forgotten about even there, at that library, until recently, when scooped up and cared for by two representatives from the Pennsylvania Historical and Museum Commission.

Archivists Jerry Ellis and David Shoff were called in by an astute university librarian in 2003. Ellis would call the discovery the "largest amount of material in the state on the cultural and social history of a region." He and Shoff had the archival material shipped to the state capital, and they painstakingly worked after-hours, outside their departmental responsibilities, to as quickly as possible organize, catalog, and care for what had become so old and neglected on paper.

Because these archives are now available and readily accessible to the public, perhaps the most proper look can be finally given this lost city, this society that was Allegheny.

The Allegheny City Archives indeed inform and were the basis for this book. It is not that the city had no previous written history, however, that inspired this writing. There are several source books already written on the northside region of Pittsburgh—The *Story of Old Allegheny City*, a W.P.A

Writer's Project publication of 1940, and *Old Allegheny* by Charles Dahlinger in 1918, to name just two of the major works. As well, John Canning of the present-day Allegheny City Society has in recent years prepared historical booklets on a noteworthy architect and particular neighborhoods of Allegheny City/North Side. In between these examples are others, including some modern, listed fully in the book's bibliography.

All are informative works which drew on oral histories, newspaper articles, and archival material found in records from the Historical Society of Western Pennsylvania (now at the Senator John Heinz Pittsburgh Regional History Center) and the Carnegie Library systems, mainly. As far as it can be surmised, however, none were able to draw upon the enormity of the archival material just catalogued.

That which was already written about Allegheny City, both in newspaper articles and publications major and minor, represented a competent foundation upon which to build another book—one that now tells the North Side's story with the illustrious detail provided by the lost archives, and compiles the various other source material in one sourcebook. As the Allegheny City Archives in Harrisburg provide the majority of this book's *new, detailed* information for the years 1840–1895, such sections are simply pre-referenced in the text with an introductory statement about the archives being the source. As noted in this book's Bibliography, the archives contained Public Works and Public Safety records, Housing Surveys, Common and Select Councils notes, and Mayor, Comptroller and Treasurer Office records.

The Bibliography here serves mainly as a Works Cited page to reference the variety of other sourcebooks that informed the rest of this work. However, when a particular bit of information is original to this text or not extensively-documented among the many other sources cited, a parenthetical note appears in the text to direct the reader's attention to that particular source in the Bibliography.

This work is intended to illuminate Pittsburgh's North Side. Because initial readership will likely come from those living in this area, an effort was made to provide more in-depth descriptive material, when possible, directly from the Allegheny City Archives. Surely the broader story of this great city will satisfy the reader less intimate with her, however. The hope is that it inspires residents to appreciate Allegheny's legacy, visitors to see her history, and others to want to better understand the forces behind the shaping of their own neighborhoods.

Before one would dive into the material presented in this book, it should be pointed out that it is not intended to be the exhaustive resource on all that can be discovered and understood about Allegheny City. It has, though, extensive information and detail of each stage of Allegheny's growth, paralleling the vast information greeting any visitor to the archives in Harrisburg. This book should be taken hand-in-hand with others, of course, that tell Allegheny City's story.

In-depth information about particular neighborhoods or significant historical figures, to name two examples, are best obtained from reading the broad spectrum of full works written on Allegheny City and the North Side. There is also a lot of promotional literature out there for individual historical sections of the area, usually found in neighborhood civic group records. Too, nothing beats personal family records or talking to individuals—either heirs or historians or homeowners—that know of a particular aspect, facet, or structure of Allegheny City/North Side.

Indeed this work was written as an adjunct to the oral histories and fine written material that do their best to bring justice to age-old, incomplete material. This book drew on a lot of records that at times were unfortunately incomplete or contradictory in places to other records out there. (This was surely also encountered by others attempting to sift through Allegheny City history.) It is best to consider all of the histories as attempts at a full and accurate picture—at their worst only a bit speculative when necessary and hopefully noted, and at their best unique and accurate sketches of the portrait of a place, to be taken in full.

On a personal note, because this work was written within a tightly-defined schedule and rather short timeframe of the Local History Grant, it does not draw upon *all* of the available sources mentioned that round out the picture of Allegheny City. Though the intent was for a study to more completely flesh out the records in the Allegheny City Archives, the sheer amount of historical material actually available was overwhelming, once the research in Harrisburg was completed.

Because the book's basis was to be the 'new-found' Allegheny City Archives, a cap had to be put on what could be added, for essentially the year-and-a-half's work, from available other source material out there. For that reason, the works cited in bibliography could be extended to include, for those interested, the University of Pittsburgh's Archives of an Industrial

Society, the Carnegie Library of Pittsburgh's Pennsylvania Room collections, and more.

As well, the book does not replicate many facets and geographical areas of Allegheny City/North Side that have been much written about, but rather attempts to highlight some of those that have had little or no attention.

Where the book was also not able to go in-depth was for the time period after the annexation, from 1907 to 2007. A glimpse is given at the time immediately after, at the latter half of the century when renewed preservation efforts were underway, and for the future outlook. A concentrated study, if records were available, would certainly be warranted for looking at that span of time from 1907 to about 1967, to see the social effect on the people, the political effect on government for the area then known as the North Side, and the perception Pittsburgh had of its northern annexation. Justified as well are continued histories into the twentieth century time period for the North Side, including when last remnants, vestiges of Allegheny, were finally lost—old sites, buildings, and people.

A recommendation is in order for those that hopefully become intrigued by a particular land-plot, land-owner, or structure. To further research the history, the place to begin is with the circa-1789 map with original Out Lot numbers and owner names overlaid upon Redick's survey (*Figure 7*). The book uses this as a logical starting point with which to understand the transformation of the land as it became man's 'claim.' Anyone doing independent research using that map as a base starting point, with then others that show up chronologically in this book, should be able to unlock the chronological history of a *particular* site, person, or built structure—through deed records and the like. There are more maps, some quite large, in the archives in Harrisburg than could be easily replicated in this book, though their broad (and at times very specific) information was considered. As well, the Maps section of the Historic Pittsburgh site (www.digital.library.pitt.edu) has Warrantee Atlases and the Hopkins Plat Maps for just about any section of the old city that is desired to be researched.

Certainly, this book only shapes and molds an undoubtedly malleable configuration, scratching the surface as a general history of the land. It nevertheless provides illustrious detail where possible and significant maps, the latter being *necessary accompanying graphic material that should be consulted as one is reading the framework of the text.* With the entirety of the text and these maps, the reader is potentially led to people and structures inhabiting individual places far too numerous to mention, but that had their beginnings in a place called Allegheny.

Because previous histories of Allegheny have not gone in-depth into the full land origin (including that of the geographic region as a whole) and the native people's history, this book begins with these. In particular, it addresses those natives that may have been treading on land north of the rivers, where no other written history of this region has gone, beyond mere storytelling. (Much has been written about the French and Indian War, but the recorded activities—save for Smokey Island—all take place south of the rivers. This book attempts to consolidate what is recorded, in scattered places, of that which happened, and likely happened, on the north bank.) Because these things took place before the white man tagged the land 'Allegheny' makes them no less important or fascinating in understanding as full a history as possible of the area.

For this reason, the reader is lastly encouraged to take pause before jumping into the story. It begins not in Allegheny City, Borough or Town, but long before, of a time and place out of which she was conceived, and it leads to the entrance of this northern bank of land cut by three majestic rivers.

This portrait of a place, in *Resurrecting Allegheny City*, focuses on three players in the North Side's history as Allegheny—the land, its people, and their structures. But none more important than the land, literally stealing the show. From earliest days, to neighbor to Fort Pitt, to a frontier town and far onward, what was set aside for Allegheny to sit upon was land called the *Reserved Tract opposite Pittsburg*. What this land witnessed is remarkable. Though now part of Pittsburgh for one hundred years and counting, its hills and valleys, its woods and runs, its burial ground, its overlooks and sunken islands, all seem to remember the numerous catalysts it encountered, shaping a history and a memory it will not relinquish.

The part played by the people of Allegheny is surprising, as of course no one originally Alleghenian survives to this centennial. And the remaining character, the structures, can claim the most visible stage-time in the city's illustrious and remarkable tale.

Resurrecting Allegheny City speaks from the essence of another time, tracing land-plot histories, showing a forward-moving society still centered around a town square of the 1790s, presenting life within pre-twentieth century homes, and beyond. It explains why, in 2007, many Pittsburgh Northsiders are sacredly tied to their neighborhood, their historic homes, and the very land upon which they are rooted. They are defined, still, by Allegheny City.

Prior Glance: Earliest Time
PROLOGUE

When no longer under water from the earliest epicontinental sea, the land of southwestern Pennsylvania was shaped and molded by the momentum of the glaciers. Whereas early earth-force from continental shifting elevated the land and formed the region's sediment, scythe of ice then carved southward from Canada, stopping just short of the region, but indelibly marking its topographical identity. Remnant rivers have cut hills, and valleys have been created—unique rifts and peaks among trinket springs and runs and streams. Islands, left as larger mementos, lie almost attached to the banks, stretching toward their related land. Huge ridges, table-topped, created through the push inward and upward, are stacked high above the currents below. Further inland, new mounts pile high behind the first, their roll and ripple paralleling the rivers at the base. Water-smoothed rocks, some deposited and left for later find high atop slopes, testify to this earliest transformation.

During the latter Ice Age, Paleo-Indian hunters inhabited southwestern Pennsylvania at a rock shelter later named Meadowcroft. (*Figure 1*) These earliest people of North America would camp every autumn under the impressive southern-facing rock overhang, close to the Ohio border along Cross Creek. Continually breeze-swept, the protective perch overlooked a swampy valley with lush grasses. The surrounding forest of the region would slowly evolve, however, into deciduous, nut-bearing woodlands and this contributed to the Paleo-Indians moving on southward.

Around 1000 B.C., the Adena make the land of the southwestern Pennsylvania region their home. Artifacts attributed to them from this time period have been found in Hampton, just northeast of Pine Creek. (*Figure 2*) Similarly, a large man-made earthwork at the juncture of Chartiers Creek and the Ohio River magnificently once attested to the existence of their civilization and even a later people. The Adena began the burial mound and left behind stone instruments and clay work. Their conquerors, the Hopewell, furthered the craft of using stone, as well as bone and wood implements, to perfect artful objects of necessity. They also continued to build upon the great Indian mound, at this location later known as McKees Rocks. Just across the way, within the Ohio River, would be an island's beginning. Further, with a shoreline running the extent of many miles upstream, would lie a northern bank of land cut by three rivers.

At my feet lie both *Fair Waters and Beautiful River*. The latter laps at my lowest land, the leftover sediment and continually-created silt at my southern and western lines. A few parts of my middle are unattached yet seemingly still tethered to my bank.

Before my eyes, across the way, stands a huge ridge. Not to be missed, woods on massive rock occupy my southern sight. Stacked high like the side of a bowl, beginning only slightly back from the southern bank of the other river, *Monongahe*la, this mount runs very high above and along *Beautiful River*. Its top flank, across from my middle, is nearly flat. Glancing slowly westward, I witness the giant startlingly drop to nothing, with a dramatic hollow made, but then dramatically jump up and start to not-so-much stay flat, but roll and dip in places, sloping off only slightly, with its offspring ridge popping up second-generation to the river's edge. Another hollow happens, this one seemingly cradled with more back-ridge, and land is seen high and far off in the southwest distance. A large isle, aborted, is seen lying almost in limbo between the northern and southern side of *Fair Waters* below, and the remnants of the flat mount occupy my whole western panorama—vast, descendant stretching hills, continuing far down river and inland.

Also in my view, between myself and the *Monongahela*, is land other than my own. This middle ground, between my vantage point and the giant perch across the way, had no choice but to be formed into a beautiful triangle, pierced on two sides by two strong competing river flows. It is flat, prone at its smallest area, but pointing majestically at juncture, down new river created by the approaching two.

It is only a bit eastward that this slate of land, covered in woods and bogs from an old flood plain, humps with grotesque magnitude and unique proportion abruptly skyward—a token of the creative work of ancient ice, north of my land. This whole area across the way, like my own, has also its assemblage of rivulets and ponds long left behind. This middle land that I view ever widens eastward, still between two waters that grow further and further away from each other. My eastern scope takes in sprawling ridge and flatland valley across *Fair Waters*. The sun rises and greets my easternmost vantage point, and now is seen a high eastern ridge of my own land. This ground intensely falls down so steep as to almost plummet atop my largest isle, with only a slim backwater channel between the two. *Fair Waters* is at its lowest here, nearby this isle.

Rays of warmth and light come to my westward area below only after visiting this high ground. From here westward, the view of my territory is lovely woods—forest also broken up by runs and rivulets, springs and streams. Though this first hill is flat and parallel to *Fair Waters*, there are many more, also providing magnificent views, dotted throughout—haphazard, steep and crooked of climb, where sandstone beds terrace the landscape, and limestone outcroppings surprise with their shape.

My bounty includes trees of locust, oak, hickory, walnut and chestnut. There is but one land area that stands out decidedly prone, devoid of hill interruption, up from the gently terraced bank of *Fair Waters*, near my middle. Fox, wolf, deer and beaver inhabit my whole expanse, and hawks fly and catch the gale of the wind off my ridge heights.

My area wends around westward, across from the triangle-land, witnessing the catharsis of one water to the third. Here I have a table-land, very small but with brusque hump-shape, coming between the river bank and the inner woodland. At this bank my small semi-attachments lie, formed by the buildup of silt now deposited over and over by the swift *Fair Waters* colliding into *Beautiful River*. Along with them is sandy shore almost claimed by the rivers as well. Here the southern sun soaks and blesses my vegetation. My lines then follow the *Beautiful River* downstream. And across my pastoral western flats, I absorb the setting sun as it shines rays far deep, square-down all my hilltop ridges.

I am sacred land, and will come to experience and be known for great things.

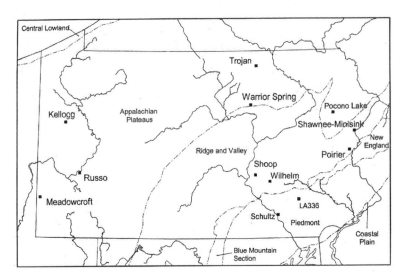

Figure 1. *Paleoindian Sites in Pennsylvania*

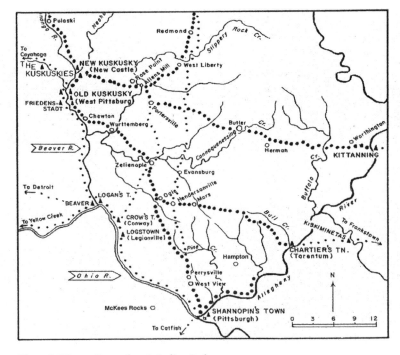

Figure 2. *Western Pennsylvania Indian Paths*

... One Hundred Plus Years Before the Christening of a City

chapter one:

NATIVE AMERICANS & THE FIRST SETTLER

Beyond the existence of Ancient Indian civilizations in the greater southwestern Pennsylvania region, modern Native American presence on the northern banks of the three rivers has been documented from about 1740 on. However, the existence of these various peoples definitely pre-dates this timeframe—to even long before William Penn's 1682 Charter of the Commonwealth of Pennsylvania, whose western boundary included the virtually unexplored land west of the Allegheny Mountains.

There are traces of a post-Hopewell people circa the late 1500s living at the McKees Rocks Mound site, that land merely across the *Beautiful River* from the northwestern bank. They cultivated the land in their village, but the visible wooded island and northern bank just beyond most certainly beckoned as hunting ground. Travel by dugout, or birch bark canoe, just two miles upstream would have them come upon a unique triangular piece of land, a river named for the above *High Banks Breaking Off and Falling Down in Places (Mo-non-ga-hela)*, and sight of a northern bank that makes a large curve around a series of small isles and wends its way far northeastward along *Fair Waters*.

The Upper Ohio territory, early reference to the land area extending from the rivers' confluence to far north and westward, would have people of its own around this time. The Eries were known to inhabit land near the far lake area, but a Minqua tribe was perhaps living much further south, closer to the northern bank of *Fair Waters* and *Beautiful River*, by the year 1662. As well, it has been noted that a Monongahela people inhabited as far north as the Upper Allegheny river valley, which began beyond Pine Creek to far north and eastward. (The Upper Ohio and the Upper Allegheny territories were essentially one connected land, extending northward to Lake Erie.)

Around the same time, the Iroquois Confederation of Six Nations, based in upper New York State, included in their hunting ground the region south of the Pennsylvania lake. Quite possibly, it extended as far south as to the three rivers, and one theory is that the speculated Minqua people were killed or driven out by the Iroquois.

By the 1700s, one of the Six Nations, the Seneca, had established some villages far up *Fair Waters*, but, like all the natives, were still wanderers. They traveled downstream into the confluence formed at the triangle-land, and it is their people who named the third water *Beautiful River*. Their cousins called it *Great River*, spoken in Iroquois tongue as *Ohiio*. It is also believed that the Senecas may have caused the destruction of the Minquas, or that they may have merged into one people.

It would be the Shawnee Indians who were predominant in the entire region in the early 1700s, however. Two Shawnee villages prospered, one far upstream and one equidistant downstream from the cut of the three rivers. A footpath, created by a mixture of the various native peoples, came to be established along the northern bank—from well up *Fair Waters* down to its flow into the *Ohiio*, only cutting inward at the place of the low-lying bank and obstructive humped land.

Indians from the eastern and western territories roamed back and forth across the collectively called *Great Path* that was cut through the woods along the bank. From the west, they stopped their canoes upon the large island in the middle of the *Ohiio*. From the east, they crossed *Fair Waters* at a low place, near the back channel of another island. In crossing the rivers, they could venture over to forest which spread east from the triangle-land.

Long before notations could be recorded about the comings and goings of the Native Americans in this region, they were taking rest from the swift water upon the north bank's small island attachments, and even venturing inland from the *Great Path*, through the woodland and marsh. Apparently even Delaware and Cayuga were visitors to the land just north of the rivers.

The other significant footpath, beyond the *Great Path* outlining the north bank, would follow northward from that very path, at a place just east of the rivers' confluence. It cut straight through flat woodland, until obstructed by one of two central hills, forcing a curve leftward to get around this sandstone abutment. From there it went through the beginning of the cleave of this hill and another even larger abutting from the left side. As the way straight forward would have been too steep an ascent, and as the second hill was tiered, the Indian path here made a sharp westerly turn, slightly back on itself, then gradually went up and around the great tiered ridge that the ancient waters had long before cut from the rock. This trail, unlike the *Great Path* on flat bank, followed circuitously along the high top of long ridges that hovered above valleys to the east and west below, and as it cut an even path to avoid the downward-sloping hillsides.

Upon this and other ridge tops of the beautiful wilderness, these Native Americans rested, and saw the great juncture of the waters from above, the magnificent views across the way of the rolling hills above the *Ohiio*. They were indeed more than visitors to this northern area of land cut by three rivers. It was their wilderness. They would continue along, making a path that would continue to curve to and fro along the highest points, and then later take a more direct northerly direction. This Indian trail, called the Venango Path, would cross with many others much further north from the river, as it cut through the land always at the most efficient spots, along dry terraces high above stream-cut slopes and at times swampy lowlands below. Some Indians even tread the Venango footpath back and forth to the far north, as they knew it would bring them upon a Great Lake.

After the Shawnee and Seneca had well established their villages in the region, and were using the north side of *Fair Waters* and the *Ohiio* as their hunting grounds, the white man began to arrive and stay in southwestern Pennsylvania. (A lone Arnold Viele, likely a French trapper, had apparently viewed the surrounding lands by canoe only, sometime in the 1600s.)

The time would be the first half of the eighteenth century, and life for Native Americans of this region would now drastically change. In nearby New York State and Virginia, as well as in eastern Pennsylvania, the white man's presence had already altered the lives of the Indians come this time;

many were even being displaced into southwestern Pennsylvania. Traveling along the footpaths that led into and out of the region as a whole, natives came upon other displaced Indians, and also the first white men (and first horses) traveling to this new frontier.

The French were the first. By 1725, they would establish a main trading post at 'the Forks of the Ohio,' what would become the common white man's reference to the triangle-land at the confluence of the rivers. From the Seneca, the traders heard of the riches of the whole land. However, the French paid no attention to *Fair Waters* delineating the Allegheny—they considered it and the Ohio as one river only, *la Belle Riviere*. They befriended Native Americans with a show of metal tools, and gifts of fox pelt were given in return. Though little known or talked about, it was from the French that the natives learned the fine custom of scalping one's enemies.

The British would be next; they arrived a bit later than the French. They recognized the trading relationship already established between the French and the Indians, and the French desire to claim the territory. Those footpaths that led to the area from the eastern part of the state soon became bridle paths for British fur traders' pack trains. Coming from the center of the Commonwealth, and like the French, the British brought liquor, guns for defense and mere trade, and other items of interest to the Indians. Trade was the basis of the bond between the Indians and either French or British frontiersman/colonialist, and whoever at any given time had the favor of the Indians, due to such trade, would significantly impact the political relationship to follow. The French fell out of favor as the British replaced their novelties, but this is only a generalization. For, in the ensuing several decades, the British/Indian and French/Indian bonds would be as varied as the native peoples had become by this time.

Looking down upon the foreign visitors from atop the north bank's hump-shaped hill, there is little doubt that the Indian, native to the land, was taken aback at the clearing of forest at the triangle-land, across the river. Suddenly it would be obvious, to any Indians on the bountiful northern hunting ground, that many people other than their own were now traveling down *Fair Waters* and the *Ohiio*.

Also with the transient French and British traders came those, fewer in number, trying to settle on the frontier territory, on land around the trading posts. Occasionally, more brave and independent souls tried to stake out land a little further from the masses, and their cabins would be erected in cleared land east of the large trading post at the Forks of the Ohio.

Native Americans surely set occasional camps on the northern land, but would more often move from place to place. Any erected structures, teepee and hut, were likely temporary, if only governed by the seasons. No large Indian settlements, like those up or down river, seem to have transpired just north of the rivers' confluence, since this land was more apt to be their beloved hunting ground.

Enough information, albeit scant, does survives to note the first occasion of a settler, a white man, upon the northern bank of land. This took place in the fall of 1740.

A frontiersman who had been living at a settlement near the Shawnee village on the upper Allegheny, Andrew Long decided to travel down river with his family. They likely landed on the easternmost of the north bank's small isle attachments, just at the bend in the river, and made their way inland to the eastern base of the hump-shaped hill. They cleared a small bit of land there—out of forest, a clearing for their cabin, the first white man's intended permanent structure, it seems, on the rivers' north side.

The land on the north side of the Allegheny and Ohio Rivers had now become home to the white man, as well as native Indian. The latter, albeit without village, still inhabited its glorious expanse, and would for another fifty years, although with great change upcoming. It is not known if any relationship, detrimental or otherwise, initially took place between Andrew Long and native peoples still hunting in this wilderness considered homeland.

Three years later, two other families who had been former upriver neighbors of Long, joined him and built nearby, just a bit further inland to the north. To settle to the north of the rivers, contrary to the advice of the time, took courage and an independent spirit. Only land within the Forks area and eastward was known to be occupied by whites, and north of the rivers was deemed unsafe. So Long and comrades were likely not involved in the bustle of activity surrounding that land. He probably began a quiet life on this northern land, uninterested in settling near the protection of the Fort. He was apparently undisturbed for the first three years, before the other families' arrival. It is certainly a possibility that native Indians encountering this foreigner exhibited gentleness to and harmony with him if indeed he was interested in only humbly living on the land. (As is documented but also lesser-talked-about behavior, opposed to the proclaimed and popular conception of always-savage natives at war with white or fellow red man.)

But in 1743, the beginnings of a war were now more than smoldering between the French and British, and the natives of the north side of the rivers, as those of all of the region, would find themselves to be used for the cause of both sides. The Shawnees living in the upper Allegheny village were manipulated first, perhaps, in that they supported their half-breed cousin Peter Chartiers in his full assertion to the French cause at this time. He led a loyal band down river to the 'Ohio territory' to help the French, and it was then rumored that the Shawnees would be making raids, as well, upon British traders and frontiersmen in southwestern Pennsylvania and Virginia.

Little other information of Andrew Long's familial encampment survives, except that shortly after the other two families arrived, the men in all three families were wiped out by an Indian raid. Perhaps seeing Long's comrades arrive was just too many settlers for the natives on the north bank to bear, foretelling them of a time to come when the whites would push out the Indians. However, this would have been about the time of the supposed Shawnee raids into the backwoods. Quite possibly, and if so, unfortunately, the fate of Andrew Long was permanently stamped by the motivations and movements of Chartiers, who easily could have used the *Great Path* on the northern bank as passage to Ohio. In so doing, Chartiers would have come upon Long, as the path followed just north of his homestead and the hump-shaped hill, and just south of his comrades' half-built cabins. But it would be Indian hands that bore the blood for the killings.

It is said that the three families tried to seek safety in Long's cabin, but all nine men would be killed. Some of the women and children apparently survived the attack and were taken to an Indian camp; only son Albert Long escaped along route. His, and their, fate afterward is fascinatingly unknown. As such, and because Andrew Long settled on the north side well before others, his story would be overshadowed, a century later, by the better-recorded actions of the pioneers of the later 1700s.

By the year 1748, some of the raiding Shawnees returned to Southwestern Pennsylvania, which was under Native American rule by two Seneca warrior chiefs and one Oneida. But the fate of the region was about to be controlled by the white man, based, in part, upon the play of the various Native peoples. Seneca Chief Guyasuta was based at a village not far upriver from the low spot in the Allegheny, and old Queen Aliquippa was at one along the *Great Path* down river. Oneida Chief Monacatootha oversaw natives within the area around the Forks of the Ohio.

In the late 1740s, the Indian chiefs would meet with trader and friend to the Indians, George Croghan at Queen Aliquippa's village. Also at the meetings was Conrad Weiser, Pennsylvania's Indian agent. In 1750, the region was still the far western frontier of Cumberland County of the Commonwealth— at least the territory from the rivers' confluence on south and eastward, since everything from the Allegheny and Ohio Rivers northwestward would not be considered part of any county until the 1780s.

The natives were unconvinced of Pennsylvania or British title to the land, and unhappy that the fate of the land was rapidly changing. But they weren't the only ones. The French, in 1753, would occupy Presque Isle, north on Lake Erie, as they prepared to make their presence far more known in the area. And the colony of Virginia had been holding meetings with the Indians, as well.

The northern bank of land now witnessed more than the catharsis of one water to another. A young George Washington and some Indian allies, sent by the Virginians to speak to the French, traveled north on horseback, to the Forks of the Ohio. He would venture far northward via a spot down river, near Queen Aliquippa's village. His path eventually took him to merge with the Venango Trail, far north. On his return trip back down that trail in December, to deliver the message that the French were not interested in leaving the territory, he and his guide Christopher Gist left their weakened horses and set out on foot. They left the trail and traveled south down Pine Creek to reach the Allegheny River. At the low point in the Allegheny, nearby the northern bank's large, easternmost isle with slim back channel, Washington and Gist crossed via raft and almost drowned in the icy waters.

The native on the middle land of the north bank, below the hump-shaped hill, could at this time make his way across the largest island at the river's bend, because it was connected by a sandbar at low water. He now peered out from the wooded bank and saw the makings of a new log structure on the infamous triangle-land. In 1754, after Washington's visit, this was built near the site of the previous French trading post. But the French moved southward rather quickly to attack this progress. They would be victorious, claiming the Forks. And they began to build Fort Duquesne.

With amazement, the natives would now keep close watch on the swing of activity and immense structure rising across the way. Upon advisement by his top men in the region, those very trees were about to be ordered cleared by the Marquis de Duquesne himself, as he worried about the British firing from this land just a pistol shot away from the French fort. As well, this little island, about to be referred to by the white man as "Smokey Island" (for the smoke rising from Indian campfire) was on the verge of becoming infamous for its own role in the intense history of the time.   (Contrecoeur Papers)

General Edward Braddock's army was badly defeated in 1755—the first attempt of the British to win back the Forks of the Ohio. Several soldiers from his army of Scotch Highlanders were captured by Indians who were helping the French in this skirmish. They were brought to the camping ground on Smokey Island, recently scalped by the French of its forestry. This island would be the main place where natives and whites would try to converse together, in order to settle differences over the land. But when the natives wanted to display their displeasure, as would be the case with these British soldiers, or talks went bad, with no bridging of differences, the island became the contraire. Macabre shows of torture of white men in captivity could be easily seen from those at the new fort. And the white man knew, whether he was French or British, that the next to be tortured could easily be himself, as the native sentiment was coming to be so fractured. For the next few years in particular, scenes like this, with various whites, were repeated in sensational manner—on this natural stage of an island amphitheater surrounded by the great mount and rolling hills around the Forks of the Ohio.

Over the next several years, the French influenced many natives to raid the settlements that spread out from the Forks, and many early British homesteaders fled back east at this time. No further white settlements after Andrew Long would be in existence on the north side of the rivers for seventeen years after the attack on his family. Smokey Island signaled one entrance to the land to definitely avoid.

Warrior leaders would oft huddle with the French, who now were persuading the Indians to see them as loving fathers who would help improve their existence. The Indians had begun building teepees, huts and log structures on Smokey Island, and the low ground between it and the hump-shaped hill, and these oft served as meeting spaces. But the Native Americans, who had traded with the French, then the English, and now fought strongly with the French (that is, many but not all of them) were wary of any white promises.

One Indian elder's proclamation to a French *father*, transcribed by a member of Celoron's campaign down *la Belle Riviere* around this time, implores the French to stop their invasion:

> The river where we are belongs to us as warriors.... M. de Joncaire had come three years ago with much merchandise which he distributed as he desired, after which he said that he had acquired the land.... That pained me. We have told our brothers, the English, to withdraw. We shall be on the side of those who take pity on us and who listen to us. Although I am small, the master of life has not given me less courage to oppose these establishments. This is the first and last request that we shall make of you about it, and I shall strike out at whoever does not listen to us.... With these four strings of wampum we tell you that we beg you to listen to the demand we make of you and our opposition to your occupying our river. We therefore beg you, my father, to take pity on our children and those to come, seeing that, if you settle here, it is the way to make us all perish.   (CONTRECOEUR PAPERS)

The tide started turning on the French advantage around the summer of 1758, when the Indians had lost confidence in French provisions and the might required to fight off the reengaging British. The latter were determined to win the land at the Forks and surrounding territory, and they were gearing up by spreading word to the Indians that the French did not have the natives' interests at heart. The British promised the Indians that they would drive out the French, and then themselves retreat back to the eastern part of the Commonwealth, which they of course had no intention of doing.

The British even sent the Moravian missionary Frederick Post to spread this word of peace and retreat. He huddled with the natives, including an influential Delaware, Chief Killbuck, on Smokey Island in August of that year—all while the British prepared to send Gen. John Forbes to lead a campaign to take the coveted land. Though the message of peace and new loyalty to the British was taking hold, many Indians still in allegiance to the French wanted blood over a premature attempt by General James Grant to attack Fort Duquesne in September. Like the first spectacle of 1755, Grant's men, too, would end up tortured on Smokey Island.

The British would shortly be victorious, however. And the French had to accept that the majority of natives were now behind the British cause, believing it to bring them freedom of their land. Forbes reached the Forks toward the end of the year, only to find that the French had abandoned and burned Fort Duquesne.

The British general would soon declare for work to commence on interim Fort Mercer, until the later Fort Pitt could be erected. He had immediately written of his victory to his commanders, stating he sent it from "Fort Duquesne now Pittsbourg." Thus what little was left of the settlements that had earlier sprung up eastward from the triangle-land were named as provincial *Pittsburg* (never again with the "u") in surviving earliest records. As well, Forbes, almost upon his deathbed, explored a bit of the Woodland Indian territory above the north banks of the Allegheny. Already long worn by Indian foot, the part of the Venango Trail past the hills' cleave, and up and around the tiered ridge, apparently held some fascination for the general. He would ask that he be brought over to that famous path and remarked about it later to his soldiers and British commanders.

As Fort Pitt neared completion in 1761, new homesteaders came to that area that would become called 'the Point,' setting up some shops, taverns and other early businesses—all as Native Americans on the north bank looked on. Even as they began to trade for novelties like chicken eggs, and cooperated on some ventures, they saw as broken promise the fact that the British transformed the land and were not leaving the area. For the white man, too, there was disappointment—the hardships of home life in essential wilderness, as well as measles, smallpox and dysentery, not to mention the bitterness and recourse of many of the Indians.

A pioneer by the name of James Boggs was the only one interested, in the late summer of 1760, in the north side of the rivers. The frontier community near Fort Pitt had a population of 151 at this time. Boggs would be that one individual above the rest that decided to move his family over to the northern bank that was east, just upriver, of Smokey Island. He chose the land that was just south of where the Venango Trail started northward from the *Great Path*. Clearing a spot here, so close to the native crossroads, might have been his downfall. His intent was to farm, and he was able to apparently erect a cabin. His homesteading efforts, though, met unfortunate end in a few short years, being prompted by Indian uprisings all around the area to move closer to the protection of the fort at the Point. He abandoned his cabin and the little land his family cleared, and moved back across river. He would not be heard of again until twenty years later, when he would again figure prominently, albeit short in duration once again.

Perhaps Boggs thought it safe to venture northward when he did because of the fact that it was a couple months earlier that very summer of 1760 when Colonel Henry Bouquet, officer at Fort Pitt, with a legion of other soldiers, crossed the river and traveled the Venango Trail farther northward than had Forbes, supposedly just to survey the forested northern ridges. Included were three companies of the Pennsylvania Regiment, a Lieutenant Thomas Hutchins and George Croghan. The latter two men left diaries of the expedition. Hutchins describes their campsite the night of July 7, 1760 as "by several springs" on a hillside that would two centuries later be identified as an area lying over a mile northward.

The British soldiers still had a friend in some natives at this time, in particular one entitled *Delaware George*. Loyal until his end in the spring of 1762, he would be the first documented native buried on the north banks of the Allegheny—directly east of the first islet, or peninsula (depending on water level). James Kenny, a Quaker storekeeper at the Point, noted in his journal that a file of soldiers and Indians attended the burial and fired three rounds over his grave, which was west and closer to the river than where Boggs still would have been residing at the time. Kenny also noted that wealthy trader George Croghan provided for the coffin.   (Traveler's Guide)

Life around Fort Pitt by the summer of 1763 was difficult for soldiers as well as homesteaders, due to Pontiac's uprising at Fort Detroit and its related effects in the southwestern Pennsylvania region. Fort Pitt would be under siege from Indians until the beginning of August, when an especially bitter attack ensued, as they crossed the Allegheny from the north side and shot arrows into the fort from fairly close range. But they would be unsuccessful at driving the white man out, with the recent attack at nearby Bushy Run.

The frontier community at the Point began to grow even more, while many Indians were beginning to leave in larger numbers, finding it hopeless to continually defend their claim to the beloved land. And the white man was now, in 1764, holding major expeditions far into Indian territory to the south and northeast, to clear the region of its natives. In the fall of that year, Colonel Bouquet and many troops addressed the north by crossing the Allegheny on a large "exploratory expedition" heading northwestward. Their number was 1500, and included were soldiers, light horse troops, and a few women nurses. Packhorses carried ammunition and supplies. As well, there were even herds of sheep and cattle droves, in order to sustain the army away from Fort Pitt.

The first night they would camp just across river, not far inland— around the area right off the Great Path and north of the hump-shaped hill, close to where Long's comrade families had settled. "Rich, level land with stately timber" was noted as having been found there. With an expeditionary force like that, the British soldiers were beginning to effectively limit any future impact the natives could hold in the region, though the frontier would still be far from free from attacks for another thirty years. (TRAVELER'S GUIDE)

A transaction took place in 1772, between two Indian chiefs who had traversed the land north of the rivers and a white man by the name of Garret Pendergrass, whom they later met in the central mountains of the state. He was apparently friendly with the Indians and wealthy; his family had been in America for some years already. Supposedly the chiefs felt the need to return some favor to Pendergrass, so they "granted him land"—what amounted, in someone's later estimation of the deal, to "a worthless swamp between the Allegheny and Ohio rivers." Essentially the low-lying northern bank, the title of this land is actually recorded in Deed Book A in the Bedford Co. Court House, and is signed by a circle within a circle, and a turtle, the marks of *Connehracagecat* (the White Mingo), and Chief Anonguit. Pendergrass would not come to claim his land... at least not in the 1770s.

(CUMBERLAND COUNTY LAND RECORDS)

Also in 1772, troops at Fort Pitt were finally withdrawn and sent back east, where there was growing colonial dissent. It was felt, albeit prematurely, that further maintenance to oversee "Indian problems" was no longer a necessity. In the next couple years, the old fort would serve as trading post, and also even be taken over ever so briefly by the Virginians, as they tried to still lay claim to the land. (Many frontiersman were indeed loyal to Virginia.)

Around 1775, both over land policies and Indian relations, white settlers in the region, now, were increasingly dissatisfied with the British. The continued infighting of the white man—surfacing Virginians and British settlers angry at their leadership—only confirmed the Indians' belief that their land would eternally be claimed by competing and negative forces. This spurred on trouble, especially with raiding Mingos, causing havoc with the intent to homestead anywhere further away from the Point, let alone the northern bank.

By this time, the area at the Point (but still not the frontier north of the rivers) was supposed to have been now part of new Westmoreland County. To be exact, Pitt Township. But the disarray of the Revolution saw only the eastern majority of the present county able to rule over territory, so it was during this chaos that Virginia actually established three counties competing in territory to the Penn's claim on the land. The area at the Point, already christened Pittsburg and recently part of Pennsylvania's Westmoreland County, was also thus called by Virginia part of their 'Yohogania County.'

To make matters worse, the American patriots were now trying to get the Indians on their side against rising anti-British sentiment. Like in the French and Indian War, one side (this time the Patriots) was now calling for Indian neutrality in the upcoming fight, and the other (this time the British) was trying to enlist their support. Also this time around, the Patriots made the very public but false promise that the natives would have sovereignty over their land after all was said and done (though the Indians were surely also getting similar old assurances from the British.)

The Revolution raged on, with the early American government being established in 1777. William Penn's heirs would thus no longer hold official proprietorship to the Pittsburg Manor of land. Soon the land would be vested to the new legislature of the Commonwealth of Pennsylvania.

In trying to win back the turning favor of the Indians, the British whipped up their fury, complementing their savagery by putting bounties out on the scalps of Patriots. Indian raids then intensified over the homesteads and ridge paths leading to the region from the south, east and northeast (the north and west entrances were still under native control, despite recent expeditions). As in the days of Fort Duquesne, Patriot munitions were now low. Wagon wheels were up and running over bridle paths from the east, but gunpowder was hard to come by, and enough could not be transported.

A large island two miles downstream from Fort Pitt (and previously called McKee's Island by the white man) had been purchased by a Thomas Smallman in 1780. He would have had wealth and connections to the patriot cause at the Point, which would dictate or overrule any activity happening on another island of such strategic importance. (Colonel Alexander McKee had been granted the land beyond the island, on the south side of the Ohio, and named McKees Rocks, for his service to General Forbes.)

Around 1778, Smokey Island would again figure prominently in the history of not only the northside land, but the land of the entire region. As well, what would happen there would signify how the motivations of the Indians, the British and the Patriots had become so confused, and typify the ambiguity of the ravages of all wars. For as it was, some of the Indians were still fighting for the British cause during the Revolution, some the American, and of course, some neither, essentially. Delawares had a Treaty to not join with the British any longer, but that did not necessarily call for siding with the patriots, either. Delaware Chief Killbuck, however, was aligning himself more and more with the patriots based at the Point.

Chief of the Turtle Tribe of Delawares, Killbuck became part of the Moravian Indian mission, and oversaw a contingent of these natives who were loyal first to the British (against the French), and then faithfully to the American patriots when they deserted the British cause. Killbuck and his followers were stationed on Smokey Island, where there was now a long row of flat-topped huts, erected by the Indians to receive traders. Killbuck's reputation with other Indians started to suffer at the end of the 1770s, when he was so influenced by a General Brodhead as to actually call for the Delaware to fight against other Indians, for the American cause. (Sadly, of course, Chief Killbuck thought the cause was not just 'American,' but somehow in his tribe's best interest, as well.) In 1781, Killbuck would be forced to step down as chief of the Turtle clan, despite his still being a Delaware, and still being followed, afterward, by many members of the tribe.

After being somewhat disenfranchised from Indians in general, but still with his own band of followers, Killbuck gave the island a new reputation of friendliness to the new American colonists. And for his loyalty, Colonel John Gibson would 'give' Chief Killbuck the island to call his own. But in the spring of 1782 something awful would happen.

Killbuck had learned that some of the Ohio country Delawares were violating their treaty obligations and joining with the British. So he took his allegiance with the Patriots one step further and informed details of the insurgency to the leaders at Fort Pitt, which had come back into existence after the attempted Virginia takeover. Patriot Continental Army officers then very brutally massacred a band of these Delawares in Ohio. Controversy ensued as to whether that particular band was really one of the insurgents, or had simply been a peaceful tribe connected to the Moravian missionaries. A lot of evidence pointed to the latter.

After this horrendous event, nearby tribes in the region threatened Killbuck and his followers, who were equally surely horrified at the event in the Ohio territory. Now Killbuck's Delawares, sitting on Smokey Island, would have to be prepared to fight for their lives. But ironically, it would not be fellow Indians but instead patriot soldiers from Chartiers Creek who were so angry that there was talk of action being taken on the wrong group of Delawares, that they decided to attack any and all Delawares of the region.

With all-around sentiment so confused by the chaos of war, these incensed patriot soldiers came upriver to Smokey Island, and most of Killbuck's followers (as well as a few patriot soldiers from Fort Pitt) were savagely killed, again with spectacle made to all those in view across river. It seems Smokey Island could not maintain its peaceful reputation.

This event would come back to specifically haunt the family of one of the patriot captains in later years. It was also well-known that the horror of it resounded throughout the new American country. Chief Killbuck himself, and only a couple others, actually managed to escape—by swimming across to his friends at Fort Pitt. Killbuck would go on to live on his little island soon again, and he would be the most prominent Native American entwined in the history of this northern land well into the next century.

The Patriots, many mere homesteaders with little or no military background, had a very hard time of it against the British loyalists who remained in the region. Despite the fighting, though, that would continue in the region until Revolution's end in essentially 1783, the little town of Pittsburg had remarkably continued to slowly grow. It had taken until 1779 for the Mason-Dixon line to be extended, but once it was, the town was formally once and for all Pennsylvanian. Though it would have beginning businesses of boat-building, a distillery, and a coal manufactory on the great mount across the Monongahela (now called Coal Hill), and new settlers even now venturing east of the Point area, the land north of the Allegheny and Ohio Rivers was still considered Indian territory in the early 1780s.

chapter two:

ALLEGHENY TOWN

Despite the fact that land on the north side of the Allegheny and Ohio rivers was considered unsafe, due to Indian tensions, the Land Office of the General Assembly of Pennsylvania began plans, in 1783, to set aside a Reserved Tract of land on this very area—3,000 acres going one mile deep, or north, from the two rivers. This Reserved Tract would be for specific use slated by the State. Namely, for the central lower portion just opposite Pittsburg to be the site of a town.

The Commonwealth's aim was that money raised by the sale of town lots, and surrounding wilderness-to-be-turned pasturage, would help pay off the state debt incurred during the Revolutionary War. As well, they eyed the land for yet another new county seat, to be carved out of Westmoreland.

Having heard word of these plans, a Revolutionary War veteran, Colonel William Butler, began plans of his own to operate a ferry business across the Allegheny. He had been granted, by an Act of the State Legislature, the right to establish the ferry, even before the town land would be laid out and put up for sale. Because the land was unsuitable without improvement, he was to have been given clearance to a title only upon showing plans for a landing and ferry house. But Butler's plan apparently would be beat out by one from another man whose chosen locale for the ferry landing would come to have an advantage

The Colonel did not pick very well. The plot that Butler staked out, just inland east of the peninsula near Smokey Island, constantly flooded. It also was land incorporating the site of Delaware George's grave. His chosen northwestern boundary was also adjacent to where Andrew Long and friends were massacred forty years earlier. And his land claim extended northeast-ward into a corner of land first cleared by James Boggs twenty years earlier.

Boggs' wife, Martha, would later write to the President of the Supreme Executive Council of the Commonwealth, that her husband had received permission by General William Irvine, military commandant at Fort Pitt, to indeed (re)settle and improve upon what was to be the Reserved Tract, still

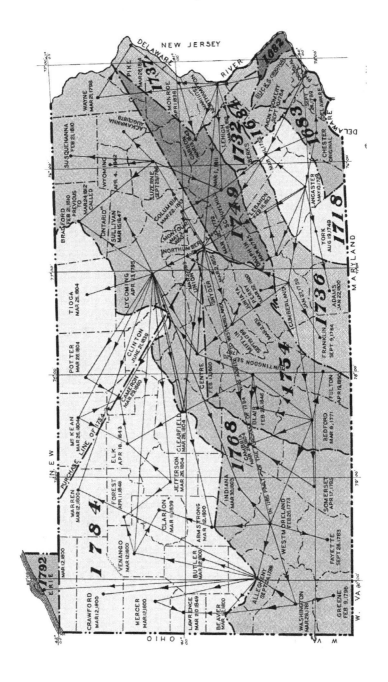

un-surveyed, in 1783. It is likely that he got to the north bank (again) slightly before Colonel Butler. He began building another log house, since his original cabin did not survive, or suffice, on about the same spot of the earlier one, and he cleared approximately nine acres of land.

Unfortunately, Boggs would be killed while felling a tree, and his widow was left to deal with the heavy-handed Butler, who tried to force her off the bank. Undaunted, the incident is what prompted her to write the State Legislature, thus having in recorded history at least the facts surrounding the 'second' landing north of the Allegheny River of her first husband, James Boggs.

> Colonel William Butler... [has] taken poseation (sic) of a part of the Lands Cleared by my husband [since dead]. I presume more than the Lot [given Butler by the legislature] & that on the back part of my house, he has lately Told me that I must turn out of the house in the Spring.... (STORY OF OLD ALLEGHENY CITY)

Martha Boggs appealed to be allowed to stay, and simply tend the business of her land, and the Commonwealth voted in her favor. But, to perhaps better protect her interests, she would shortly thereafter marry a man by the name of James Robinson.

Robinson would pick up where Boggs had left off with the land, but he would build a new log cabin for himself, his wife and stepchildren. This would be closer to the river and slightly east of the original spot of Boggs' rebuilt cabin. Also undaunted by Butler, Robinson built yet another structure adjacent to his new home—a ferry house. On firmer land than Butler's portion of the bank, it is with this structure that James Robinson won the favor of the early ferry business across the Allegheny River to the northern bank.

The setting-aside of the Reserved Tract came about officially through the *Last Purchase*, in 1784, of Native American land by the Commonwealth of Pennsylvania. This was all part of the larger plan to secure the remaining

Figure 3 (opposite). Pennsylvania in 1784, with the Last Purchase

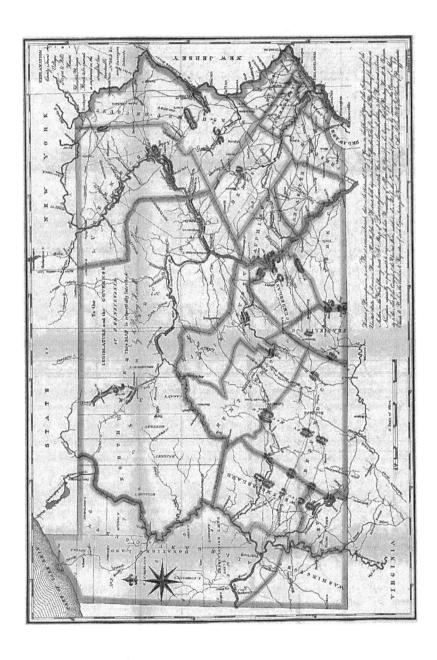

lands in the state for use by the post-Revolutionary government, and to compensate those soldiers who served.

Pennsylvania would have an obligation toward its soldiers, but no money to pay them. So within the *Last Purchase*, the Commonwealth provided for the Reserved Tract, but also division of other land north of this, into two sections, The Depreciation Lands and The Donation Lands. (The Reserved Tract was actually just the southernmost portion of the Depreciation Lands.) The available Depreciation Land tracts would begin just north of the Reserved area, and would be assigned in exchange for depreciation pay certificates held by soldiers for their service in the Revolutionary War. (During the War they had been given regular pay, but in depreciated currency, so the difference was made up in these certificates for that value.)

The larger boundaries of the Depreciation and Donation Lands were described by the Supreme Executive Council as early as 1783, but their survey, lot division, and sale would not be fully completed until the end of 1785 and 1789, respectively. (The Donation Land tracts started just north of the Depreciation Lands—essentially *gifted* as land grants of varying sizes to officers and other soldiers, based on rank, who would serve longer, closer to the true end of the War that would come about in 1788, with the Treaty of Paris.)

Not every soldier wanted a piece of wilderness territory, and many opted for cash, selling what could have been their land to professional speculators, who took every advantage to grab up land parcels. As would be widely later documented, many Land Companies with connections to the Land Office would pursue unethical means in claiming large plots for themselves.

Even though Pittsburg was considered part of the Commonwealth of Pennsylvania's territories, the state followed William Penn's earlier footsteps and only formally made land its own after "purchasing" from the Indians. So, come 1785, the town of Pittsburg, recently acquired in the *Last Purchase* by the state, became *officially* a part of Westmoreland County, even though already in the works was the plan to carve out further government seats and thus have this county area soon renamed.

The earliest map of the region directly north of the three rivers is a Warrantee Atlas drawn up by anonymous surveyor in April of 1785,

Figure 4 (opposite). Depreciation & Donation Lands

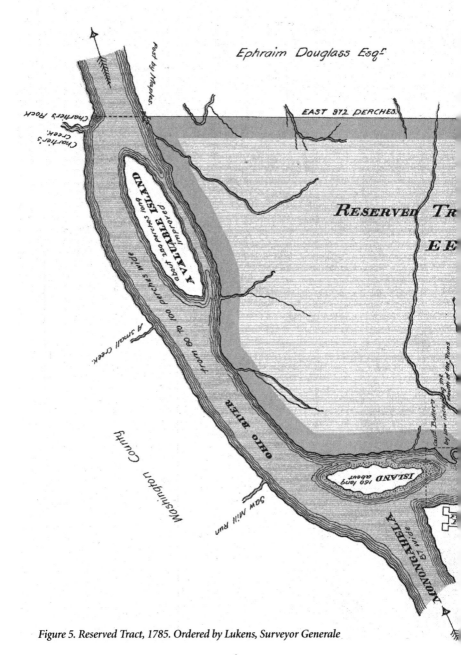

Figure 5. Reserved Tract, 1785. Ordered by Lukens, Surveyor Generale

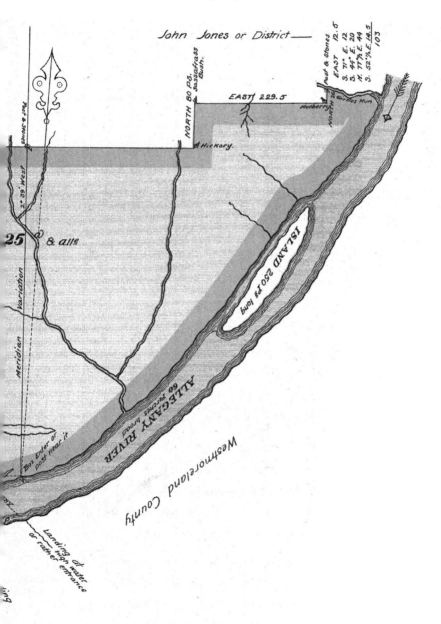

"pursuant to the instructions from John Lukens, Surveyor Generale of the Commonwealth. (*Figure 5*) The Reserved Tract is shown in its entirety, and Westmoreland County is clearly shown at bottom right (for the area east of the Point) as well as Washington County at bottom left (extending into the area southwest of the Ohio River at the time). Distinct are the names of two assigned surveyors of the Depreciation Lands just above the Reserved Tract— Ephraim Douglas, Esquire and John Jones. Spreading out further west down river would be a district covered by A. McClean, Nathaniel Breadin, William Alexander, Samuel Nicholson, and on a later map, the name Hoge and extensive territory by Daniel Leet. To the east upriver would be Col. James Cunningham, Colonel Joshua Elder and, according to a later map, the name Gappen. (The Depreciation Land maps, not unlike other documents from this early time period, indeed differ with each other.)

The Reserved Tract itself is devoid of surveyor assignation on this map, but clearly shows the drawn plan for the desired ferry across the Allegheny. It is evident on this map that Pittsburg settler James Robinson (misidentified as *Robertson* on map) indeed won the ferry contract. Colonel Butler's name, however, also is visible on the lower end of the Reserved Tract, for that swampy area of land *called Butler's by law, including the Mouth of the Runs*, which would be the streams running northward from the peninsula, and extending northward.

This 1785 map shows the runs, streams, and ponds of the entire Tract, cutting inland from the river banks, as well as three mid-size islands, one across from the Point, the one upriver and the one down river. The little islets east of Smokey's Island were under water as of this date, making Butler's *Mouth of the Runs* area look quite unusual, surely due to excessive flooding.

No name is attached to Smokey Island on this map, but corn was said to be planted there by Killbuck, who had returned and was living quietly, watching events unfold as Boggs returned, and then Butler and Robinson crossed the river. Peace had finally come to the isle, and it would be better known from this time forward as Killbuck's Island.

The large island down river in the Ohio is identified on the map as *A Valuable Island, about 280 perches long*, and *Improved*. That would be McKee's, bought by Smallman in 1780, and by a John Hamilton at some early point in its history as well.

It would seem that the business of the ferries operating across river from the Point was delicate indeed. Across the Allegheny, and the Monongahela as well, problems were encountered with regard to water level and level of land at the landing site. (This early map even shows *low water level*, as well as the fact that two sites, one for arrival and one for return trip, were required.) Apparently the river hit the Allegheny bank quite rapidly, and it was often extremely muddy at the ferry's landing.

Crafty Colonel Butler must have also claimed ownership (*called Butler's lot, improved*) of the very spot where Robinson built his ferry house and new cabin, although [Robinson]'s name is put on the line across river marking the return trip, as if to clarify any discrepancy. (But discrepancies could still be claimed. It is quite possible Butler and Robinson collaborated, with one collecting toll for ferry arrival, and the other ferry's return.)

It would be mid-1785 when James Robinson had the ferry house built, and it appears to be the first structure on the north side land to show up on a map, as a small rectangle where the ferry arrived and departed. Robinson would go down in the history books as the one businessman successfully carrying out this business of transporting individuals across the river, even though it is Butler's granting by the state legislature that is recorded. It would indeed be another decade, however, before settlers would slowly start to come to the Reserved Tract by any ferry. In 1785, it was still uncharted wilderness.

But James Robinson and Martha would start a family of their own almost immediately. He would later popularly be called the first white settler on the land north of the rivers, and their first child, William, born December 1785, was supposedly the first-born white of the area (Long and comrades' children, as well as Boggs,' were simply unknown and thus not considered.)

About the same time that Robinson's ferry house was completed, John Jones would complete the survey of his Depreciation Lands district, in July 1785, dividing it up into three large areas—going as far east as the Allegheny River just above Girtie's Run (named for half-breed Colonial-times traitor Simon Girty of that area), and as far west as the *post & stones* marking the meridian line. (Surveyors would show significant geographical features when available, but physically mark the corners of land when needed. Boundaries were often shown simply by *Hickory*, or a *Post by Maples*. Notches were put in trees and rocks were heaped up—whatever could be used to show boundary markings.)

A few more names would soon dot the map showing the Depreciation Lands. Later transposed northerly onto the 1785 map would be the completion of surveys, first patents, and warrantees of that land come

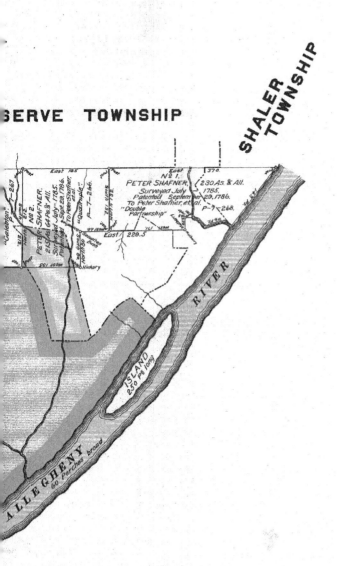

Figure 6. Depreciation territory above the Reserved Tract, circa 1786

years immediately after, starting as early as 1786.

The three lots divided by Jones were patented to Peter Shafner in 1786, and given names, as plots quite often were. In this case, he owned *Double Partnership, Quadruple* and *Calebton*. With this map transposition, the Reserved Tract is somewhat different in shape from the 1785 'truer' map— the later transposition showing an extension northwestward into Douglass' territory and being chopped into a smaller area on the eastern boundary. (*Figure 6* is the map showing the Depreciation territory above the Reserved Tract. Compare to *Figure 5*.)

But the yet-uncharted area of wilderness termed the Reserved Tract would indeed seem to follow along the boundary lines of the original, as an upcoming full survey of the territory shows. Interestingly, many years later, the bits of Reserved Tract territory 'subtracted out' in portions from the original map (and thus not highlighted in *Figure 6*), would show up at various times as part of adjoining Reserve Township, and would come to have their own unique histories connected to, but separate, from the Reserved Tract.

As well, some of the Depreciation land appears on separate later township maps as also having been patented in 1786, in a few cases to family names that would later show up in the northern portions of the Reserved Tract. Needless to say, a few early settlers (before survey) and wealthy land owners (with influence) were getting into some of the northern areas before full jurisdiction and true ownership could be determined. Those making it to the northern areas would have to be getting there from an easterly route likely via the upper Allegheny, and then crossing Pine Creek, because nothing seems to document whites yet traveling the Venango Trail northward, and as the lower Reserved Tract was simply peopled by Robinson and Butler in 1786.

As for the Donation Lands, furthest northward—completed surveys show that a couple land histories began also as early as 1786, but generally more toward the end of the decade and beyond.

It was in September 1787 that the State Legislature ordered a survey of the proposed town, and in so doing, a survey of the full Reserved Tract. Surveyor and lawyer David Redick, a resident of Washington County, was given the job. The same month of the same year, announcement was made of plans for the new county seat—to be called "Allegany," after the mountain chain, but spelled as the river, *Allegheny*. It was announced, surprisingly to those in Pittsburg, that the new town about to be surveyed, in the wilderness of the Reserved Tract, would be the seat of that government, and would officially take on that role as soon as public buildings could be erected.

Redick began his survey the following winter, but wrote, in February 1788, a letter to Benjamin Franklin, President of the Supreme Executive Council of Pennsylvania at the time, protesting the assignment. In it he describes a land virtually unfit for housing stock. "I went with several gentleman [sic] to fix on a spot for laying out the town opposite Pittsburg... I took a general view of the tract and find it far inferior to my expectation.... There is some pretty low ground on the rivers...there is only a small proportion of dry land which appears valuable, either for timber or soil...it abounds with high hills and deep hollows, almost inaccessible to a surveyor. I cannot believe that small lots on the sides of those hills can ever be of use... to farmer or settler."

Redick added that he felt some of the rougher land "not fit for inhabitants of the moon." He graciously declared that he would of course continue the work laid out for him if expected, but asked the legislature to reconsider their town survey plans.

It is not clear what response Redick got back from Franklin, but the bottom line was that he was not dismissed from duty. He finished a survey, *Plan of The Reserved Tract opposite Pittsburg* that spring, for which he was to be paid 100 pounds. He laid out the little town based on early colonialist models that followed English custom, with a town square, surrounded by *common land*, and outlying lots. (*See Figure 7 & Close-Up Figures 8–13*)

Redick laid out the square not on a direct north grid, but centered pointing northwestward about 20 degrees. He centered it on the crossing of the Venango Trail and the *Great Path*. There would be four central blocks set aside for public buildings, with the other blocks each divided into four long lots.

The town square began just north of that acreage claimed by Robinson, and as far west as almost to where Long had settled. Its northern boundary on the west would have brought it to the land settled by Long's comrade families that followed him down river. Staring down at Redick from the north, above the town plots, was the cleave of the two hills faced by the Indians as their northward trail began ascent. To the direct east of the town plot was flat land, as was the west, or at least that area above the hump-shaped hill.

The four central blocks, plus 32 more around, added up to a total of 36 for the town as a whole. 102 more acres outside the town would be designated as common pasture land. This would be around the square in different proportion, and Redick drew both the square and the surrounding Commons together in rectangular dimension on his survey.

Also on the survey (which by approximately 1789 would have names of property owners transposed upon it), within the western side of the rectangle, he wrote the total acreage and title *Commons and Burying Ground*. There was 1400 feet on the west (the most expansive area of ground, including a good portion ot the hump-shaped hill and land north of it); 250 feet on the east and just slightly less on the north (right before the hills shot upward on the latter); and the least amount, 60 feet, on the south (apparently allowing for Robinson and Butler's claim and plotting the town enough inland so as not to be just on the river bank). The far reaches of the western area, right at the base of the hill, would indeed serve the early town as burial place, just a mere distance northward from the Indian burying ground, down by the bank of the river.

Streets would emanate from the center of the town square. A dirt road had already sprung up on the bank, through the middle of Robinson's farmland, to directly connect with the Venango path that would become the town's main north/south road. And the dirt of the Great Path, too, would make up the east/west road, what had been a shortcut across the land at this latitude.

Outside of the rectangle that comprised the town square and surrounding Commons, Redick drew up a grid of remaining land of the Reserved Tract, divided up for the purpose of assignation of the out lots.

Each *in lot* of the town would be paired with a surrounding *out lot*, the individually-designated farm land provided each town settler. Only one out lot would be assigned per owner, except in cases where the land was rough and hilly. In that case, it appears that several lots were grouped together in parcel, and referred to as farms. Thus in total, it was prearranged that anyone who would purchase a Town Lot of the Reserved Tract would also receive an accompanying *Out Lot* for individual use, and usage of collective *Commons* ground for pasturage.

The runs, streams, and ponds detailed by the earlier map are visible and elaborated upon in Redick's survey, as well, with some of the the area previously designated as Colonel Butler's acreage looking under water, with quite a further dip of the land to the east of the sunken islet. As well, even Smokey Island's eastern end is obviously under water, with the appearance of much shorter length, when compared to the early map.

Uniquely drawn on Redick's survey is the area northeasterly of the town square, for it is the only area not divided up by grid lines, and shows special delineation. Starting around the eastern hill met just before the cleave, and proceeding as far north as the Tract boundary, is a huge rectangular parcel of land comprising 312 total acres. Redick simply called it *High Rough Land*.

Sections of land were tackled by apportioning where primitive lanes, or streets, could be laid out (but would not be, for at least a decade) and then dividing within, forming lots. These lanes were drawn very straight for the most part, quite unlike the terrain could actually support when, and if, each of the lanes became a reality. Trying to lay a grid to unusual land, Redick simply surveyed the area somewhat linearly, not attempting to mark lots according to the multitude of curves of the sandstone hills. It is obvious, though, that he did try to incorporate their general interruption of the land into some areas that were clearly hilltops, and others valleys. Perhaps Redick saved the High Rough Land area to be apportioned lastly, but then abandoned the idea within the time available to survey, for, although this land contains the highest northside peak, there are others whose elevations come close, yet they appear apportioned just as was flat land. Thus, to look at the survey is to suggest that only the *High Rough Land* is the hilly terrain of this northern land, and such is not the case.

It is unclear as to whether Redick named the lanes he drew to appear on his survey, or more likely, if they were assigned by the legislature shortly after. Most are straight northwest/southeast and northeast/southwest, but there are a few exceptions, accommodating early settlers.

The only already-existing dirt road connecting with the Venango Trail, through Robinson's property, was drawn but not named. Also south of the town square, there is an unnamed lane designation drawn in yellow, accounting for boundaries of Butler's and Robinson's already-settled property, and thus it jogs around almost as if a private alley to the both. (A short little stretch of road east of Robinson's family homestead is termed *Sandusky Lane*, however.) As well, in the furthest western area of the survey, a staggered lane pattern was chosen, likely according wishes of another early land squatter, John Woods, who had come to hold some interest in this and other northern areas just before the time of the survey, in the late 1780s.

Just north of the town, Redick surveyed a section of lots three across—two to the west of the hills' cleave and one to the right. Continuing a line northward from the town square (but with no respect to the Venango Trail's adjusted western route, due to the sandstone outcroppings) is a lane simply entitled *External Ally*. The western boundary of the Commons land, drawn northward, is more evocatively named—*Pasture Lane*. And *Ferry Lane* would be the northwestern-most lot dividing line, suggesting Redick knew of plans soon to come of another ferry across the Ohio River, operated by a Robert Elliott.

The other major north/southward dividing lines (notwithstanding the twenty degree axis skew) are *Last Lane*, leading straight to the area of High Rough Land; *King Lane*, marking the eastern boundary of that area; and *Sasafras Lane*. Running relatively west to east across the survey are the following Lane names: *Castle, Back, Island, Strawberry*, and *Bank* on the west, and *Huccleberry, Chestnut* and *Spring Lane* on the east of the Tract.

Allegheny County officially came into being the fall of 1788, and it would be divided up into seven townships, with Pittsburg and all areas north of the rivers part of Pitt Township. Because no activity but a survey had so far taken place across the Allegheny River, however, the new county duties were decreed to take place temporarily in Pittsburg. From the first public announcement that the county government was to permanently settle across the river, citizens of Pittsburg protested, because their land was already supporting a town. Lawmakers voiced their opposition, stating "there is not a soul living on that side of the river." (They were not counting James Robinson, Colonel Butler and John Woods, of course.) As for housing the county jail, the public outcry was that "the only miscreants to be committed to jail would be beasts from the forests."

But the lots, themselves, on the north side of the river (vis Redick's imminent plan, and apparently based on the total square footage from Lukens' ordered survey) had already gone up for sale in Philadelphia when Redick was just assigned to begin his work. The state would hold a public auction, with appointed commissioner, and one of the main selling points would be that the land would hold the county seat, increasing the lots' value. Simply titled *Town Lots in The Reserved Tract opposite Pittsburg*, the public auction was held on November 1787.

The Town Lots (measuring 60' x 240') and connected Out Lots of comparable size (5–10 acres) were sold to highest bidder, and many would indeed sell relatively cheap at the time of the auction. The four central blocks of the square were left empty, in reserve for such public buildings as a city hall, court house, and market house. A majority of the lots were known to be purchased not for the purpose of settling, but for land speculation, especially due to the coveted county assignation.

Completion of the auction was recorded by Presley Neville. In a random order, the archaic surviving document lists the Town Lot number ascribed, the corresponding Out Lot number, the purchaser's name, the price sold for, in pounds, and a fifth indecipherable column. Separate pages described individual lots in detail. At the end of the archival papers is a summary report:

**Total acreage: 252 3/4 acre; In Town and Commons: 163 acres;
High Rough Land not Surveyed and not fit for Cultivation: 312 acres;
Whole amount surveyed, exclusive of Roads: 3,000 acres.**

This sale of lots in what would soon be called Allegheny Town transpired in that fall month of 1787, but it would be another year before Redick finished describing, dividing up, and drawing the land, and two years before the names of the buyers at auction were transposed onto a survey map. It would seemingly be available for public perusal by 1789, complete with original survey in background and original buyers' names transposed atop each lot. As well, the lots were numbered in two colors— Out lot numbers are in red, with corresponding Town Lot numbers, that go with it, in black.

Once sold, building and occupancy requirements would have to be met, and then a patent would be formally warranted in the name of the landowner. This would be considered ownership by settlement and improvement in the Commonwealth. It incorporated the idea that those rare land "squatters" (settlers like Robinson and Woods) who arrived before land survey, could also put forth their claims alongside those later purchasing.

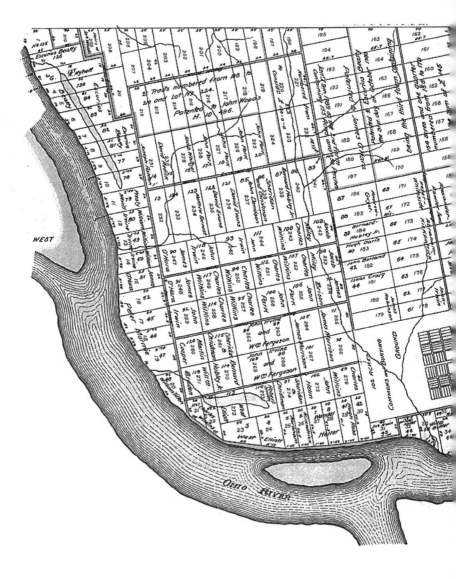

Figure 7. Plan of the Reserved Tract opposite Pittsburg. *Redick's survey with original owners transposed, circa 1789*

TOWN OF ALLEGANY

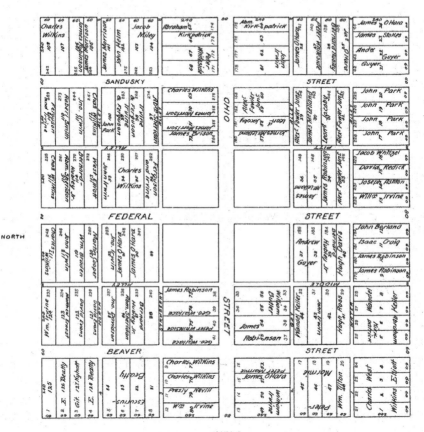

Figure 8. Close-up: Allegheny Town center, with original owners' names

Figures 9–13. (opposite and next 4 pages). Close-ups: Allegheny Town with Out Lots

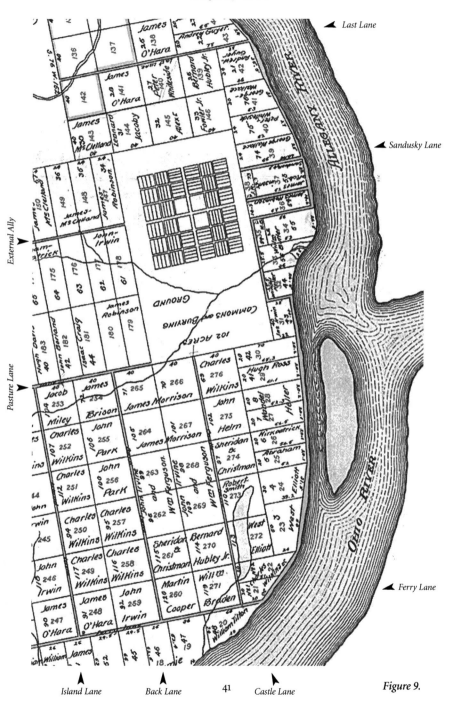

Last Lane

Sandusky Lane

External Ally

Pasture Lane

Ferry Lane

Island Lane

Back Lane

Castle Lane

41

Figure 9.

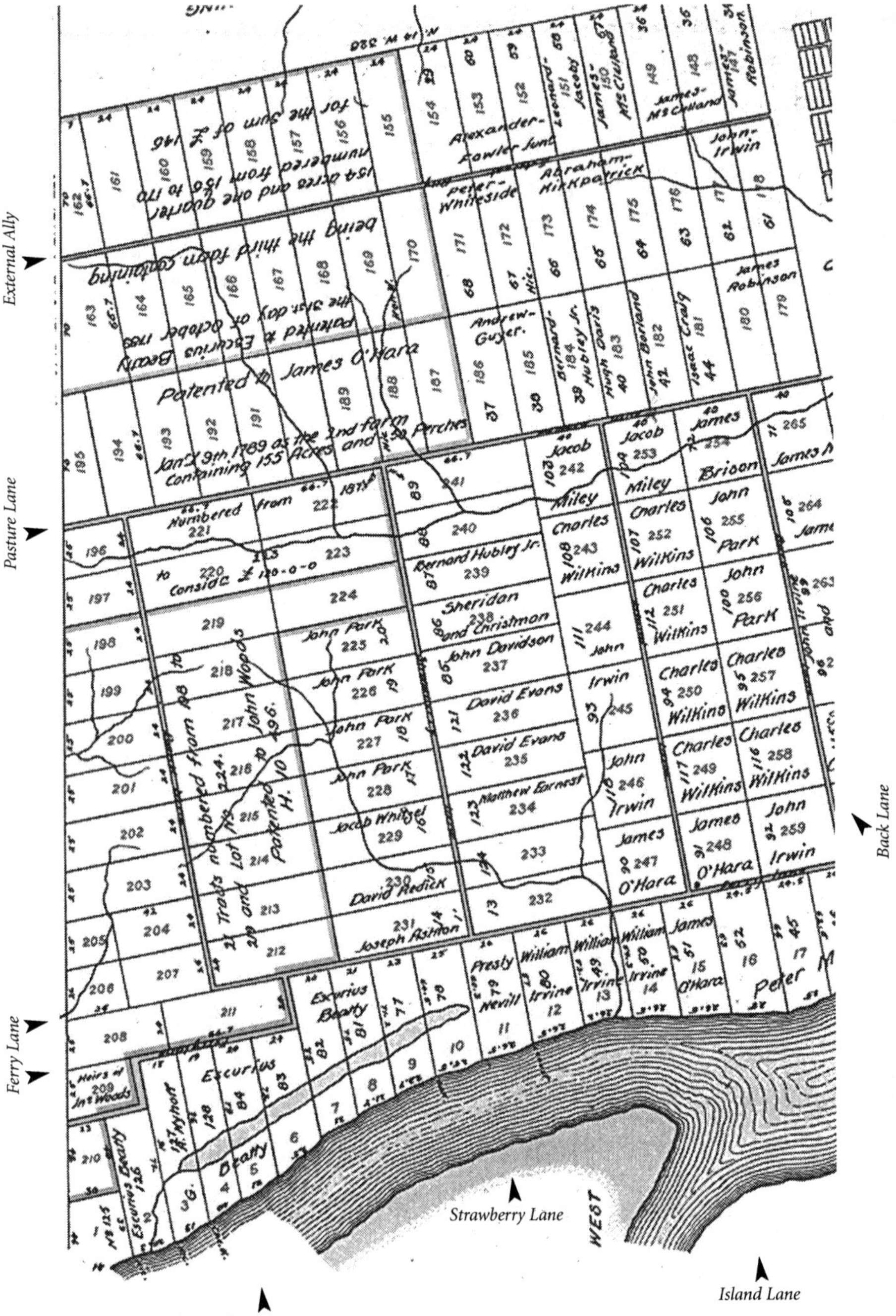
External Ally
Pasture Lane
Ferry Lane
Back Lane
Strawberry Lane
Bank Lane
Island Lane
Patented to James O'Hara
Jan'y 9th 1789 as the 2nd farm
Containing 155 Acres and 50 Perches
Alexander Fowler Junr
Peter Whiteside
Abraham Kirkpatrick
John Irwin
James Robinson
Andrew Guyer
Isaac Craig
John Borland
Hugh Davis
Bernard Hubley Jr.
Sheridan and Christman
John Davidson
David Evans
Matthew Earnest
Jacob Whitsel
David Redick
Joseph Ashton
John Park
Charles Wilkins
James O'Hara
Jacob Miley
James Brison
Presly Nevill
William Irvine
Escurius Beatty
Heirs of Jn Woods
WEST

Figure 10.

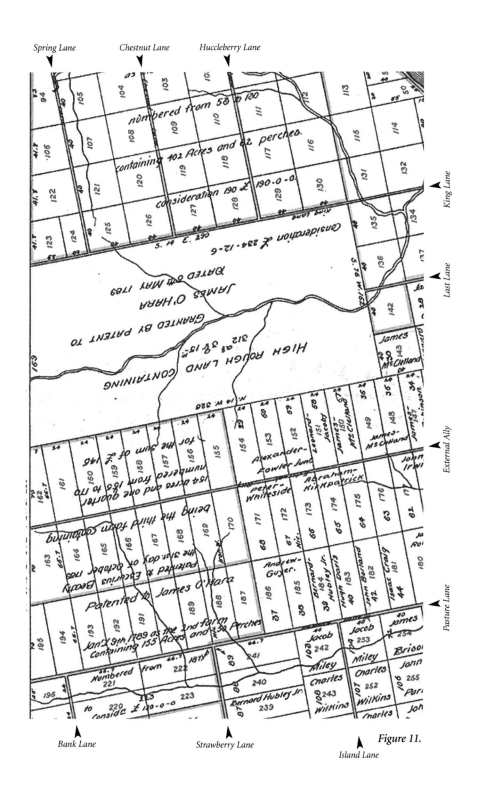

Figure 11.

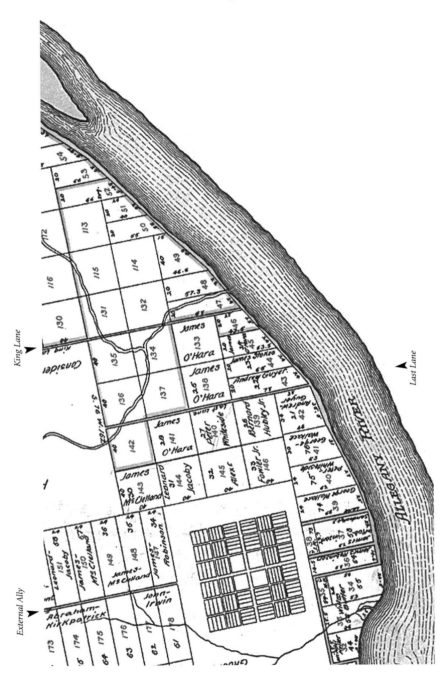

Figure 12.

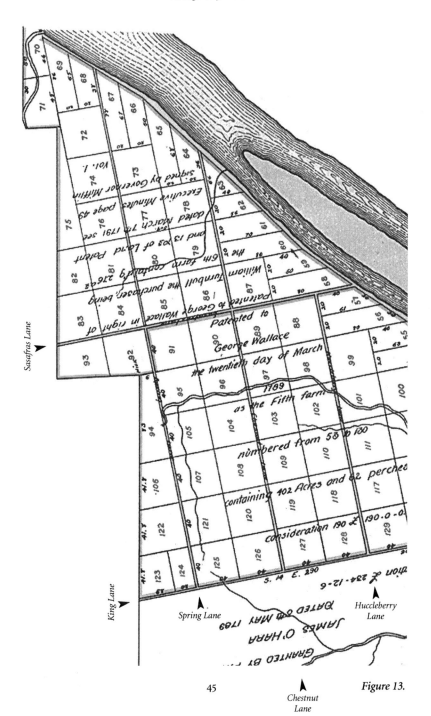

Figure 13.

The state would thus consider all purchases alongside unusual scenarios in the process of application for warrant, survey, and ultimately patented deed.

Colonel Butler's name shows up on two town lots, primely located adjacent to the central public square. He also retained the property he originally squatted on, which was designated as two out lots next to James Robinson's two on the bank.

Robinson also has two town lots assigned, very close to the main square, as well. Like Butler, he was given them as town-lot complement to his squatted land. In addition, he apparently bought four additional lots, spread all around the central square. Complementing these were three out lots just north of the Commons. He would thus have his original farmland on the bank, plus more acreage north of the town square.

Perhaps not unusually, "old claims" to land started surfacing after Redick's survey and eventual settling of the town. Butler and Robinson had become certainly comfortable in their land holdings on the banks of the Allegheny for several years now, and their claims were also confirmed by the Commonwealth. But old Garret Pendergrass would surface to claim what the Mingo Chiefs had given him fifteen years earlier. Valid as his land claim was, given its documentation in Bedford County archives, when Pendergrass went to claim his new land, "he was dispossessed by squatters already living on it." (Butler and Robinson did not budge, and apparently Pendergrass did not press the issue with the Commonwealth.)

As well, an Indenture of 1787 shows a claim by Thomas Girty and his wife, Anne, of Pittsburg, to General Richard Butler (also described as of Pittsburg):

> Whereas Johonisse Scanayadge and Cosswantinace, Chiefs or Sachems of the Six United Nations of Indians, by deed of 2 Aug 1749, did bargain and sell unto George Croghan Esq. in fee, a parcel of land situate on Eastern side of the River Ohio to the northward of an old Indian town called Shanopin Town at the mouth of a Run called Two Mile Run....

This land, though it apparently wasn't granted Girty, would have been the strip of land near Girtie's Run (the stomping ground of Thomas' renegade family member), near the back channel of the island in the Allegheny, all the way down, apparently, to Butler's (and thus Robinson's) property.

Girty tried to establish that Croghan gave the property to him, but neither that, nor the intrinsic claim that Croghan had any proprietary hold on that north bank, changed the state's mind. (CUMBERLAND COUNTY LAND RECORDS)

General William Irvine, Commander at Fort Pitt during Revolutionary War times, held at least five town lots and John Irwin, Esquire, would buy at least four—with out lots stationed toward the west end of the Tract, including along the edge of the Ohio.

Even David Redick, skeptical of the practicality of the land he was forced to survey, bought a lot—number 15—with corresponding out lot not far inland from the island in the Ohio River. And four lots, comprising a whole block near the southeast corner, as well as another northern lot, were purchased by Judge John Parke of Pittsburgh.

Nearby some of Parke's lots, an "Andrew Guyer of Philadelphia," who was involved in the shipping business of that city, purchased two, as well as two more considered prime, in the southwest of the public square. In purchasing the first two town lots, Guyer was given two out lots just to the east, by the river. For the prime town lots, he was assigned out lots up a westward hill, above Pasture Lane and Robinson's northern farmland above the Commons. This hill was actually the sloping westward perch of the great ridge to the west of the cleave above the town. So some out lots were indeed hillside lands looking down upon the Commons and other flat areas of the Reserved Tract. And like some other men buying several town lots, Guyer thus had both flat and hilly pasturage available to him.

That is, if Guyer and others ever moved from Philadelphia. Many who bought at the auction would find to their dismay, one year later, in 1788, that the citizens of Pittsburg protested far too much that the town across the way (now surely termed 'Allegheny Town') would get the county seat. Instead, it was decreed in this year that Pittsburg would forever be the fixed locale of Allegheny County. With that news, many who bought, especially being from the eastern area of Pennsylvania, renounced the pursuance of their warrant patents. They not only did not move out to the area, but lost interest in renting out or selling their land speculations in an area they deemed isolated and still of the wild.

James O'Hara of Pittsburg, who had earlier worked with Indian trader-turned-land surveyor Ephraim Douglas, would buy perhaps the most town lots, six in number. O'Hara would bear the title of quartermaster general with the army, with work that took him to the Ohio region. His interest in the land was certainly for speculative purpose, since he was quite successful with his munitions dealings. O'Hara had many out lots, dotted throughout the Tract. In addition, he had patented to him, in January of 1789, 155 acres and 50 perches (approximately 8.5 lots), entitled the *2nd Farm* of the Tract. As well, O'Hara would be granted patent, in the spring of 1789, to the full 312-acre *High Rough Land.*

Major Isaac Craig was a successful businessman who, along with Colonel Stephen Bayard, bought the land at the Point from the Penns. At the end of the 1780s, he also bought the eleventh town lot, next-door to one of James Robinson's. His out lot would thus be near those of Robinson's that were bordering the North Commons and Pasture Lane.

Escurius Beatty was another landowner of great proportion. The *3rd Farm* belonged to him, patented in October 1789. He also purchased numerous town lots and was afforded the very first (in numbering system) of the out lots—way up river furthest west in the Tract. As well, he owned a great number near that first out lot, to complement all his town holdings—all strung along the Ohio River's edge, including the pond in that area.

In some instances, it would appear that there were some land owners of out lots who did not hold corresponding town lots. One such case is that of Woods, who claimed that northern Reserved Tract land that was then numbered as out lots 198–218 and Lot 224. All would be patented to him—likely considered, but not labeled as, the *1st Farm.*

George Wallace would hold out lot 39, eastern neighbor to James Robinson's original land settlement, as well as several town lots. Also, on the eastern side of the Tract, a *5th Farm*, containing 402 acres and 62 perches was patented to Wallace in March 1789. (A *4th Farm* is oddly not shown.) A last, *6th Farm*, furthest northeast of the Tract, and extending to its eastern boundary beyond Girtie's Run, was *patented to George Wallace in right of William Turnbull the purchaser... containing 276 acres and 13 perches of Land Patent dated March 7, 1791.*

Wandel Keller and Hugh Ross would hold out lots that sat just in from the banks of the Ohio River and Smokey Island—the western end of the hump-shaped hill. They, however, did not reside there. Its only known inhabitants for years would be wild turkeys.

The last out lot of the Town of Allegheny, numbered 276, would go to Charles Wilkins, a man who held numerous town lots. It would be situated bordering the far west side of the Commons.

After the 1787 auction in Philadelphia, but before any activity would be seen taking place in the *Reserved Tract opposite Pittsburg*, Colonel John May and eleven others from the Point area rowed across the Allegheny in the Congress barge. It was May 1788. They visited the farm of Colonel Butler and, "among other objects of curiosity... went to see some Indian graves," lying west of his house on the property, toward the bank. This would have been Delaware George, two other natives buried in the previous 25 years, and a chief Kimtony, who apparently died a few days earlier. As grave markers, they found poles "daubed with red," according to May's journal, "left out of the ground as tall as the dead." (TRAVELER'S GUIDE)

chapter three:

FRONTIER TOWN &
RURAL COMMUNITY

For about five years after the auction of Allegheny Town lots, and the fixing of the locale of Allegheny County definitively in Pittsburg, the land north of the rivers was still anything but settled. The plots of land were now fixed, for the first time being apportionments claimed by the white man. No more would the wilderness there, which managed to come through the French & Indian War and American Revolution unscathed, be undisturbed. The land would slowly go through transformation according to the varied needs and desires of its individual inhabitants and collective intended purpose. But remnants of both thick woodlands and the native peoples who called it home remained for a little while longer.

Historians have found the early spelling of Pittsburg, the new county seat, to also be with an "h" at the end, and this is how the city, itself, formally presented itself. But the vast majority of pre-1800 maps and documents generated outside the city (from the State of Pennsylvania and in correspondence from those in other regions) spell the name with simply a "g" at the end. (See for example Figure 4 and Redick's correspondence—the latter taken directly from *Commonwealth Colonial Records*.) Then about half of such documents post-1800, up until about 1830, continued to show a "g" only at end. (For this reason, that the majority of primary Commonwealth sources cited in this text show only "g" until the additional "h" became evident at the later time, this text reflects that same "evolution" of the spelling used by Alleghenians and others outside of Pittsburg.)

The *Last Purchase* of 1784, which cleared the way for the making of a town in the Reserved Tract, did not convince the Indians that the land now belonged to individual men, part and parcel. Though most had now left, in despair over the staking of land by the whites, many still roamed this area. And some could not put the events of recent times past, when they were not only stripped of their land, but manipulated against each other as they tried

51

to sort out the ways of the white man. In particular, the awful event of 1782 stuck in the souls of several natives looking for retribution against Revolutionary War captains.

James Sample was one man targeted. He lived in a cabin with his wife and children in a remote, forested area just northeast of the Reserved Tract, near Peter Shafner's land. One day when Sample was out, some Indians arrived at his cabin and kidnapped his wife and children. Brought back to an Indian camp in a clearing in the woods, they were bound and forced to experience a torturous lead-up to death, not unlike that which Smokey Island entertained so much of. But apparently one of the Indian squaws recognized Mrs. Sample as someone who had paid her a recent kindness, in the brief dealings the natives of that area had with the whites. So, the family was luckily untied and led to safety by this squaw.

Chief Killbuck continued to exercise a different kind of control over his Killbuck Island, now—a peaceful coexistence with the new happenings on the north banks, planting his land with seeds of corn and grass. Once Allegheny Town would be birthed, he would even occasionally rent out portions of his land to the white man.

But because there were still Indian tensions for the expanse of land on the northern bank, the Commonwealth government and President George Washington put in action a soldier known for his willingness to combat the remaining natives. Starting about 1789, General "Mad Anthony" Wayne worked toward driving out remaining bands of tribes and individual native warriors on the frontiers of western Pennsylvania. In the early years of the 1790s, he was backed by munitions supplies and other support from James O'Hara. Toward the end of 1792, in the Allegheny Town area, his efforts were considered close to complete and successful. The only natives seeming to remain, a handful in number, were those willing to assimilate into the white man's vision of the land of the region.

Along with Mad Anthony Wayne's success had came the passage of another act that would enable more settling in all of southwestern Pennsylvania. The *Settler's Act of 1792* provided that anyone desiring land could easily apply for a specific parcel and obtain a warrant. After meeting specific conditions to cultivate, improve, and settle the land, within building and occupancy requirements, a patent would be handed out, showing final claim and ownership. With regard to Allegheny Town, this Act was a specific attempt to fill in the gaps of unpurchased land, but also address all the land bought at auction, which five years later was still not seeing human face nor gathering tax revenue.

And though Wayne had worked his way through the region, it would still be until the end of 1795 that Allegheny truly started becoming a town. Finally, then, the little center square of land saw some initial landowners arriving. The first would be those who had lived across the way in Pittsburg. They came across on Robinson's ferry and began to clear their plots and build timber structures for their homes. Those coming from Philadelphia way would arrive shortly thereafter, as the all-clear that had been given, was finally believed—that the land was free of natives. The speculators, those less interested in inhabiting, but rather renting out their land, would come, too, from both areas. They began to build, in order to make money off those taking ferry's and Conestoga wagon's passage to start a new life.

A small but steady influx of settlers began arriving to the north side of the river. About this time, in 1796, the Commonwealth laid out the first real road in Allegheny Town, on top of the dirt road through Robinson's property and up through the town square. Except for its middle section right through the town, it was named the Franklin Road, because the Indian path it was laid upon, the Venango Trail, extended all the way to Fort Franklin (once past the cleave of the two hills and followed upward along the ridge).

But it seems only a smattering of individuals whose names would be transposed onto the Reserved Tract lots as *owners* would actually end up peopling the north side of the rivers. Many had just given up the idea of seeing their claim through, after the letdown that Allegheny Town would not be bestowed 'County Seat,' and was essentially not known as much of anything at that point. Apparently their claims to the land were now difficult to sell off even to those looking for a speculation.

To the few settlers who were now in Allegheny Town, however, the seed of what would be their town was planted, and the land was far more than *nothing* to them. Their focus was on clearing the land as per Redick's survey and putting up houses. Their thoughts would soon turn to the public structures that were to make up the town, as well.

The wilderness of the Reserved Tract would begin to thin, slowly, and just in spots at first, with the beginning being the town lots and Commons. The commons land would be their only pasturage space, until time permitted exploration and transformation of the out lots assigned each town lot owner.

Settlers were specifically granted, by an act established when the survey

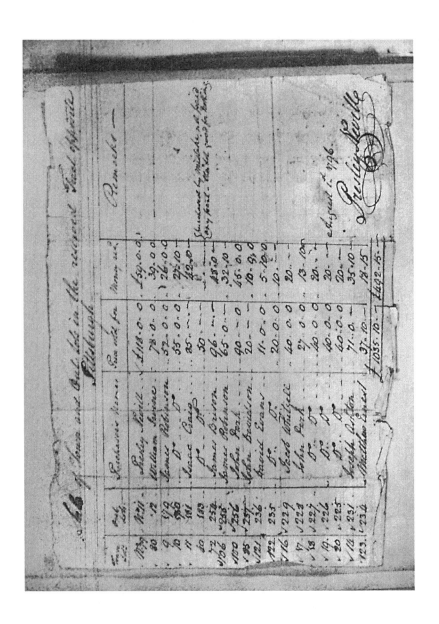

was decreed, the right to graze their cattle, collectively, in the Commons, as well as mutual right of passage. Slowly, the actual land of the Reserved Tract was starting to look like the survey on paper that Redick had drawn up a decade earlier. The population would soon reach about 150, the same as frontier Pittsburg of three decades earlier.

Approaching the year 1796, the remaining Reserved Tract land would be auctioned off in Philadelphia. Records would continue in the manner of the previous auction listing. Also in this year, Allegheny Town, as it was north of the rivers and west of Pine Creek, temporarily became part of Pine Township. (Previously having been of the larger area known as Pitt Township.)

It was in 1796, as well, that Mad Anthony Wayne's forces, still working in areas further west of the Reserved Tract, camped for a few weeks before winter on the northside land, around the West Commons area. Part of the territory just to the northwest of the Reserved Tract at this time was still referred to as *Indian Incamping Ground* on some regional maps, and it was this ground that Wayne was on his way to.

Across the river, Pittsburg had become a borough in 1794. And by the late 1790s, it had been seeing the gradual dismantling of Fort Pitt, and the rise of the primitive coal industry, especially across the Monongahela on the great mount, named Coal Hill. Only the brick redoubt of the Fort, and the lines of earth marking the walls, remained.

In 1790, Robert Elliot and Eli Williams had been granted patent to McKee's Island (the one purchased by Thomas Smallman a decade earlier). It sat in the Ohio, just off the bank near the western out lots. At the turn of the nineteenth century, they no longer would own the island. But Robert and a relative, Daniel Elliott, would be known for operating a ferry across the Ohio, at a point a little east of this island. Pittsburg surgeon Felix Brunot, born of French father and Native American mother, would acquire the island in 1797. With this acquisition, it would ever be known as Brunot's, even though he, too, would sell it a few short years later.

The rivers in the middle of the decade were at low water level, as a little island west of Butler's property, and east of Killbuck Island, showed again on

Figure 14 (opposite). 1796 Allegheny Town auction record

a map of the time, but with just a peninsula (and not a third island) on the far eastern end.

Islands, and one hundred acres at-a-time of riverbeds (the latter with valuable mineral deposits) were treated as separate land parcels of the Reserved Tract. Attention to their sale would be a short time after the In and Out lots were sold, and with the provision that both navigation on the rivers would not be disrupted, nor the underlying beds themselves disturbed. Being that two of the Reserved Tract's islands already had a lineage of sale, only the easternmost island, with slim back channel, would be available around this timeframe.

As Allegheny Town was in its earliest years, other areas of the Depreciation Lands, northeast and northwest of the Reserved Tract, began to be populated, but at an equally slow pace. Large swaths of land were patented as farms to a handful of individual men who would later divide up the land into small plots. The Venango Trail was the artery cutting northward through the wilderness and hills, connecting with some of this land.

Following the footsteps of Peter Shafner in the Depreciation Land area (just northeast of what would be George Wallace's out lots), men such as William Wilson and George Wallace, also, bought more land surveyed by Douglas. Just as within the Reserved Tract, there were competing claims to some of those lands, since there had been infamous trappers in some of those areas.

Caspar Reel was one such trader surely known to those beginning to people the land north of the rivers. He was a skin dresser far beyond where the Venango Trail cut through Escurius Beatty's and General James O'Hara's property, then passed Wilson's and Wallace's land, into further wilderness. He would soon enough, especially under new Commonwealth guidelines, be granted a 727-acre farm for his claims to some of the land.

In fact, in it had been recorded in 1786 that the Penn heirs had sold that very land to Casper Reel, "of Pitt Twp., Westmoreland Co." for 10 pounds. Apparently, though, this land was once claimed part of John Wood's acreage. If so, Woods' land interest actually extended further east than would end up being granted to him after the auction. It likely was co-opted by interests purchased by the influential O'Hara and Beatty.

John McCaslin, too, was a hunter and trapper who had roamed the surrounding wilderness and would come to be known by early Allegheny Town inhabitants. His home territory was north beyond Peter Shafner's land.

In addition to his accompanying out lots 179 and 180, James Robinson had also participated in buying more land, in the early 1790s. He had land patented to him further northwest, down-river along the Ohio, which began to slowly be another route used to stake out Depreciation Land territory. The name for Robinson's first additional tracts were *Sandy Bottom*, immediately northwest of Hugh Brackenridge's territory, and just northeast of that, *Rigmaroll*. Those that could afford it, like Robinson, bought up parcels as they became available, even though the land would long be attended to.

At the end of the 1790s, a very early industry developed just east of Robinson's original farmland. Close by the river, William Hays established a tannery. The Reverend Joseph Stockton also came over from Pittsburg to teach in a frame schoolhouse nearby, on the east side of the Franklin Road, which would be across from the Robinson homestead. Close by where Andrew Long's cabin had sat, west of Robinson and Butler's homes, would be the First Presbyterian Church of Allegheny, and this lay just south of the *Burying Ground* that Redick established and which served as potter's field to the entire early town.

In 1798, the State Legislature considered raising money for much-needed piers where Robinson's ferry landing was. This was due to the great height differential between the landing spots on the bank and the shore, which was rapidly eroded by current. James and Martha Robinson were beginning to do so well, in the business of transporting people to and from the area, that they would be able to have the first brick structure of the town erected. Their new home would sit on a northern portion of their land in the early 1800s. At this residence, they would also maintain an inn for the visiting public. The ferry house sat on the east of the Franklin Road, along the bank; the log cabin built in the 1790s stood on the west side.

The land plots of Allegheny Town and immediate surrounding, based on Redick's survey, would suit the town well up until about 1815 or so. There was no need to divide up larger land holdings into subplots yet.

Allegheny Town at the turn of the nineteenth century was attempting to reach 300 in population. On lots long before earmarked for them, humble log houses had sprung, as well as early structures for business. By this time, the out lots in what had still been wilderness were beginning to be cleared of

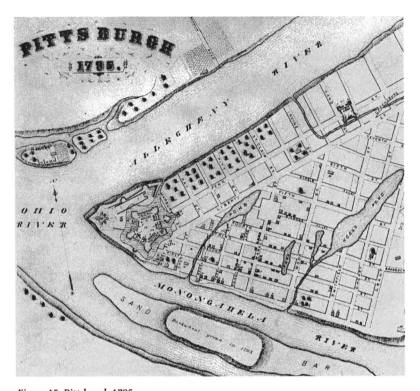

Figure 15. Pittsburgh 1795

dense trees and made useful. Settlers were traveling out, on dirt lanes marked by Redick's survey markings, to areas furthest out from the center of town. Pasture Lane, heading northward on the west of town, would have been foot and horse-traveled at this time, and the out lots westward were explored.

On out lot 13, one of many of General Irvine's lots, a glass works was started, considered the first of any industrial plant west of the Allegheny River. This was just opposite the tip of Brunot's Island in the Ohio. The point where it stood was called 'Glass House Riffle,' where dangerous, fast water flowed inward from the Ohio River (nonetheless good for the making of glass). It was first operated by Dr. Hugh Scott, but sold in 1801 to Ebenezer Denny and Anthony Beelen. Dr. Scott would then have a drugstore in the area.

Scott was a busy man; the same year, he had just been elected post-master. As for the glass factory, it would not survive beyond 1802, perhaps

Figure 16. Hump-Shaped Hill, First Presbyterian Church & Barlow House, circa 1800

because both Denny and Beelen wore many hats, as well, in that era when enterprising businessmen were chomping at the bit to start fortunes on the virgin land.

Though little survives to officially document it, Allegheny Town in the early 1800s had started organizing itself collectively as a town. In addition to setting up structures to live and work in, the few early settlers pulled together a Town Council, and it was this Council in 1801 that gave Scott his new title. Town officials met at Robert Campbell's White Horse Tavern, until a town hall would later be built.

Roads in the town square were named. The short part of the Franklin Road that went straight through the square was patriotically named Federal Street. Running east to west was Ohio Street (along the other Indian trail, the *Great Path*), and bordering the town were Union on the east, Montgomery on the north, Webster on the west, and a road already referred to as 'Second Bank' on the south, as the land there echoed the lower river bank, with a rather abrupt, small embankment.

At the turn of the century, two more counties were carved from Allegheny—Butler and Beaver, in the north regions of the Depreciation and Donation Lands. Areas just immediately north of Allegheny Town also had their share of early pioneers and were beginning to see the seed of small frontier communities. The land north and east of the Reserved Tract would, by the end of the first decade, come to be Ross Township. This happened as the Franklin Road slowly introduced people to the northern reaches of the wilderness, and as settlers also slowly came from regions along the upper Allegheny River to settle there.

In 1801, mail delivery via stagecoach came once a week to Allegheny Town. A plow works, near Robinson's inn and the White Horse Tavern on the Franklin Road, would soon begin operation. And apparently a primitive block house for some remaining Native Americans was built on the far West Commons at this time. It would later become a school.

Chief Killbuck decided to sell his island in 1803, but he had no official paper title to the land. He drew up a deed, himself, however, that November, showing the sale for $200. It would be to Abner Barker, who was related to a descendant of Thomas Smallman, through marriage. Killbuck's deed described the land as, "A certain island situate in the Allegheny River nearly opposit to the Point in the Borough of Pittsburg known by the name of Killbuck's (or Smokey Island) containing about thirty acres." Felix Brunot also sold his island this year to Charles Cumming, who cleared the land, fertilized the soil, and started a truck gardening business.

Killbuck's deed, however, went unrecorded, and something would go wrong between the Indian chief, Barker and the State. For, just fourteen months later, Killbuck petitioned the governor that "an indisputable written title for ever to Killbuck's Island near Pittsburg" just be given to himself. Apparently, he was addressing the State's claim that he was never entitled to the land in the first place. Killbuck defended himself, writing that Colonel Gibson had given the island to him, "in the name of the Commonwealth of Pennsylvania," as "sole property" on which to clear, plough and plant, and that the island is "known to this day by the name of Killbuck's Island."

(BOTHWELL)

Killbuck even declared that Gibson's successor, General Irvine, recognized the land grant. Before Gibson granted it to him, the chief mentions that all the people of his Nation had already considered it his land. Most importantly to him, though, was that he "remained faithful to the Americans as long as the Revolutionary War continued... in the service of the United States; and I have continued to be their firm friend ever since." He stated that he never thought his original title to the land could ever be in dispute, as he thought a written title "not necessary after having heard the words and promises" of the "great men" who assured him of the land. Killbuck expressed toward appeal's end that he wanted nothing but "the little island" that he truly felt had been his for some time.

To get word back and forth, to and from the State Legislature would take some time, and years would would pass before Killbuck's situation regarding the island would be resolved. He did hear word from the Governor by June 1806, when he was instructed to make application to the Land Office of the Commonwealth for his island. Meanwhile, his primitive deed to Abner Barker was somehow on its way to being recorded in Allegheny County land holding offices. The whole matter, confused, and like others related to northern land claims, simply did not resolve in any neat fashion. Nor would it resolve before Chief Killbuck would die, in 1811. He would be buried underneath a mulberry bush high on the western bank above the Ohio, not far from his cherished little island—one that was symbolic of the last real tie to the Native Americans and the unbroken wilderness.

Beyond mail delivery, a regular stagecoach service would be established from Pittsburg to Philadelphia in 1804. Here, fifteen years after the sale of Allegheny Town lots, would some of the original landowners (whose names appeared on the overlay map circa 1789), or their heirs, finally come to southwestern Pennsylvania to see their purchase on the Allegheny River's north side. A great deal of the land that was assigned purchaser in the earlier years indeed still sat vacant come this time.

The majority of Allegheny's earliest settlers, unlike the few that set up businesses and early manufacturing, were farmers, living off the countryside. Once cleared, the land of the town site, including Commons and nearest out lots, would appear as flat, sunshine-filled pasturage. A transformation was occurring over the thick woodlands that spread across the whole of the lower Reserved Tract. The hillsides, too, very slowly, were thinning of woods, as out lots were tackled here and there by those landowners who could easily make it up to those areas. The livestock brought to the land included chickens, cows and pigs, and they grazed on and roamed about the Commons land. The settlers lived, simply, off the land. Their life was centered about their town. They were proud, early on, of their town businesses and industrial efforts. When a family member perished, they were buried, simply, in the part of the land assigned as the *Burying Ground*.

In 1809, an early market house was deemed a necessity, since Allegheny Town's population had reached 450. Across the way, Pittsburg already had over fifty stores open to the public. Blacksmiths and butchers began to establish themselves around Allegheny.

Allegheny Town's existence was uniquely urban/rural around this time— small business interests in its town center that would be found in any early American town or village, with the addition of impressive early industry, but also distinctively paired with country life.

By 1815, the town had begun to shed its frontier image, and slowly established itself as a rural community known for its farmland and early industry, surrounding a sound town center. It would be different in identity to the town of Pittsburg across the river, which was far less rural, with town center more built up. Pittsburg, within the Point area, was decidedly urban and would even remain a garrison town until after 1812. Due to lingering Indian fears, a Fort Fayette was erected up near the Allegheny bank, around Penn Avenue at 9th and 10th Streets, after Fort Pitt was demolished for good. Only further out its east end would Pittsburg have land area similar to the look and feel of the land just north of the rivers.

William Robinson, the declared first-born of white northside settlers back in 1785, was a young man of twenty-five in 1810. Like his father, he now purchased desired land further north. Immediately east of *Rigmaroll* would be the son's *Pine Grove*. This land was part of the wilderness that the fur trader Caspar Reel traversed and was given title to many years earlier. But Reel that same year, in 1810, would be apparently satisfied by being given official patent to two tracts, entitled *Caledonia* and *Reel Hall*, just northeast of the young Robinson's.

Transportation by steam boat along the rivers had begun in 1811, and provincial Allegheny Town would continue to slowly expand. Though the steam boat was appreciated, aspirations had been surfacing for a bridge to be built between Allegheny Town and Pittsburg, though it would be a decade in coming. Transportation to and from Pittsburg was still time-consuming.

In the early teen years of the nineteenth century, a 'Rope Walk' was relocated from Pittsburg to the west side of the town area, not too far from where Elliott's ferry was now operational. John Irwin would be the proprietor of the business.

In a long, narrow building on the very last out lot, number 276, rope was made by walking the strands the length of the building while weaving. The map of 1789, which transposed original owners' names onto Redick's layout, has Charles Wilkins, Pittsburg merchant, owning this property. But he sold it a mere three years after the auction, in 1790. The new owner would be John Irwin, Sr., though the Rope Works would not go up until twenty-one years later by his son, John Jr. He would do so well as to expand it over the years to adjoining lots that he rented from Harmar Denny. (Denny had purchased the four large out lots, and even others, owned by James Morrison, just west of the Commons.)

During the War of 1812, Allegheny Town would again witness military forces en route to areas north in the Commonwealth, since war materials were being shipped north to Lake Erie. Two thousand soldiers needed to camp on the North Common and all the trees still left standing in the pasturage of the Commons were cut down.

Commodore Perry was commissioned to build a fleet in the Great Lake during the War of 1812, and he had cordage made at Irwin's Rope Walk. He would travel the Franklin Road north, numerous times, through the cleave of the hills and up and around the old Indian trail.

John Irwin did very well with his business, not just with Perry as a customer. Irwin had a large house bordering the West Commons. In 1816, he would partition and give some of the land to his daughters, Elizabeth and Margaret. The Rope Walk was a well-known fixture now of Allegheny Town. Its success helped influence the period after 1813 to be one with more early industry starting up and succeeding in that area west of Pasture Lane. Even though America was in a postwar depression, with Pittsburg industries certainly feeling the crunch, Allegheny Town was finally on a growth spurt, so many years after its conception. In fact, many enterprises began moving from Pittsburg to Allegheny at this time.

Not far from Irwin's Rope Walk, but north of the Commons (in what was out lot number 181 of Isaac Craig), a very early Allegheny subdivided plan of lots would be drawn up by Neville Craig in 1815—*Mechanic's Retreat*. It would be for worker's housing, accommodations for the many who were about to be employed in Allegheny's blossoming industrial sector.

Abner Barker's residing on Killbuck Island had come to a close not long after Killbuck's death, and a mere ten years after being granted the disputed title. By the year 1817, while the island still resembled in some ways the wilderness that the whole area once was, David Morgan, along with his pregnant wife and child, arrived from New York City, built a shanty and camped there. They were at first not used to the owl hoots, and the "melancholy cry of the loon sporting in the waters of the Allegheny." (Maps of the area around the island, from about 1815 to 1832, would show it having company once again, with not only *Kilbuck* listed, but *Low* island, and a small unnamed island, as well as a *Sand Bar at Low Water*.)

In a few years, a terrible fire devoured the family's shanty, witnessed by neighbor Jacob Cupp and his wife. Morgan and his wife lost their four children, and would be gone from the area by about 1829.   (BOTHWELL)

In 1818, Allegheny Town had seen the building of a state penitentiary on the West Commons. The Commons was unique land. Only in New England states could other Commons land be found. But the specially-designated land, with its benefits to the town's residents, created a buffer—only *beyond* that area could the town expand.

With the decision to build a penitentiary, the original purpose of the Commons land was essentially co-opted by legislators. Instead of keeping the area solely for pasturage, the legislature had opened the door for it to be divided up for even private usage.

The West Common, which had already been used as a military station, now would see further public service. The penitentiary would sit right beyond Sherman Street, at about the spot where had the partially-built homesteads of Andrew Long's comrades. The octagonal building was built of the gray sandstone so prevalent in the area, in Norman style, with two circular sentry towers. There were high exterior walls enclosing an open courtyard for prisoners' exercise. The first prisoner would enter in 1826.

With precedent set just a year earlier, trustees of the Pittsburg Academy asked for land in 1819, in order for their school to come across the river from small buildings near the Point. But it would not happen that the Academy would relocate at this time, because they saw major protest coming from the citizens of Allegheny regarding the Commons land infringements. They would continue to try, however.

The Academy, established in 1787, would have its charter redone that very year of 1819, when they became the Western University of Pennsylvania.

The charter actually read that the University should "be erected and established near the town of Allegheny." It went further to posit that the State Legislature had long ago intended for the educational institution to be on the Reserved Tract, just as they had intended for Allegheny to be the county seat. The Academy should sit, the charter stated, on "forty acres of the vacant land belonging to the Commonwealth, bounded by or adjoining the out-lots of the town of Allegheny." Written histories later would support this, as the University was to have been "the first chartered school of higher education west of the Allegheny Mountains and north of the Ohio River."

Sometime between about 1815 and the end of the 1820s, original land plots, as described by Redick, began to slowly evolve into subdivisions. Maps from the latter end of this timeframe show residential and even light manufacturing uses for much of the land area south of the town proper, especially that belonging to Robinson. At first glance, the new subdivided area appears even more tightly condensed than Allegheny Town's grid. Robinson obviously decided to section off parcels of his farmland to new settlers and businesses desiring to be established there. Structures went up rapidly, with a later map showing much development having occurred during this timeframe.

Robinson sold his holdings from the Franklin Road east to Sandusky Street, to someone named McDonald, who then rented out the land. This would be from river's edge, or Bank Lane, north to the South Commons. Isabella Street would be a new road, parallel to Bank Lane, that would be named early on—likely after a wife or daughter in someone's family. Beyond Sandusky Street, Robinson continued to maintain holdings which he had picked up from Peter Whiteside and George Wallace, at least through 1830. The eastern boundary here was Guyasuta Lane, to become Anderson Street.

Robinson's holdings directly north of his homestead, up to the South Commons, would be subdivided as well. In the middle block of the land, in a large area, he would allow for the Pittsburgh Cotton Factory to be established.

Evidence of Butler's presence on the land, except perhaps for a lot off Pasture Lane, disappears after about 1810. Many divided lots extended over to where the hump-shaped hill began. Kilbuck Street was laid out parallel to the river in the far western blocks of this area, dead-ending at the curved inlet of water that, if there were a footbridge, would take one over to *Low* Island and then on to Killbuck Island. The Juniata Rolling Mill and the Allegheny

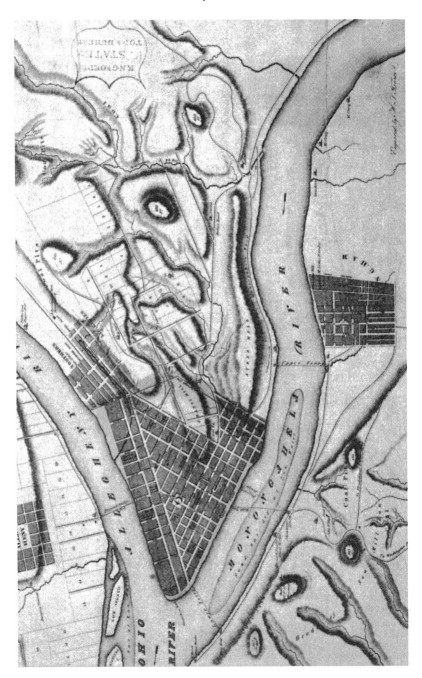

Steam Saw Mill were located within these many small blocks. As well, Irwin's further property at the southern foot of the hill was subdivided. Just south of these new property lines was another (western) *Bank Lane*, close to the high-water mark.

The year 1819 saw the opening of the Pittsburgh-Butler Turnpike. It was a dirt road that followed Ohio Street eastward out of Allegheny Town (over top the *Great Path*), paralleling the Allegheny River up until the large Pine Creek Valley where Guyasuta once ruled. From there another roadway would extend due northward. Far south of Ohio Street and east of the Commons, over to East Lane and previous holdings of George Wallace and Andrew Guyer, would now be many residential blocks, as well. These were tenement-type structures, even more tightly condensed perhaps than *Mechanic's Retreat*, and they were built to house workers from the Hope Cotton Mill. This factory was nearby, close to Bank Lane. The little development was called *Hopeville*, after the factory.

Southeast of the town square, north of Second Bank and just south of Ohio Street, was an area of development that was also subdivided about this time. Lothrop (narrower), Washington and Liberty were the names given three streets sectioned out on property originally belonging to Fowler, Hubley and Whiteside.

Close to 1820, public debate intensified over the necessity of an appropriate bridge to span the Allegheny River. General William Robinson was the preeminent citizen (and perhaps the only one with adequate financial resources) to advance capital, foreseeing a return on his investment. He had a few years earlier formed the Allegheny Bridge Company, which was granted a state charter in 1816. In the year 1820, the first bridge between Allegheny Town and Pittsburg was built, a wooden structure with six arches over stone piers. Costing $75,000, and called the Allegheny River Bridge, it joined the Franklin Road with St. Clair St. across the river.

With the bridge built, the town no longer struggled with transportation problems, moving into an era beyond ferry and steamship transport alone. (The ferry house was still in existence, and likely operational, however, until about 1827.) The population around this time would be approaching 600.

Despite its limited early industrial success, Allegheny prior to this time would still be best known for its agricultural-based economy. The building of

Figure 17 (opposite). 1815 "Darby" map

the first bridge marked the end of a time when the mention of "Allegheny" evoked images of pastoral land.

The northern bank of land in the 1820s saw the area open up industrially—especially far west by the Ohio River, and in areas right along the Allegheny River, southeast of the town. Small-factory cotton mills opened in the early 1820s, and the end of the decade witnessed the start of the iron industry. The Juniata Rolling Mill was established not far from the Robinson homestead.

The mid-1820s brought a variety of activity in and about Allegheny Town. Adjacent to the site of Chief Killbuck's burial place of 1811, a Reverend Hopkins built a mansion and named it Killbuck to honor the famed native. As well, he built a school adjacent. Activities at this grand home were surely written about socially in the pages of Allegheny's first newspaper, the *Allegheny Democrat*. Also on the west side of the Town, far west of Pasture Lane and heading toward the Ohio River, the Borough of Pittsburg bought a coveted ten-acre lot for a Poor House, as they had been eyeing land areas of Allegheny Town for this purpose.

Backed by citizen protest, in 1824, the question of rightful possession of Commons land was put before the Supreme Court of the Commonwealth. The court favored the citizens and ruled against the Western University of Pennsylvania, which had still been trying hard to get land appropriated to them, and did not want to stop even with this judgment. Despite the ruling, amazingly, Commons land would *again* be wrongly given for private use just one year later—to a different entity, one that had ties, in the Reverend Joseph Stockton, to the University. What was granted was a tract of land to the Presbyterian Church for a theological seminary. This was southwest of the Penitentiary, running along the northern base of what had started to be referred to as "Hogback Hill" come this time, by the citizens. Its resemblance was supposedly too similar to the animal that was in large numbers running rampant not only on the Commons, but on the town streets.

A new small church was also built right past the northwestern edge of Allegheny Town, and south of this, at the eastern base of the hill, a log cabin school *also* presided over by Reverend Stockton would be even further out onto the Commons. (When Stockton first came to Allegheny, he preached a sermon under a tree just north of the new church site, then likely helped establish a supposed blockhouse to teach Native Americans nearby, before having the First Presbyterian Church erected at the base of the hill.) The log cabin school of the 1820s was considered the Allegheny Academy.

A few years later, trustees of the Presbyterian Church inflamed citizens by having some lot owners somehow sign over portions of their Commons rights, which legally was impossible, since the Commons was cooperative in nature. The land they targeted now was atop the Hogback Hill.

It was also looking like forty acres of Commons ground, at the same time, was about to be formally granted to the Western University of Pennsylvania by the State Legislature. Unfortunately, after the several infringements unto Commons land, some private citizens living and working in the town square also started extending their homes into Commons territory, or boldly erecting new, adjacent structures on the bordering Commons land.

Things would come to a head when the Presbyterian Church formally announced its desire to expand on the Commons, and citizens of other faiths, including Methodists, Episcopalians and Roman Catholics, who had been arriving in Allegheny Town, protested. The furor caused the town council to declare that any property infringing on the original decree of Commons land for pasturage, short of the penitentiary, be relinquished. The private infringements had to go, the Presbyterian Church gave up its advance (except for plans for the land atop Hogback Hill), and the Western University also realized it needed to stop looking at Commons property across the river for their promised land.

At this time, Presbyterians were the majority in Allegheny Town; most of those who signed an act allowing the expansion in the first place were indeed Presbyterians. Around this same timeframe, St. Clare's Academy for Young Ladies was established by Sister Frances Vande Vogal—on sixty acres northeast of the Franklin Road, before the cleave of the hills. The majority of land that this Academy held was on what had been James McClelland's land and the southwestern corner of James O'Hara's *High Rough Land*.

It was here that likely the first structure on one of Allegheny Town's many peaks was indeed erected. The school was actually a convent, with fourteen nuns, founded by the Flemish order of St. Clare, and the building was a long, gray structure that sat on this hill which they named Mount Alvernio. The citizens of Allegheny Town would more simply call it *Nunnery Hill*. As the religious order was faced with internal disagreement, Mt. Alvernio was left deserted by 1835—but not before Maximilian, Prince of Wied, commented favorably upon the institution, seen from below as he passed through Allegheny Town.

By the mid-1820s, other areas close to Allegheny, including one named for Commodore Perry's numerous passages, were seeing their small populations growing as well. Perrysville, just north of the Reserved Tract via the Franklin Road, and closely tied to Caspar Reel's history on that land, blossomed as a village at this time.

By 1825, Allegheny certainly no longer felt like a frontier town. And it hardly felt, too, like the rural community it had been in its recent past. Socially, it would enter into an early golden era. That year, General Lafayette was on tour of America. He was lavishly entertained at the home of Thomas and Frances Preble Barlow, which sat on the western edge of the Second Bank, not far from the eastern foot of Hogback Hill. In attendance that night were all of Allegheny and Pittsburg's political and social elite.

chapter four:
THE BOROUGH OF ALLEGHENY

The Second Bank, especially closer to the town center, was where many of Allegheny's wealthy had built beautiful homes just before the cotton mills moved in, adjacent southward, in the early 1820s. But by mid-decade Allegheny Town was growing rapidly due to new neighbor, industry. Approaching the year 1828, the population reached over 1,000. An influx of workers came with the additional commerce, and some of the affluent industrialists and merchants began to build both more elegant town and 'country' homes, those past the Commons. This occurred especially on the west, near Ohio and Webster and past the West Commons on Water Lane. (This was Redick's *Castle Lane*, which never seemed to retain its originally-conceived name.)

Though considered far more civilized than of forty years prior, Allegheny (and even Pittsburg) was still thought of as quasi-primitive to those living in the eastern section of the Commonwealth. That is, until travel would take them to the newly-prosperous town. In the late 1820s, Allegheny was a nice stopover to points westward, now the new frontier.

On April 14th of 1828, Allegheny Town filed papers with the Pennsylvania State Legislature to incorporate into a borough. This would be granted, changing Allegheny's status forty-one years after the town survey. Not all of the out lots, connected to the original Town Lots, would be included in the new boundary lines. Only about one-third of the Reserved Tract—all of which had indeed been surveyed into farms or out lots of Allegheny Town— would be included in the borough's markings. This was likely due to lack of development, still, of the land furthest north, east, and west.

Allegheny Borough would end at East Lane, and just below the hills' cleave at the north of town. The western boundary was unusual; its northern end on the far west end of town was very shallow into the Tract, just north of the Rope Works at Water Lane. But after cutting in at Pasture lane, it extended further northward to a line that would extend to just below the hills' cleave.

In May, townsmen met still at the old White Horse Tavern, since a Town Hall had not yet been built. There, they appointed borough executives and elected council. John Irwin was named Burgess; President of Council was James Brown. Among the other eight councilmen was Robert Campbell, whose tavern had played such a large role in Allegheny's politics and identity with travelers to the area. It had a wide porch where visiting farmers would offer their produce, and a large side-yard where horse and cattle were displayed for sale. Above the tavern, there were lodging rooms. The White Horse was still popular through the 1830s, as was Hugh Davis' store and tavern, on lot number 40 at the northwest corner of Federal Street and Water Alley. Other taverns, come this time, were also doing good business. There was the W.H. Tavern, the Slab Tavern that went up across from the White Horse on Federal Street, and the Bull's Head Tavern, southwest of Ohio and Arch Street. (As such, the latter crossed over into Commons territory.)

With the opening of the Erie Canal, up north, a noticeable lack of commerce traffic had begun to affect Allegheny businesses. Soon there was talk of another needed canal through the Commonwealth.

Thus at the same time that Allegheny became a Borough, another major development happened for the people living in the *Reserved Tract opposite Pittsburg*. Construction of the Pennsylvania Canal through to the southwestern section of the state began and was completed in 1829.

The western destination brought the Canal right to the Borough of Allegheny. It came in along the banks of the Allegheny River, with locks and a Lock Tender's House on the east, and ended in a 90-degree turn into a basin, not far northwest of James Robinson's homestead, at that point in the land that had been Colonel Butler's swampy land. The area around the basin would fast become a commercial hub, with the location of warehouses associated with shipping and commerce, as well as numerous transportation company offices. After the southward turn at the basin, the Canal went through a lift lock and an outlet lock, and then ran straight into the Allegheny River, just about where the evident stream was in Butler's land circa 1780.

Pittsburg once again complained that Allegheny was granted something that they, instead, should have and political pressure was exerted on the Canal commissioners to have the terminus end in Pittsburg. Though a route on the southern, or Pittsburg, bank of the Allegheny was not as economically or geographically feasible (as pointed out by engineers who had worked on the Erie Canal) Pittsburg still disputed the proposed route and delayed the project. But this time Allegheny would win out, with the original terminus basin being granted.

Pittsburg protested enough, however, that, at a spot just after the canal's entry and locks in Allegheny, an aqueduct, "an enormous wooden trough with a roof," ran southward across the river into Pittsburg. With the aqueduct in place, yet another basin was added on the Pittsburg side.

The massive canal project employed many workers, who at times had to deal with making a major embankment for where the Canal was to pass over low ground. As well, the embankment would be along both sides of the Canal, separating it from the early lanes and streets laid out in the area.

Certain streets, only in their infancy in Allegheny, were dislocated, and many small bridges were built to carry other streets over the Canal. This included a bridge over Anderson Street, and the Franklin Road below the town square, where the Canal was 12 feet below street grade. The latter initially had a wooden bridge, but later a stone arch that at present day still lies buried underneath modern change to the area. After the Canal turned due southward beyond the basin, there was another bridge over Robinson Street (what the unnamed lane marking the northern boundary of his homestead came to be known).

A lot of these workers came to the area from a variety of european countries. From an etching of the period (from the same series as upcoming Figure 23), it appears that the workers were housed, again tenement-style, in row structures tightly condensed, particularly east of East Lane and north of Liberty Street. But much of the entire area east and south of the town housed canal workers. Eventually, even with the work completed, many settled in Allegheny and the surrounding land.

The Canal meant many things to the people of Allegheny. Passengers came down river to visit or pass through the city, and barges of coal, lumber, hay and other materials came en masse. This opened up manufactory and the marketplace for the Borough of Allegheny, and all of its adjacent territory in the Reserved Tract. Tremendous job growth was evidenced, as now even more warehouses, shops, mills and factories sprang up.

In 1829, on a day just before the Canal opened in Allegheny, a street was graded near where the Canal dumped into the river, beyond the the basin. Something fascinating was unearthed there for several schoolboys watching the construction. The remains of four skeletons, along with copper rings and other ornamentation, were discovered. That ground, transformed in the last couple decades from Colonel Butler's original property, was the very spot of the Indian cemetery that sat south of the town burying grounds. In the years when it had been divided into subplots, it obviously lost its once-decorative poles, which marked the spot of a forgotten time, where Kimtony and several others rested, on land to them forever sacred.

On this day in the fall of 1829, testament of the original residents of the land, long before the white man took over, had indeed surprisingly surfaced. One of the skeletons, in fact, was not plainly in the earth, as the others, but was in a wooden coffin "secured with iron nails." This would have been Delaware George, buried twenty-five years before the others, in 1762, with a coffin provided for by George Croghan.

The first canal traffic made its way ceremoniously into the Borough in 1829. Close to four million tons of freight were shipped on an average week. Paper, iron and saw mills, as well as brick-making plants and numerous tanneries, would come into existence. More taverns and stores also began to open about the town center.

The borough council and other executive officials realized they were very behind in constructing the official public buildings required for a prosperous town. Early construction bonds were taken out and plans began for the long-talked of Town Hall, which, when completed would be called the 'Town House.' A new Market House, to replace the structure of twenty years earlier, and a Fire Company were planned.

The borough politicians also looked at passing ordinances dealing with new, and in some cases, continued nuisances around the turn of this decade. Hogs were ordered to be securely on their owners property, and a boy was employed in the Commons to oversee the townspeople's cows. The governing of the Borough fell to the Burgess and Council, as well as numerous others including the Constable, Tax Collectors, Street Commissioner, Clerk of Market, Weigh-Master, and Inspector and Measurer of Coal.

There are other land areas that are shown, on an 1830 map, to have had major subdivision occur around the time of the Borough's making. This would be the area north of the town square, and north and east of Robinson's original out lots numbered 179 and 180. Father and son had not yet done anything with either, beyond maintaining pasturage. Small in area, north of the town square, intense residential development with subdivided lots took place on what before was mostly farmland, except for the developed *Mechanic's Retreat*. (Similar development would also then occur in this area on lots owned by John Irwin.)

Residents of these new sections above North Commons would be tenants on Robinson's and Irwin's land. The majority of structures that were built were very modest, for stable hands and others who maintained livestock and worked other sections of the surrounding land plot, for the town's wealthy. The houses sat on dirt roads the size of alleys, and the farmland they worked occupied the rest of the area. Jackson Street would be made, running east to west from the Franklin Road to an area on Pasture Lane known as Snyder's Hollow, after a man who owned a couple land parcels in that area by this time.

North and east of the town square, James Robinson's other property, as well as land originally held by James McClelland, had been sold to a Fleming and Boyle by about the 1830s. And George Croghan now owned property northeast of the town, instead of the Leonard Jacoby shown on the original map. (Croghan would be related, through marriage, to James O'Hara, whose property this was originally.)

In other sections of the borough, land-plot changes had been taking place as well. West of Hogback Hill and beyond the Rope Walk, large tracts were now held by Towne, Ekin, Leichtenberger, Denny, Evans and Hopkins and Parks—all on land originally designated to other men. In the northwest, major holdings belonged to Denny, Gray, Page, Young, Anderson, Snyder, and Cameron. These would all be different from the original landowners names. However, because no map exists that shows an area far enough north of Allegheny until about 1830, it is especially difficult to discern whether the original owners, whose names were transposed on the 1789 map, really ever owned the land or immediately sold after the county designation was lost.

Near East Lane, Charles Avery, an influential man who helped African-Americans in the area receive education, now held property. Another man, Nicholas Voegtly, had bought a lot of land at the early part of the decade, east of Avery's holdings. He established a church beyond East Lane, to Long Lane. (The latter road had been Redick's *King Lane*.) Less likely to be changed than the names of those who originally bought at auction were the original surviving street names, but in some cases the latter would not last or ever be

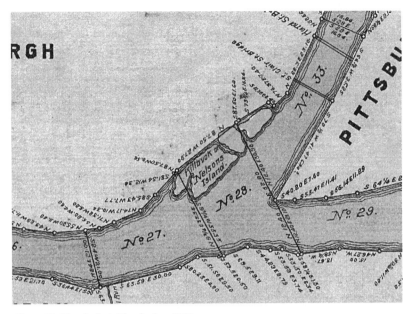

Figure 18. Riverbeds & Islands circa 1828

used. Slightly beyond Voegtly, in Allegheny's adjacent land on the east, Rickebaugh's property sat on and below the area's easternmost hill. Further beyond was land also soon to be scooped up—in the area where there were no buyers at auction or immediately after, and thus not original names but only designated out lot numbers in the overlay map of 1789.

The United States census listed the population for the Borough of Allegheny to be close to 3,000 in the early 1830s, with eight slaves, one of whom belonged to William Robinson since the early part of the century. This compared to Pittsburg's numbers at the time of 12,500. Scotch and Scotch-Irish had always been the predominant group in Allegheny, but now rising numbers of Germans, Swiss-Germans and English were immigrating to the central and eastern portions of the town, in and outside of Borough lines. Many of these early settlers, though, were American-born, coming to Allegheny from the eastern American states. Especially at the southern end of East Lane, the Germans and Swiss families congregated, and even divided among themselves, with the southernmost land parcels, closest to the river, being known as Schweizer Loch ("Swiss Hole").

In the northeastern area of Allegheny, outside the Borough line, there were a couple rolling hills (in addition to the mount furthest east) that led northward. On the lower hillsides and in the valleys in between, butchers set up shop by the numerous springs and runs there, and farmers tilled the top peaks. Meatpacking in this area became so noteworthy, including the famed Henry Zoller Meat Packing Company, that the main stream through the valley was termed Butchers Run.

Just to the west of the butcheries and "Swiss Hole" was land immediately north of Ohio Street, which had been part of George Croghan's holdings of late. But in the 1830s, three streets would be laid out running north to south, as well as three east to west. The latter three were *First, Second* and *Third*.

Once again, the Borough Council looked into public outcries over the Commons land infringements, mainly those by the Presbyterian Church, in the early 1830s. They forced the church to relinquish the Academy building (which sat south of the *Burying Ground*) to the Borough, and it thus became the first free public high school of Allegheny.

The Presbyterian Church continued on with its plans, from the 1820s, to expand and build upon its holdings in what essentially was the extreme southwest Commons. Upon Hogback Hill in 1831, they would open a massive theological seminary structure, and the hill's reference would now change to 'Seminary Hill.' A Seminary Road apparently curved down the eastern side of the hill, despite the crag of the sandstone outcrop. As well, Seminary Avenue ran atop, and Columbia Avenue just below, at the north foot of the hill.

The next year, 1832, would bring cholera and a massive flood to the southwestern Pennsylvania region, and effects of the latter appear to have begun the indelible alteration of Allegheny's three connected little isles. Three years after the unearthing of the Native Americans remains close by, now much of Killbuck's Island and *Low Island* were temporarily under water, and the small unnamed island, as well. The latter, which often was just a peninsula anyway, never appeared to resurface—the floodwaters washing away the sediment that used to peak above the surface.

The floodwaters even narrowed the back channel which separated the two other islands from the bank, only 70 yards wide to begin with,

Figure 19. 1828 map

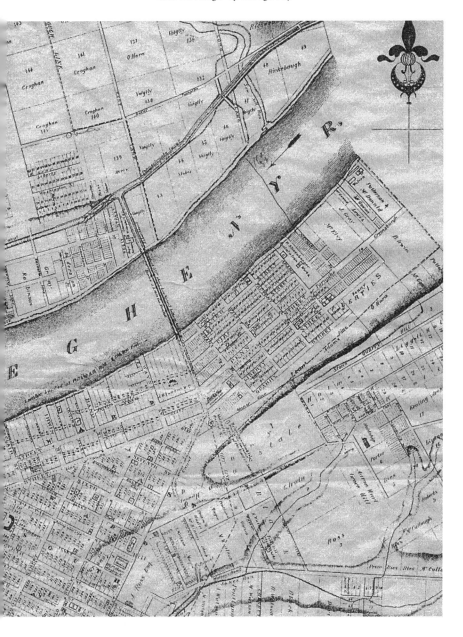

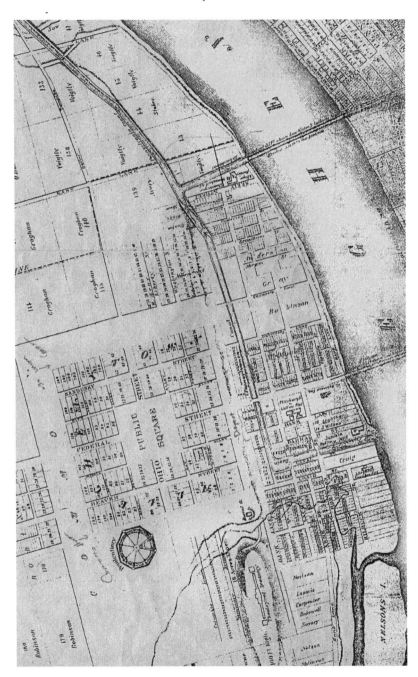

to negligible. But in a few years this little stretch of lowland, essentially 'above' Killbuck and other Islands submersion, would forever take on an amusing new place in Allegheny's history.

Low Island had just recently been bought in 1829 by Ezra Nelson. During its short life with this title, and and even after its sinking, it would be referred to as Nelson's Island.

Zenas Neel claimed possession of Killbuck Island that same year, and he put up a small foundry. But it was destroyed in the flood, and the island itself, as well as Nelson's, would from this point on be little more than large sandbars. Seemingly not content with any man's intent on the tract, little Smokey Island had a mind of its own.

Much of the lowest portions of Allegheny were also submerged under thirty-three feet of water, including where the Canal emptied and the aqueduct area. General Robinson kept a steamboat anchored in his garden to attempt rescues around the southern end of town. Barns were seen floating down the Allegheny and downtown Pittsburg was also under water.

The Town House was finally completed in 1833. It was a two-story brick building with center cupola, at the southeast corner of Ohio and Federal Streets, with the first floor occupied by the newly-organized fire company. *Hope* and *Columbia* were the two christened hand-operated engines that, along with bucket brigades, fought off town fires. The new fire engine house and volunteers, as well as the bell ringer, were put to use in a particularly noteworthy fire of 1836, when the Irwin Rope Walk burned to the ground. It would be rebuilt, only to suffer similar fate again the next decade.

Allegheny's first primitive Market House, a roofed shed that was open on the sides, for farmers and gardeners to show their goods, still sat in the town square, nearby the Town House. On the southwest of the square was a hay scale and weight-house.

There was other new construction, as well. William Robinson spurred early development on Federal Street this decade, both in the town square and just south. At Federal and Robinson Street, he built a very fashionable row of buildings named Colonnade Row.

The eastern side of the Borough of Allegheny experienced much development during the Borough era. The far reaches of Ohio Street, which began the Butler-Allegheny Turnpike, saw its share of new settlers. The Straub Brewery

Figure 20 (opposite). Close-up of 1828 map: Allegheny Borough center

Company built underground vaults and started a successful, long-lasting business on a spot that would become home to other breweries in the future.

Industry in the Borough took off even beyond what it had earlier in the 1820s. Generally west of Federal Street, now, were forges, machine shops, and iron works. The firm of H. Spang and Son, to be notable in the iron and steel industry, located on nearby Sandusky Street. East of Federal were generally cotton, woolen and paper mills in increasing number. There was the Arbuckle and Avery Cotton Mill near Sandusky, Robinson and Isabella Street. This was a cotton yard mill that later would become the Eagle Cotton Factory, and only one of several that greatly benefitted the economy of Allegheny Borough. Nearby, and equally successful, was the C. Kingland Engine Works on the corner of Sandusky and Lacock. Scattered also throughout the Borough were lead paint and wagon factories. The lumber mills usually were closest to the river boatyards, and this business skyrocketed since there was a great demand for housing on the many vacant land plots long ago surveyed by Redick that now were seeing development and in some cases, direct subdivision.

Structures for families of moderate means were to be found right along the Canal as it came into town, near the "Butler 'Pike," as it would be clipped to. Fine homes also continued to go up on Water Lane, as the wealthy living at Second Bank had seen so much change of late, with the dirt and noise of the Canal, new commerce and industry so close at hand. But what was not good so close to home life of the privileged was especially good for the vibrancy of the town. Business was bustling close to the town center.

At the northern base of Seminary Hill, new lanes were worn over to Pasture Lane and continued west, by Water Lane and Irwin's Rope Works. In 1833, the Borough appropriated early money for the improvement of the Borough's streets, including putting a bridge over a troublesome gully in the West Commons. Sandusky Lane, which would meet and join Union Street in the town square, was improved, as was Craig Street, just west of the Canal. Also the section of South Bank, where it adjoined the East Commons, was attended to. And land was for the first time sub-divided in what had been out lots 146 and 139.

The Borough of Allegheny began such rapid expansion and industrialization in the 1830s that, within Borough boundaries, its image was simply no longer the rural community that so marked its existence for most of its young life, and that had also set it apart from the bustle of Pittsburg across the river. But what did set it apart, from any spot in America with such commercial and manufactory growth, was the Commons land. As a buffer around a town exploding with industrialization sat a land area marked mainly by animal life and vegetation that, despite infringements and now visible deterioration, still seemed to set a pastoral tone for the geniality, civility and pride that marked Allegheny citizens, whether the wealthy or workers. This land area represented a stake in *community*—of mutual responsibility, purpose and respect for the last vestige of the wilderness that originally comprised the northern bank of land cut by the three rivers.

Of course, all the property immediately surrounding the Borough, that was still considered part of the town as originally conceived, also still retained its rural flavor at this time. And it would be visible farmland just beyond the view of factories, because the flats of the lower portion of the Reserved Tract could be seen near, far and wide from the river bank in Pittsburg. And the lush Allegheny hilltops, hovering above the success of the town below, certainly were in view to any and all traveling down the rivers or about Pittsburg across the way.

Pasture Lane on the west side of town, and East Lane on the east now linked townspeople to farms and countryside in the far out lots, the hills and the land north of the Reserved Tract, referenced as "north of Allegheny." By the year 1835, Reserve Township was officially formed in what had been part of Ross Township originally. This was northeast of the Reserved Tract, but also included some eastern portions of Allegheny that lay further east of East Lane, left out of the original Borough designation. So, the land in this area, now co-opted per se by Reserve Township, was starting to accumulate multiple identity histories, as it would forever be linked to the Reserved Tract and Allegheny, but now was under the wing of a new municipality. This situation would also be the case for a few other areas originally designated as Reserved Tract/Allegheny land.

In the northern area of Allegheny, just outside the Borough line and up the rolling hills above *Mechanic's Retreat,* was a plan of Lots by John O'Hern, called the *Plan of Mount Relief.* And adjacent, but right within the City Line boundary, was George Ledlie's properties, originally out lots of Abraham Kirkpatrick.

These plots would incorporate the ridge that the Venango Trail followed up and around, later to become the upper, primitive portion of the Franklin Road. And though this land was very visible as directly hovering 'above' the town, it was not officially part of it at this time, being outside Borough designation. But this ridge that was so integral to the native's way of life, and its top peak that they so frequented, would soon play a colorful and prominent role in the white man's existence.

Because the Borough had stopped almost prematurely in its northern boundary on the western end of town, just north of the Rope Works at Water Lane, it too precipitated a separate history. The town of Manchester came together in 1832, named for the industrial/manufacturing city in England. It organized municipally, as a town, and began to develop its streets, mainly based on Redick's original model. The bulk of families were Scotch or Scotch-Irish.

Manchester's early commercial hub was Ferry Street, shown on Redick's layout, but a curve inward toward Water Street had been worn into a lane by this time. Redick's *Back Lane* would be Ohio Lane (not to be confused with the Borough of Allegheny's Ohio Street, however). It ran from Pasture Lane, near Robinson's out lots, to Ferry Street. The opening, in 1835, of the covered Union Bridge, from Pittsburg across to Manchester, was significant to further development for the area.

The earliest political resolution to survive from Allegheny's youth, from the Borough era, speaks of its own street development. It is an Article of Agreement dated 1836, referring to a land parcel just northeast of the town square, before the rise of what had been O'Hara's *High, Rough Land*:

> We the undersigned do hereby covenant, and agree to open and surrender for the use and purpose of increasing the width of White Oak Alley so much as the ground thus surrendered will increase the same... to Allegheny. All our Right interest and claim in and to all that portion of ground situate and contained between the [indecipherable] line of White Oak Alley and a line running north from a Point on Chisslet Alley six feet from, and east of White Oak Alley to the southwest corner of the frame house belonging to R. B. Mowry, which house corner is about 100' south from Locust St. and said line being about 108' 6" from and east of Boyle Street.

> And we further agree to pay our private share of the cost of
> Grading and Paving said Alley as thus increased, Provided the Eastside
> Walk shall be made not less than 5' wide so far as the width of said
> alley is increased to 26'.
> Witness our hands this 19th day of July in the year 1836 in the
> presence of Thomas Payne, George Dinney and R. B. Mowry

Allegheny's first bridge was demolished in 1837. With much acclaim, an
iron suspension bridge designed by John A. Roebling would replace the old
wooden structure. One year later, the Mechanic's Street Bridge would be built
from what was called the "Northern Liberties" section of Pittsburg over to
what was then still east of the Borough line, at Chestnut Street. Bridges were
a definite necessity between Pittsburg and Allegheny Borough, as commerce
between the two had stepped up incrementally over the passing decades, and
dramatically within the last ten years.

Also in 1838, the land delineation of the Borough was on its way to
being enlarged. Final clarification of this would come in the 1840s. Another
bridge in remarkably short distance, the Hand Street Bridge, would open two
years later, connecting Pittsburg's 9th Street and Allegheny's Anderson Street.
For this, Anderson Street, which was east of Sandusky, was widened and
renamed from the earlier Guyasuta Lane, running between Robinson's and
Colonel Anderson's property. As well, all the wooden bridges on the streets
over the Canal would be now completed. And, for the first time, primitive
early sewers would be constructed for the Borough.

Definitely a swift transition had taken place in the *Reserved Tract opposite
Pittsburg* by the fifty years that had passed since Redick's town layout.
From forested terrain, mere wilderness at its onset, to farms and lush
countryside with a provincial, frontier town center in its infancy... to early
industry matched with rural community outskirts in its youth... and now to
burgeoning commerce center and shipping point, with numerous well-built
homes and still the retention of a land set aside for the community, in its
young adulthood. All while only a portion of the original Reserved Tract was
currently being given full attention, while surrounding area, forever to be
considered 'Allegheny,' was biding its time, waiting for its turn at
transformation.

Population of the Borough skyrocketed by the end of the decade of the 1830s. 10,000 souls were now residents on this land, over three times what it was at the start of the decade alone, and now closer in comparison to the city across the river that had quite a head start. Pittsburgh's population was at this time 21,000; its total land area was about twice that of Allegheny's.

Though it was growing and modernizing, Allegheny was a bit behind in some areas when compared to Pittsburgh, which had begun to have early concert halls and theatres, for example, and by this time had earned an "h" by all outsiders that previously resisted and were still using the provincial spelling. Though it had not yet attracted the fine arts, Allegheny did attract, about the year 1835, other traveling entertainment, which settled in transient caravans on the low area below Seminary Hill (where the islands used to cling to the shoreline.)

As well, Pittsburgh had begun an early water-works system, bringing water to the city structures, as opposed to in Allegheny, where the farmers, housewives, commerce leaders and even firefighters still had to go to springs to retrieve their supply, or rely upon pumps and wells and the timing of water-carriers arriving with their pushcart barrels.

But Allegheny had begun to make up for lost time and lost opportunity that had started with the county re-designation. It would soon rival Pittsburgh in just about every way—at least enough for visitors to the area in coming decades to remark of the twin, or sister cities occupying south-western Pennsylvania, at the confluence of the Monongahela, Allegheny and Ohio Rivers. Ironically in 1838, however, a southwestern Pennsylvania newspaper expressed that the whole region encompassing Pittsburgh and the Borough of Allegheny "began to have the appearance of one large city, divided by the rivers." (KELLY)

Allegheny City

chapter five:
FOUR WARDS & EARLY GOVERNMENT MEASURES

By 1840, the population per land area of Allegheny Borough was commensurate with Pittsburgh's, which had been incorporated as a city in 1816. And commercially and industrially, Allegheny's larger mills and factories were already rivaling Pittsburgh's. (Allegheny certainly felt no inferiority socially and culturally, either, despite lack of concert halls at the time.)

Borough officials were prompted to apply to the Commonwealth for a city charter. The State Legislature easily recognized that Allegheny at this point had grown to city proportion, of the third-class ranking, and would grant the charter April 13, 1840, birthing Allegheny City.

Elected as first mayor in July of that year would be first and favorite son, General William Robinson. A seal and flag for Allegheny City were created, the former depicting Robinson's father's homestead as *First Log Cabin* (conveniently forgetting Andrew Long's), and in the foreground, a figure traveling down river in canoe.

Two legislative bodies were formed—the Common and Select Councils, with representatives from each of four created wards, at this time of the city's origin. The state also recognized Allegheny's ability to control its own land. The *Reserved Tract opposite Pittsburg* no longer had tight restrictions placed by the state over the governance of roads, and such things as the Commons land. By law, the right to grant commons land for public use was now transferred from the State to the Select & Common Councils of Allegheny City, making further outcries about infringements there solely in the hands of the city executives.

The City of Allegheny would begin issuing its own money, one and two-dollar bills. It also began to spend on all that was deemed necessary. Various Committees were formed to deal with a variety of issues—the Canal, Wharves & Landings, Fire Companies, Markets, Water, and Streets (formation, grading & paving).

The very earliest legislation deals with matters likely pressing, though somewhat less weighty than one would expect from a new city government. A motion came on Select Council table, just at its onset, which was "relevant to dogs running at large." As well, there were motions to consider the "measurement and inspection of shingles," to "prevent nuisances," one "concerning shows, plays and theatrical entertainments," as well as the very significant "regarding City Limits," looking at "streets leading to the Markethouse," and a formation of "Night Watch and Special Constables."

On March 18, 1841, a clerk presented an invoice of $8 to the Select Council from Mayor Robinson himself, for the hauling of cinders in order to make a foot way across the East Commons. There was also introduced an ordering of window shutters for the Town House, and an Ordinance "regulating roofs, steps, cellar doors, and awning poles in the City of Allegheny."

Other legislation and political discussion that survive from archives of the early city and Select and Common Council minutes:

1841   "Whereas it has become necessary that Robinson Street should be... opened up to the aqueduct... extend[ing] Robinson Street and Lacock Street."

"Who is entitled to a right of Common? Every owner of an In Lot or part of an In Lot—that right extends to every part or parcel of the Commons... and can not be extinguished except by his own consent... it is an interest in the land, inextinguishable."

1843   *Permits to the Public Graveyards* were discussed in Council, with a list of names, detail of death, and "$ 1 paid" toward expense of digging a grave, and furnishing a simple marker, at the old town Burying Grounds. These would have been for poor citizens, and those with no church affiliation

Figure 21. Seal of the City of Allegheny

Figure 22. Allegheny City currency, 1848

(as there were also church cemeteries in Allegheny). "Boy drowned in Allegheny River" was one entry on the list, and another, "Woman killed by plow accident."

1845 Discussion of the situation where a property owner's lot is lower than a proposed bounding street:

> "it is at [that property owner's] own proper cost and expense... to be placed upon the line of said lots and the street, a fence or other protection, sufficiently high and strong to protect from accident the citizens... and to prevent the material of the street being washed into such lots."

> "[In response to] Petitions in relation to the Penitentiary Sewer, the Committee says the evil complained of can only be remedied by the owners filling up their lots."

The third mayor, Hezekiah Nixon, had finally authorized a new Market House to be built. It would be completed in 1845; the wooden building would sit on the southeast corner of the town square, as the last. The intersecting streets, Ohio and Federal, were widened for ease of vehicle passage. The Market House would be open at both ends and along the sides. The butcher stalls would be located inside, with the west end of the structure reserved for secondhand goods, and the east side for the farmers. Legislation and regulation in a few years would call for everything from putting new shingles on the north end of the roof, and for country men to not cut up the meat before arrival to market.

The canal aqueduct, in the same year of the Market House opening, would be under repair, with another contract awarded to Roebling. A span had collapsed in 1843 and the structure was closed for awhile, greatly hurting business in Pittsburgh. Roebling's new structure was equally celebrated, as were all the bridges over the rivers at the end of the previous decade.

The four wards of Allegheny City were determined by the split made by the town square's two Indian trail crossings. The four quadrants made by the intersection of Federal and Ohio Streets would be directionally extended outward to designate areas of land incorporated within each.

The First Ward was *west* of Federal, *south* of Ohio and outward to the old borough marking that stopped at Manchester, and the rivers.

The Second Ward would be *west* of Federal, *north* of Ohio and outward to the Manchester boundary, but to a more northerly point than was the old Borough marking, and drawn "virtually" across the land to a point where a straight upward extension of Federal Street/Franklin Road was met. Thus, Pasture Lane slightly further north would now be included, to an area around Snyder's Hollow that would become better known as Pleasant Valley, near Island Lane. And even though the term *City Line* would be used by the Councils to also refer to the western and eastern city boundaries, this new, slightly extended northern boundary is what citizens would most popularly call the *City Line*, or where the "city limit" of Allegheny ended within the Reserved Tract (and Reserve Township began). With the new upward extension, the infamous ridge of the Venango Trail, the ascending curve back upon itself that was now the Franklin Road, would be within the City Line.

The Third Ward was *east* of Federal, *north* of Ohio to the same northern mark that was the extension in the Second Ward, and on the east, to Butcher's Run at the foot of the eastern hills.

The Fourth Ward was *east* of Federal, *south* of Ohio, to East Lane at the lower end of Butcher's Run, and to the river.

In 1843, more of the area directly north of the North Commons would be subdivided. This would be the land that was out lot numbers 176 and 183, owned by Hugh Davis. As well, three separate stone quarries, on the northeast side of the *High Rough Land*, began to be mined. This was the eastern edge of what for a short time was Nunnery Hill, abandoned by the Flemish order about ten years prior. An early prominent stonecutter was Robert Henderson. With a partner, he bought land below where the nunnery earlier sat, essentially the approach to the hill, and then portions of the northeastern slope.

Mount Union Cemetery came into being in 1846. It would be located just north of the City Line, west of Pasture Lane as it started a slow but steady climb at the far reach of Pleasant Valley. This had been land that was originally the *First Farm* of John Woods, but was now actually considered part of Reserve Township, as it wrapped around from the east and north of City Line boundaries. The cemetery would be on ten beautiful acres of hilly land on out lots 238-241, near Strawberry Lane. They, too, like some of the lots on

Allegheny's far east side, did not have an assigned owner by the time of the transposed map of 1789.

The year 1847 brought Allegheny City Common and Select Councils hearing arguments about sand washing off Federal Street into the Canal. It came down to the query, "Is it clean?" After entertaining discussion, it was decreed to the Street Committee that "it was hereby forbidden to happen."

That same year, a site was finally secured for a much-needed but expensive municipal water-works. Allegheny citizens had been asking for this for a decade. It would be located in what was about to be called Duquesne Borough, the adjacent Reserved Tract area running as a long and narrow parcel of land along the Allegheny river, just east of the city. The water-works reservoir would sit atop the long mount that hovered above the large isle. The construction, for which the city had to borrow $100,000, was completed in 1849. Gravity would feed water down into the city, into 5/8th-inch lateral pipes, and from there, it would be fed to specific buildings and only particular, subscribing households.

The new infrastructure benefitted citizens of Allegheny, but also led to a financial crisis that very year for the new city. With the power to now sell land at their own disposal, Allegheny City legislators tried to alleviate the financial predicament by selling public land. This actually led the way for some of the lots, previously part of the public square, to be sold off privately for those looking to establish business in the lucrative center of town.

Conrad Reel, son of the fur trader, would take advantage of this. He had established a successful woolen mill in Perrysville, just north on the Franklin Road, but he would now relocate it to Allegheny City's town center. About the time Allegheny became a city, the central square began to be formally, and then colloquially, referred to as 'the Diamond,' due to the design and placement of recent buildings, and likely just a fresh outlook at the pattern made by the old town grid. Streets would be renamed to accommodate the outlook—for example, Gay Alley became South Diamond.

Reel's business was named the Allegheny Woolen Mills, later to become C. Reel and Company. It would specialize in blankets and knitting yarns for several decades to come.

Besides being the city's first Mayor, General William Robinson was busy, still, with land matters in the 1840s. He finally attended to out lots which originally belonged to his father, that were just north of the West Commons. He had the land subdivided, now matching the look of the adjoining land around Jackson Street, which had been divided and settled earlier. These lots started at the base of the hill and then traveled upward toward a magnificent view of the rolling hills of the Ohio River Valley across Manchester. As Robinson was enamored of the Mexican War of that era, he named his plan of lots *Buena Vista*, which was the decisive conflict in that war. The whole section of streets that passed through *Buena Vista*, even some that had come into existence surrounding the earlier settlement of the 1820s, took on names that evoked the Mexican War battle sites, including Taylor (for General Zachary Tayor), Sherman and Monterey. (Robinson had actually been taken with Mexico as far back as to when he was a young man in 1806, becoming intrigued by Aaron Burr's scheme for Mexico's conquest.) Once divided, William Robinson began selling individual 20' wide lots for $200 or more.

In a few years, around 1852, Palo Alto and Resaca, two streets east of this land recently subdivided by Robinson, would also be built up. Structures sitting on the lots, completed about 1850, were considered small and plain, but with early Italianate or Greek Revival style in evidence. These home-owners were mostly skilled blue-collar workers; many were in fact self-employed tailors and dressmakers, catering to the myriad of fashions now popularly displayed in the newspaper classified ads. Cabinet makers, stair builders, machinists, blacksmiths, and shoemakers were all to be found in this neighborhood, which collectively with Robinson's new lots, would a century later come to be creatively (and most efficiently) referred to as "the Mexican War Streets" of Allegheny.

By the end of the first decade of Allegheny's existence as a city, a dozen elementary schools, as well as two public high schools, were accommodating children. As well, a lot of infrastructure was being attended to for the first time. By 1849, the Councils passed a Resolution to grade the east side of the East Commons, were examining ways in which to remove the dangerous pond on Ohio Street, and likewise the pond on Grantham Street, east of the town square. As well, the the next year, there was discussion to "repair fence around grave yard" (the *Burying Ground*), an "Order to collect better wharfage," and a "Resolution against depositing stones on the beaches." The latter referred to the low-lying areas of the northern river banks, where some citizens occasionally were gathering to catch the various circuses and other shows traveling through town.

Two Resolutions went before council, in 1849, regarding the seminary ground. The first was to buy and level the land, and the second, successful, was just to buy back the seventeen acres. A fire five years later, however, before the legislature had even acted, made the decision a bit of a mute point, since the seminary building was destroyed and the church was forced to leave the land anyway.

The Councils also enforced rules in 1850 for the cleaning and disposing of waste from backyard privies and cisterns, which were the norm in the early city. An understandable extension, then, of this concern was a Resolution, as well, for the formation of a Board of Health.

Concern for the needs of the poor and indigent was also on the agenda of the new city's councilmen. The Borough of Allegheny had first addressed such concern, establishing and funding a Poor House in the early 1830s. Known as the "Work House" to Allegheny citizens, it was located outside Borough limits—just up the Allegheny River. There survives a record, in 1849, of the Annual Report of the Directors of the Poor, regarding what by now was called the City Farm and Poor House:

> To The Select and Common Councils of the City of Allegheny. The undersigned, Directors of the Poor for the city of Allegheny, respectfully lay before the Councils... the present condition of this benevolent institution, established and maintained by our citizens, for the relief and comfort of the indigent and unfortunate, whose lot may be cast among us....
>
> [There was] the necessity of erecting a barn, suitable for housing the animals and farming implements of the establishment, and preserving the hay, corn and general products of the farm...
>
> ...the class of paupers bereft of their reason was greatly on the increase, and [there is a] necessity of having some proper provision made for the confinement and management of such as were maniacs, and dangerous to themselves and others.... The Directors of the institution felt themselves called upon, by considerations of humanity and benevolence, and by a sense of duty, to delay no longer to make a suitable provision for thee unfortunate fellow beings (many of whom are females), that they might be liberated from the chains found necessary to confine them, and enjoy that artificial warmth necessary to their comfort during the winter.... It was concluded to erect a second story

on the brick outhouse in rear of the main building... The Board
contemplate inviting the townships to send their paupers, either sane
or insane, to be supported at fair compensation, until our house shall
have the complement of inmates it is capable of supporting—thereby
greatly reducing the ratio of expense to each inmate. They are also
endeavoring to reduce, as far as it is practicable, humane and proper,
the amount of outdoor pauperism [found in the city].

There was the first recorded Remonstrance by citizens, in 1851, against
the city's need to survey and lay out the Second and Third Wards. This was
just the first of many remonstrances that Allegheny City, like any municipality, entertained—as street openings and the like always provoke citizen
discussion and outcry. There would also be a Remonstrance against opening
Ridge Street, which would run along the southern side of the West Commons,
at the base of Seminary Hill, toward Manchester. It was unsuccessful, and
thus soon enough, this street would 'open' officially. (A dirt lane had already
existed, delineating the northern boundary of some of the first well-to-do
homes there.)

In 1852, fifteen years after the St. Clair Bridge was already illuminated
by gas lights, the Allegheny Gas Company was incorporated, with a plant
erected one year later on Water Lane. Finally Alleghenians could move away
from hand-held lanterns for making their way about, because gas lamps
could be found on several streets. And Agreements between Allegheny and
other boroughs continued. One year later, the Street Commission of Allegheny
City and the auditors of Reserve Township dealt with "the erection of a stone
culvert on Chestnut Street across from the *City Line* at Butcher's Run."

The Street Commission also authorized, the same year, the erection
of locust posts, for the protection of pedestrians, at the crossings of
"foot pavements," and where carts and wagons ran up and down Palo Alto,
Resaca, Monterey and Buena Vista Streets near Shannopin Lane. (These trees
grew prolifically on the hillside area just above, northward.) This section of
Allegheny was fast becoming a Drover's area, where peddlers of farm goods
from areas north and west of Pasture Lane stopped and stabled their horses,
and parked their goods in carts, wagons and buggies, en route to other
sections of Allegheny.

There was much discussion and public testimony in Council, in the early
part of 1854, regarding the continued help of the poor of Allegheny City. The

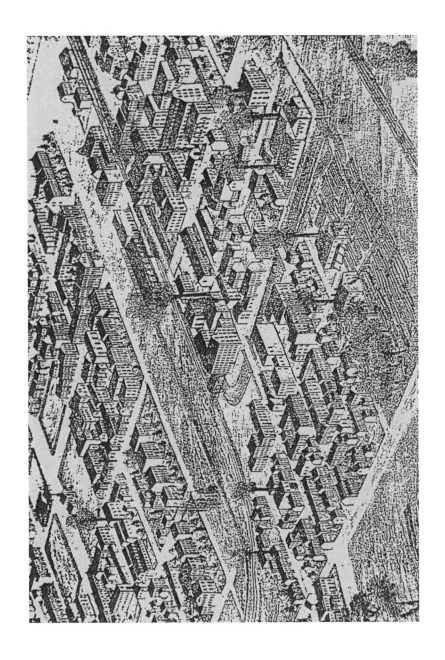

extent to which a community should concern itself on this issue would be continually called into question by future citizens living on Allegheny's land.

Alleghenians were extremely involved in their city, as archival records attest. They petitioned the Councils to direct a fence to be built across the Diamond, parallel with Ohio Street, below the Scales. Its purpose would be to confine livestock from wandering into the street, after being weighed. The crowded state of the market area during the fall months also prompted civic discussion. Council minutes reflect persuaded city leaders, who had "come to believe that there must be some better arrangement for accommodation of wagons from the country." Their remedy would be that the wagons would have to unload first and then be put southwest of the Diamond.

In the late summer of 1854, there was talk in the Councils of paving Pasture Lane—what would have been a real change to modernity for citizens who traveled the little dirt road that extended through the countryside, on the northwest of Allegheny City. The proposed paving would go as far on Pasture Lane as to the *City Line*, or the south end of John Taggart's property, where it hit Island Lane. Citizens felt they did not need it; even by 1856, there would be a "non-concurrence" in Council on the paving of Pasture Lane.

John Taggart was the son of an R. Taggart, who, with his sons, operated a successful store at 129 Federal Street. (An ad from the 1840s declared, "The Wisest Folks in town cover their Feet with our Reliable Footwear. New Goods, Late Styles, Prices Less than Others.") Taggart's northern line, just north of Pleasant Valley, would have been the southwest corner of James O'Hara's *Second Farm*—starting from a valley on the northwest side of the hilltop that delineated the end of what was once one of Andrew Guyer's out lots. His property would continue northeastward along the long valley.

In addition to the Franklin Road north of the town center and up to the separation of the hills, what was Shannopin Lane would serve as another main road to the later-known Mexican War Streets area. Shannopin Lane was soon-to-be North Avenue, so-called for likely two reasons. It served as the northern boundary outside the North Commons, but it also was an extension of little North Street in Manchester Borough, which had been in existence years earlier. A direct line from the older North Street could be directly drawn, cutting through four of Harmar Denny's lots, to become North Avenue above North Commons.

Figure 23 (opposite). First Ward of Allegheny City, by the river, circa 1850

Arch Street ran north to south from North Avenue, but in the early 1850s was called Beaver Street (and Division Alley where it narrowed northerly). De Haven and Son, also shown as located on Arch, by the latter 1850s, specialized in stove production, and would be among the most successful at this business after its establishment in 1857.

The *Mechanic's Retreat* section of the Mexican War Streets started to be subdivided in the 1850s, with skinny Davis Alley (later to be called Dawson Street) running from Pasture Lane to Beaver (soon-to-be Arch), to where it connected to the wide Sampson Street, over to the Franklin Road. The lots were no longer owned by Neville Craig; the area was now entitled *Reverend Campbell's Mechanic's Retreat*.

Despite citizen nostalgic protest here and there, streets and alleys of Allegheny began to change for the better—from uneven dirt to brick and cobblestone paving. The year 1856 would have the city spending $200,000 for grading and paving with cobblestone. Federal had been the only paved street prior.

In Allegheny's major valley, east of O'Hara's *High Rough Land*, would be the first major paving assignment beyond Federal Street. East Lane, into the wider section of East Street, was done. Then further, as East Street became the Township Road, running north to the *City Line* at the start of Reserve Township. By this time, major tracts of hillside land westward of this road, were owned by O'Hara's granddaughter , Mary E. Croghan. (In 1842 she eloped with and married British Captain E.W. Schenley and was living in London, but still held her Allegheny land parcels.)

Ohio Street, too, where it ran east of the Commons, would be paved fairly early on in cobblestone. These field stones would continue out to the start of the Butler 'Pike and Duquesne Borough, lying beneath later road surface, on a long stretch of this main road paralleling the Allegheny River.

Another cemetery would come into existence in 1857, on a hill just adjacent northward of Mount Union Cemetery. Its name was Hilldale Cemetery, and it would be across Strawberry Lane, on what had been out lots 223 and 224.

The same year brought the establishment of a Gas Committee and thus an extension of gas lamps for far more streets. Allegheny City entered into an Agreement with the private Allegheny Gas Company, to pay $20/yr. "for each and every street or public city lamp which should be lighted up." Lamplighters would go about the city, with street lamps lit 11 hours/night for no more than 210 nights a year. As well, there was an Agreement drawn up to "keep the lamps clean and in order and at all the expense necessary to keep the service pipe clear from condensation and all other obstructions."

The numbering of houses in Allegheny City was also a concern at Council table, as mail delivery had become chaotic. The delivery reference had only been to the description of a house—for example, "the house standing at the northwest end of a certain lane." The city realized this would need to change, and that a numbering system would soon need to be worked out.

In records of the Allegheny City Treasurer's Settled Accounts of 1857–1859, much can be discerned of business about town at the time. The mayor's office had a water cooler that was not working properly; the repair needed, at 75 cents, came before Councils and was approved. The city also paid for a variety of services, including having 38 loads of cinders hauled to the Scales on the Diamond. McIntyre & McNaugher were hired for grading and paving work near the Water-works, and in the First Ward. Both lived in the hilly countryside beyond the Second and Third Wards, where the Franklin Road leveled off above the ridge and began to curve around northward. McIntyre also was involved in the business of crafting lampposts.

James McBrier & Company hauled joists for the city—hemlock and locust posts, and R. H. Davis would provide 210 of those posts at the end of the decade. Locust tree trunks were extremely hard and strong, perfect for literally holding up the frames of houses. Since they were plentiful in the hilltop area where many of these men lived, they were prominently found in building foundations about the city.

B.A. Pressly provided ink, turpentine and gale alcohol to the city, and a gentleman by the name of Lockhart provided brooms, brushes and pitchers. Both lived in the southeast corner of Allegheny City limits, and two streets would later be renamed for the prominent businessmen.

Kirkpatrick was the name of a man who lived up Pasture Lane, south of the cemeteries, and he was contracted to provide cotton ropes. John Irwin and Sons provided the more heavy-duty bales of hemp. Boyd and Murdock, early lumber merchants, provided planks for some of the roadways.

The William Eichbaum Company from Pittsburgh provided sundry repairs as needed to Allegheny City Engine Companies. As well they would craft bell clappers, cranks and pencils. (His family would be connected to the history of Oakland, in Pittsburgh's East End, as the translation of Eichbaum is Oak tree.)

Unlike the early days when dismissed as primitive frontier, it had become apparent to all Pittsburghers that the land across the river's way was every bit as attractive and rival to their own attributes. For the legislators there, it became a coveted extension of land. Allegheny had arguably better industrialization than Pittsburgh at this time, better rail and water transport, and desirable homes and pasture space that was prime and rare to many Pittsburghers. The only problem in trying to expand onto its boundaries was that Allegheny was now a thriving city in its own right, not just a mere borough. Instead of having a population equally covetous of a close city's identity, Allegheny had quite an identity of its own. Its citizens were fiercely proud of what their land had become in short term, and were outraged to hear glimmers that Pittsburgh was wanting to advance upon them.

In the past, Pittsburgh had always dismissed Allegheny, when it was not going after what Allegheny had been granted. Now there was subtle murmur of Pittsburgh praising Allegheny, and using language to try to sweeten a potential bond. But the citizens of Allegheny, those that even heard it at this time, would have nothing of it. And even Pittsburghers were not well aware of their City's recent new interest.

A bill would be introduced into Pittsburgh's legislature, in the late 1850s, to effect the annexation of Allegheny to Pittsburgh. It would be unsuccessful at this time.

chapter six:
LABOR, THE RAILROAD &
SOCIAL LIFE

Before the financial crisis occurred at the end of the 1840s, the first decade of Allegheny City had been an economic boon, with even more industries flourishing. It was an especially good time for the lumber industry, which had set up shop on the large island in the Allegheny (officially, for now, part of Duquesne Borough, but still considered part of Allegheny City). Benjamin Herr had purchased the island and planted fruit trees and extensive gardens. He also operated a water-powered mill in the back channel, during the 1830s, but sawmills, as well as a boatyard, would share space in the late 1840s.

New small businesses, as well, took off in the first two decades of the new city. Among the successful would be one established by Henry Anshutz and Son on Ohio Street, in 1844, and the Lafayette Stove Foundry, which served many households in Allegheny with their iron grates and heating stoves.

Considered in full with the number and variety of industries that were established in Allegheny since the 1820s, it became impressive to both Alleghenians and outsiders that industry and business could flourish so well in such a short time as an organized town. Everything was coming together to point toward dramatic achievement for this locale planned by the state legislature slightly over fifty years prior. Though it did not become the center of politics for southwestern Pennsylvania, as originally planned, it had taken off on a trajectory no less prestigious or successful.

Businesses began to meet every need, and most desires, of Allegheny City citizens. Needed for the housing boom to come would be the products offered by Faust, Jackson and Company at 57 Federal Street. They manufactured tin (to be used as roofing, and on sills and ceilings, through the 1890s), copper and sheet iron ware, as well as dealt in stoves and household furnishings.

Conrad Eberhardt started a brewery in the year 1846. It would be on Vinial Street, not far from where the Straub Brewery had gotten its start two decades prior. Its building and business would continue to be notable for over a century. And to accommodate business, and its effect upon wages of Alleghenians, the first bank of Allegheny City opened in 1849—the Allegheny Savings Fund Company, on Federal Street.

Around this time, a map of Allegheny City shows that what is left of Killbuck Island indeed is at high water—really just a peninsula attached to the north side of the river. It had never recovered from the 1832 flood, but nevertheless, Zenas Neel's heirs conveyed the island area to John Parke, William Reed and two other individuals in the year 1849. They did nothing with it at this time, and Allegheny City itself seemed more interested in using it, by allowing the traveling spectacles passing through Allegheny to camp and set up their temporary presentations there.

New Kilbuck Street, and surrounding ones at the low end of the Allegheny river bank, comprised a new residential section on the north bank. In 1848, a young teen who would soon completely shape the course of industry for Allegheny and Pittsburgh, would move to Kilbuck Street in Allegheny. His name was Andrew Carnegie. This neighborhood was affectionately called "Barefoot Square," perhaps related to the nearby spring just north, at Spring Alley nearby Ohio and Marshall Streets in the West Commons (and just west of the *Burying Ground*). It was much frequented by children and housewives looking to get their supply of water before the water-works could service their area.

Soon the young Carnegie would move to the foot of Seminary Hill (closer to the spring), on a newer street, Reedsdale. It would be in the 1850s that he would be befriended by Colonel James Anderson, who let Carnegie utilize the extensive library in his home, west of Pasture Lane.

The summer of 1848 in Allegheny City was notable for labor's uprising, an inevitable and necessary response to the intense industrialization the city was going through. The ten-hour day had just been enforced from the State Legislature, down from the twelve-hour previous mandate (and in contrast to the thirteen-hour law that was still in operation in states on the eastern seaboard). The Cotton Mill Riots started, in an unusual twist to labor stoppages, when the *mill operators* first closed down operations, in protest that work could not be adequately done with the state-mandated reduction that was essentially looking after the workers.

Many workers were anxious to be back on the job and, going against Commonwealth law, mills were actually about to reopen with long hours. But a little-publicized iron mill worker strike had just been in progress, and newfound, organized solidarity prevented the proposed re-openings of the cotton mills, but in one case. A riot ensued, against the owners and workers of the one mill that reopened unlawfully. Allegheny's Select Council actually passed a Resolution condemning the actions of the rioters, and approved any additional means the mayor, Henry Campbell, would need to keep the peace. Amazingly, not considering the possibility that this would likely inflame the situation, he would then appoint citizens as temporary police officers. Somehow the city made it past the difficulty, as temporary concessions were had.

Just two years later, a similar situation sprang up again, continuing to put Allegheny City in the labor spotlight. This time it involved a ten-hour strike by the female employees of just two factories, the Eagle and Hope Cotton Mills. Here, twenty-seven years before Pittsburgh would encounter its major labor trouble with the Great Railroad Strike, and later the Homestead Steel Strike, Allegheny City had its taste of the required sensitivities to manpower that would be necessary for industrialization to truly work.

Labor troubles for the city would get settled just as a novel approach to some city roadways was being put into effect. The year 1849 saw wood planking used to upgrade two heavily traveled dirt roads going to areas outlying the city. Planks eight feet long and three inches thick would be put on the Butler 'Pike. And to now better accommodate wagon wheel, the same type of plank would also be used on the ascending portion of the Franklin Road beyond the hills' cleave. Here, where the road turned back upon itself and curved up and around the great ridge, it would take on a new name—the Perrysville Plank Road, after Commodore Perry who so traversed it almost forty years earlier. At a terminus in the pastoral northern ridges beyond, it reverted to the name Franklin Road, which continued even further all the way through the northern hills.

Both roads, also, were privately-owned, with the planking not paid for by any government body. The private corporations that formed to control them were enabled to do so in that the roads, for the most part, were just outside city jurisdiction. The Perrysville Plank Road started just within Allegheny's new *City Line*.

The organizing companies would collect tolls every five miles, but be regulated by the State. The Allegheny and Perrysville Turnpike Road

Figure 24. Circa-1852 map   104

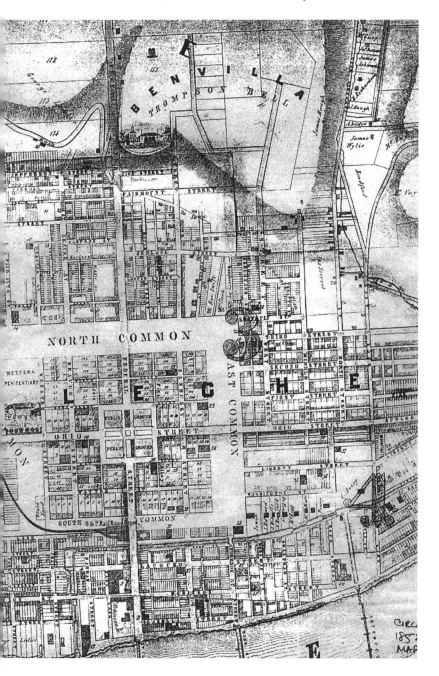

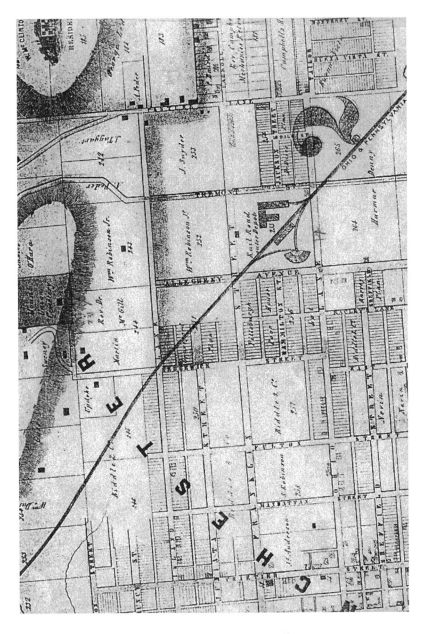

Figures 25–28. Close-ups: Circa-1852 map   *Figure 25.*

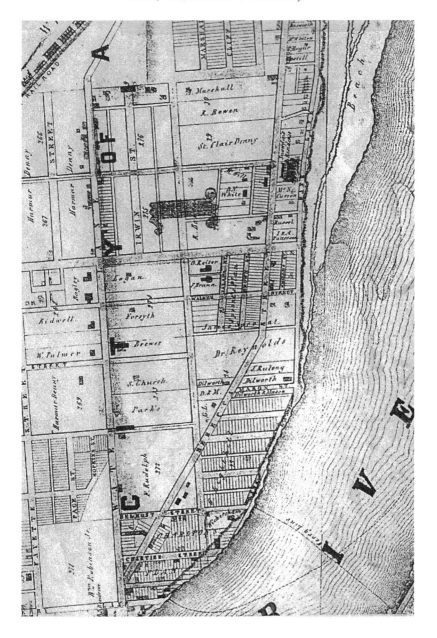

Figure 26.

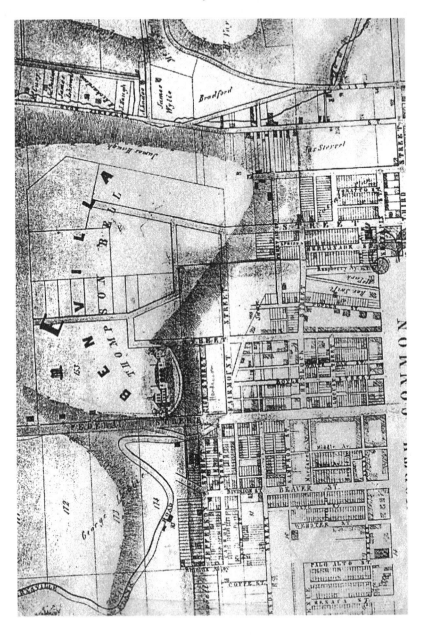

Figure 27.

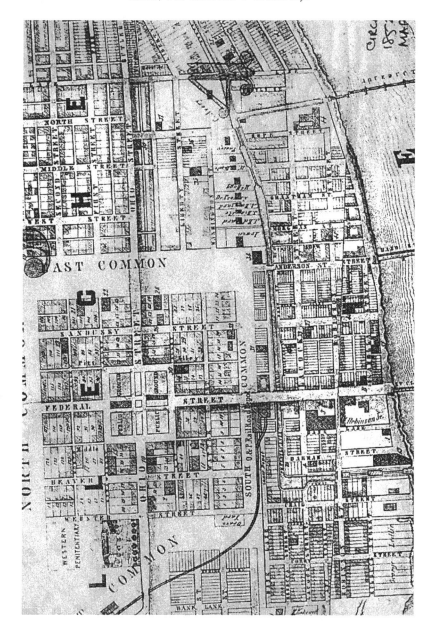

Figure 28.

Company, controlling the Perrysville Plank Road, had as its President Samuel S. Shields, who was the son-in-law of the owner of the W. H. Tavern in Allegheny City.

Different rates would apply, relating to the cargo and the vehicle type. (All kinds of cargo, including cattle, sheep and pigs, had begun to be transported along this route en masse after the Canal came to Allegheny.) Carts and wagons that had wider wheels were charged less, since they did less damage to the road surface. Sometimes Conestoga wagons driven by six horses would drag as much as three tons of cargo up and around Perrysville Plank Road and through the northern reaches of land. And stage coaches, for 3 cents a mile, would be the means for travelers between Pittsburgh and the new northern community of Warrendale.

Toll gates would fall across the highway as a barrier to travelers, and toll collectors sat in little toll houses along the side of roads. One toll house on the Perrysville Plank Road would stand for many years, located about halfway in-between the start of the toll road, near the *City Line*, and the town of Perrysville, at just about the start of Ross Township.

There was a bit of controversy surfacing in Allegheny City Councils, apparently, that the Perrysville Plank Road traversed the northeast corner of Reverend Campbell's land, adjacent north to the Buena Vista land plots of Robinson. But it seems from an 1852 map that this is really not the case, that the road curved around and just demarcated the boundary north. The road does, however, then curve through the land owned by George Ledlie, and the Mount Relief Plan of John O'Hern.

The native spirits who roamed this central ridge top would never have thought claim to the land could extend any further than what they had already unjustly experienced, and yet it had, here, with their great Venango Trail being termed a privately-owned road.

The year 1848 was marked by a huge development, the approach of the railroad for the first time in Allegheny, and it would signal the death-knell of the Canal, just a mere twenty years old at the time. The very land of Allegheny City would soon be forever altered by this far-reaching mode of transportation, and battles between the city, its residents and the company (which essentially rented land from the city) would reach into just about every decade to come.

The Ohio and Pennsylvania Railroad, connecting western Pennsylvania with the West, was granted a state charter and incorporated as a company in 1848. William Robinson, prominent still, was elected president of the company. This charter would allow for the railroad to come right into Allegheny City from the west end. It began with the granting of a 50-foot wide right-of-way through the West Commons, to Federal Street. The railroad would be simply laid across the land on the Commons, with no depression or elevation of tracks at this time.

The rails began to be laid in late 1850, and the first rail cars to arrive that same year, in celebration before actual rail service could begin, came over the Allegheny Mountains via a canal barge. A large rail yard and repair facilities were constructed just west of Pasture Lane and south of Island Lane, in out lot 255, once belonging to John Park.

The allowance of the railroad's infringement, and now the financial predicament of a city needing revenue, could have easily led the way for other potential West Commons infringements, to the point where there the West Commons might not have survived. The city councils certainly recognized this, so in 1849, one year after the announcement of the railroad's imminent arrival, they put out a "Resolution for the laying out of the West Commons and calling for a Report of the Plan Of."

They would soon see that the decision to have the railroad pass through Allegheny City, though ultimately and essentially good, would stir up decades of trouble—now not so much between city government and its citizens over land usage, but between city government and the railroad over the ability to work well together within upcoming guidelines that would be protective of the land.

By the year 1851, there was established rail service from New Brighton, about 30 miles down the Ohio River, to Allegheny City. The railroad followed a path into the city that somewhat paralleled the Ohio River, further inland. Thus it cut a path from Manchester heading southeasterly into the city, and hit the major rail yard west of Pleasant Valley. Just beyond this point, before its arrival onto the Commons, the tracks bisected, at a forty-five degree angle, where Pasture Lane intersected North Avenue. From there, they passed through the West Commons to its southernmost point just below the *Burying Ground*, and then straightened out easterly right above the canal basin.

The Canal was still in operation, but its era almost over. The Canal, itself, and all of its structures were sold to the railroad in 1857, and indeed its eastern line out of Allegheny City would utilize the line of the land where the Canal cut through town. For a short while, the railroad maintained the rest of the Canal, but when it was beginning to be abandoned statewide in a few short years, all of it would go. The railroad, alongside the Canal pathway, was elevated.

As well in 1857, a railroad bridge was finally constructed across the Allegheny, close to the aqueduct, which too was still in operation, albeit waning. Only then, six years after Allegheny City, did Pittsburgh receive its first rail cars.

In the interim, passengers went across to board in Allegheny. They could make it to the Ohio line by 1853, and all the way to the Chicago depot come the end of the decade.

There would be five stations in and leading to Allegheny City from the west. The main terminal was where Federal Street cut through the South Commons. Here would soon be constructed a beautiful station, reflecting the new corporate name—the Pittsburgh, Fort Wayne & Chicago Railroad Depot (PFt.W& CRR). Other stations were at Woods Run, the area as it was becoming known around John Woods' original Farm, and Jack's Run, also named for a stream, close by the prior. These stations received passengers traveling from Allegheny City to the countryside north and west, as they looked out window views of Pasture Lane and Pleasant Valley, perhaps their city's last vestige of true countryside, disappearing behind them. The railroad would help to further develop the outlying countryside areas as well.

Certainly, there was outcry over the co-opting, once again, of the original agreement for the Commons land to be for the citizens who owned original town lots. Talk of the council Resolution calling for plans to protect the land did little to silence claims, in particular, that passenger platforms, across Second Bank on the South Commons, were interfering with the grazing of cattle. Interestingly, the judge decided in favor of the railroad here; he proclaimed that portion of the Commons to have not had grass growing on it for some time!

By the 1850s, there were plenty of people living in Allegheny who were on lots that had lost any connection to the in/out lot pairing. Most importantly, it seems this particular collective outcry, along with the judge's eye-opening public remarks, marks the end of a time when the original purpose of the Commons would be fought for, as common grazing land, but the true beginning of a time when the citizens, themselves, decidedly embraced a turn toward beautification and possible formation of a future park on the land.

What certainly aided this cause, ironically, and prompted the thoughts that something must be done with the Commons land, was that it was so visible outside the windows of passing trains coming into the city. And in addition to the railroad, in the 1850s, there was now another means of transportation affording optimum comparison of the decrepit land with the lovely countryside still in existence off Pasture Lane. The modern transportation convenience afforded those who lived northwest of the *City Line*, and in Manchester, was the Pleasant Valley Passenger Railway—trolley cars pulled by two horses, or occasionally mules. When first established, it ran as far north as Woods Run. (Horse-drawn private coaches and carriages had been the mode of transportation prior, but with the improvement of the roads, this more public transportation could benefit many citizens.)

The tracks of the passenger railway were made up of strips of iron attached to wood embedded in the middle of the roadway. The cars had no heat, so straw was strewn across the floor bottoms to keep the feet of riders warm. Illumination at night came from oil lamps hung inside.

The bells on the horses and mules could be heard coming from a distance, and would be a welcome and familiar sound through the next thirty years. And with the tails of the animals clipped for supposed efficiency (but more than likely not to annoy the driver stationed at their rear, right before the car), the railway cars became known as *Bob-Tails*. Various routes would be depicted not by number but by the color of striping on the outside of the cars. Around 1859, Allegheny councils gave consent for the construction of rails to the center of the city, by way of West Ohio Street to Federal. A decade later, they would extend to beyond the East Commons.

With the established railroad and passenger trolley service, as well as prolific, successful industry, Allegheny City's common grounds looked nothing like they had even a couple decades earlier. Largely, and especially in the west and east, they had become industrial dumping grounds no longer fit for animal grazing. Soap manufacturers and butchers had moved in along the Allegheny banks by the 1850s, and the stench now filling the runs through those areas was overwhelming. The West Commons, in particular, had ravines that held stagnant water, prone to overflow. Garbage from regular citizens, who followed the model of industry, had been polluting the land as well.

Remarkably, only a small picnic area was left of the original pastoral green space.

The majority of citizens could see their own shameful neglect of the land. So in 1856, Allegheny City councils appointed trustees to raise funds to better all of the Commons. They decided to tackle the smallest area first, the Southeast Commons. One year later, the Southwest would be attended to. This was the area around Second Bank (now being also referred to by its new name, Stockton Avenue) at the railroad depot, and was considered priority.

The first newspaper of Allegheny's city era, the *Allegheny Morning Express*, came out in 1843. Classified ads that still exist show the flavor of the times. And the range of real estate available just north of the Commons is evident in a detail of some structures:

>A two story frame house on Jefferson Street, with stone cellar—containing four rooms; house 20 by 30 feet; lot 20 by 50 feet. Rent, $50—price, $550.
>A two story frame house on Whiteoak alley, 15 by 25 feet; 4 rooms; lot 15 by 90 to a 10 foot alley; with a stable on back end of lot for six horses. Rent $72—price $600.
>A two story brick house 19 ft. 8 in. in front, by 72 ft. back, containing 9 rooms and cellars—well finished and papered—with a well and pump in the rear. Rent $125 per year. Lot 23 by 96 to a ten foot alley. Situate on Federal Street, north of North Commons. Price, $2,000.

William Irvin, who was living at the corner of Robinson and Correy Streets two years earlier, ran his own extensive detail of available properties in an ad with the title caption, "**Rare Chances!**" In it he delineates several of his land holdings and desires, including

>"A FINE HOUSE AND LOT, situated on the second bank, just above the canal locks, adjoining Judge Warner, in Allegheny City. The lot is 50 feet front by 280 feet deep, to a street. The house is large, convenient and well finished, and recently put in complete repair. This property will be sold very low, or exchanged for Pittsburgh manufactured articles.

The next is a desirable piece of vacant ground, suitable for a factory or private dwellings, but about minutes' walk from Old Bridge, in Allegheny City. It is 95 feet on Craig Street, 30 from corner of Robinson, running back 120 ft. to a 50 feet street, on bank of canal....

There are also four other vacant lots, eligibly situated on Bank Lane, fronting the river 25 feet by 140 each, to a 20 ft. alley...."

Other classifieds also show Allegheny's character:

LIVERY STABLE REMOVED
Mr. John Oliver has removed his LIVERY STABLE to the premises lately occupied by Mrs. m'Kelvy, deceased, on Federal street, above the Diamond, where he has fitted up a large and commodious Stable. His stock of CARRIAGES and BUGGIES are entirely new, of the first quality and most modern styles. HORSES, of the finest make, and can go wither in harness or under the Saddle. Terms moderate.
N. B. Also, an elegant HEARSE, which, with any number of CARRIAGES, will be furnished on the shortest notice.

THOMAS FARLEY, Cabinet and Chair Manufacturer, and Undertaker, next door to Mr. J. Price's Confectionary, Federal street, Allegheny.

G. LAMB, FASHIONABLE TAILOR, Robinson's Row, Federal st. Allegheny, is now prepared to receive orders for making every description of gentleman's garments in the most durable manner and according to the latest style of fashion. He respectfully solicits a share of public patronage.

Besides, he keeps constantly on hand a choice and general assortment of Cloths and Cassimers, suitable for pants and coats, together with a variety of beautiful vest patterns. Also, Shirts, Shirt Bosoms and gentleman's Handkerchiefs and Cravats.

CLOCKS! CLOCKS!!—J.M. Gillett, successor to A. S. Burwell & Co. informs his friends and the public generally, that he has opened with a general assortment of the best modern improved Eight Day and Thirty Hour Brass Clocks. Also, an assortment of Alarm Clocks, to awaken a person any hour of the night. The clocks will be sold, wholesale or retail, as low as they can be purchased in Pittsburgh, or at any other place in the west.

Also, constantly on hand, Prints, Looking Glasses, etc.
Clocks repaired and warranted; Clock Trimmings always on hand.
J.M. Gillett, Federal Street, first house in M'Lane's Row, and
opposite Blackstock's Cotton Factory.

Word would be placed in Pittsburgh newspapers, in addition to those in
Allegheny, for public notices of all kinds. Formal ordinances and calls for
proposals for Allegheny City, its available real estate, and various other
business advertisements would all be found in the *Pittsburgh Gazette*.

It would only take about ten years for the new city of Allegheny to rise
to 21,000 in population, essentially doubling its size and reaching what
Pittsburgh had been just ten years prior. But after this point, and for the first
time, the city would level off, and even experience a slight decline—in large
part, due to several cotton mill closures after the riots of 1848–50.

Culturally, things had finally begun to blossom on the north side of the
river, with literary societies the first to form. Included in the ranks would be a
young Stephen Foster, resident of Union Avenue just above Stockton, and to
be the nation's beloved folk music composer. As well, though hardly 'high
society,' among the many ordinances Allegheny City government was drawing up at this time were guidelines for the numerous entertainments—
"Shows" and "Exhibitions" that wanted to encamp on the river bank. Various
circus-like fare mainly, the area that continued to seem best suited for their
staging was that infamous lowland, which also happened to be just to the
west of the "Barefoot Square" neighborhood. To the north and west of this
area, was Ridge Avenue, the area slowly becoming known as where the ultra-
wealthy built homes. Separating both ends of the spectrum was Seminary
Hill—a barrier between the rich, and the most colorful elements of society,
the traveling artists and entertainers.

Since the water-works opened in 1849, houses were able to at least start
looking toward accommodation of primitive plumbing. But this was to be
found only in homes of the wealthiest for the first few decades. In particular,
Ridge Avenue and parts of Manchester, due to the successful rise of industry,
had an inordinate share of the wealthy now, and some families, despite being
all the way across town from the water-works in Duquesne borough, made
arrangements with Allegheny City to have water pumped their way.

Early records show two families specifically making this request for their
home structures. As recorded, "a certain two-story frame dwelling house

fronting on Beaver Street," (formerly Ferry Lane) and belonging to a Simpson family, "containing 10 rooms," requested water for "culinary and household purposes for $9/year." Permitted by the Councils, their structure would be outfitted for that same price with "one bath tub... for one year."

As well, "water for the use of one horse for two years" was granted the family, and "a hydrant for the purposes of washing the pavement for duration of two years." The Agreement went on to state that, "the supply of water to be always in the pipes for the above uses unless of some unavoidable accident with the water-works or bursting of the pipes."

The other family benefitting from a similar arrangement was that of John B. Kennedy, who had the same type of house but with only 9 rooms, "fronting on the bank" of the Ohio, in a section that would later become known as Chateau, but at this point was relatively undeveloped. By 1859, ten years later, there would be a slew of others in nearby Manchester who would be granted similar privilege.

One early Allegheny industry, in fact the first that had any staying power, just could not quite benefit from the availability of water being pumped that way, and would not make it to 1860. The Irwin Rope Walk, in the hands of heir John Irwin and wife Abigail, had experienced a series of fires since the 1830s, the last being 1859. They sold the property, but Allegheny City's indebtedness to the Irwins' vision and loyalty would be honored in the following decade.

It seems one of the the brightest new industries in the city, around the late 1850s, would be lumber. Six or seven sawmills, as well as boatyards, operated along the Allegheny and Ohio river fronts. One of the largest was Brewster and Watson. In 1854, the largest barge ever built in the area was constructed near the site of old Killbuck Island, for George Ledlie, who was a coal operator. Many barges of the time would be loaded with coal and ice at this location, sharing the space with the entertainers' tents. From here, the raw materials (as well as some hobos, surely) would be drawn down the Ohio and Mississippi Rivers towards New Orleans.

Several Alleghenians in the 1850s built large estates just outside the *City Line*, with wealth comparable to some of the early families of industry in Manchester. Two estates in particular rivaled others around Allegheny City in their view. Two men who had structures that sat prominently illustrative on an early 1852 map of Allegheny City were Thompson Bell and Washington McClintock.

Bell's home, just outside the City Line above the Third Ward, sat upon the spot formerly occupied by the nunnery, as well as an area northward. Sometime after 1835, when the Flemish order of nuns left Mount Alvernio, Bell, a stockbroker, purchased the land. The structure he would build looked villa-like, with a cupola-adorned building in the rear. His house style surely informed others in later decades on the spot, as the hilltop would come to have a few other elegant villas for those of wealth, but also cottages in similar style for those of more measured means. He named his plots of land (which encompassed original land plots belonging to Fowler and McClelland), "*Ben Villa*." Just to the east of his estate would have been where James O'Hara's official *High Rough Land* began, even though Bell's land was a high, rough perch in itself, one of those areas just not defined so by Redick's survey map.

A few years after his purchase, Bell's neighbor would be a young Robert Henderson. He began operating stone quarries, with approach from the west side of the hill, just before the terminus of the Franklin Road (and before the start of the Perrysville Plank Road). This would lie just below the *Ben Villa* property. James Andrews, a wealthy bridge builder, also purchased an adjacent piece of land, to the north and west of Bell's, looking down upon where the road was aborted straight northward and curved instead up and around the Perrysville Plank Road. He built a fine home on that very hill, east of the hill's separation, that caused the original Indian trail to swerve from its straight path. Fronted by a large and ornate iron gate, it was known to hold several slaves in the 1850s.

Washington McClintock's fortune came from a dry goods and carpet business in Pittsburgh, but he chose for his home Allegheny City. He built his estate atop the western side of the central hill, on the other side of the Perrysville Plank Road. He would be neighbor to McNaugher, whose more modest home was further around the bends of the Perrysville Plank Road, and who lacked the spectacular view down upon Allegheny that McClintock had. His other neighbor, in the woods below his home, was another contractor, James McBrier.

McClintock had the most elaborate residence of the time in what was just outside the *City Line* above the Second Ward. At the top of the ridge, as the Perrysville Plank Road had just finished rounding toward the peak, a gated drive sat off to the left, which brought one onto the McClintock property. His house sat on a flat area of land just above the westward slope of the hill that had been Andrew Guyer's original property. Of Scottish descent,

Washington and his wife Eliza lived there with their seven children and his elderly father. In the vast orchards on the back of their estate—filled with pear, transplanted peach, and many locust trees—the children would play on a hillside that looked downward toward a serene Pasture Lane.

Spearheaded by a Mr. L. Bradley, the Allegheny Telescope Association would come into being in 1858, and Washington McClintock was one of a number of Alleghenians who was a founding member. News of the finding of Donati's Comet this year had spread about the country, and a significant number of men in Allegheny were sufficiently inspired to search the heavens as collective amateurs. Within a year, their group would grow to thirty, and included physician and famous Allegheny citizen, Felix Brunot. Their objective was "to collect sufficient funds for the erection of an observatory, and placing in it a telescope of sufficient magnifying power to bring the heavenly bodies near enough to be viewed with greater interest and satisfaction."

The start of the new decade to come would have the State Legislature, no less, granting this affiliation of men a charter for an Allegheny Observatory, whose purpose was the pursuit of astronomical observations. The established new board would be comprised of five individuals, one of whom was another famous man and landholder (but nonresident) adjacent to McClintock's holdings on the hill—William Thaw. Thaw was wealthy and educated, but as equally enthused by astronomy and scientific inquiry as the self-made businessmen in the association, like McClintock, and others of far more humbler means.

Being that an observatory building would be required to house the desired telescope, Thaw financially supported, and the year 1860 would see this facility a reality in Allegheny. Designed by architects Barr & Moser, it was a simple two-story building with a "central domed hexagonal observation room" and quaint shuttered windows. Eight acres of the land was donated— by neighbors Matthew Ferguson and Washington McClintock. A small portion still had to be bought, from Robert Ashworth's holdings. The chosen spot, on the combined land, was across the Perrysville Plank Road from McClintock's estate.

It would be approached by a sharp right turn from the Plank Road just before the sight of McClintock's gated drive at the peak. It would thus be a spot at the highest point above central Allegheny City, that area above the Perrysville Plank Road that was the sole reason, in effect, that the earliest natives had to go up and around the great tiered ridge to commence northward, since this land jutted outward and high above the ridge below.

As it were, even though the Perrysville Plank Road had some inhabitants living along the route upward, the land on the ridge still above it had not yet been developed, only claimed as owned by various landholders over the decades beyond which James O'Hara had any more claim to.

The very high hilltop would not yet have any structures built on it, except for what would here be Allegheny's first Observatory. It would be a place where more than just the heavens above would be observed and contemplated—as citizens interested in ideas and inquiry would soon come to gather around a facility here that all started with inspired, amateur affiliation, one that harmonized the intellectual, business and even social spheres of Allegheny upcoming.

In the same spot where natives took in a majestic view of the surrounding land, the Observatory triumphantly sat. Seen from below, in Allegheny City and Pittsburgh alike, it was a crown high atop the tiered land long trodden northward by so many. Unlike other modernizations that had been stripping the land of its original beauty, the native spirits haunting this hill perhaps found no fault with the white man's reach, here, toward understanding the heavens.

chapter seven:
OLD CITY LINE &
ORIGINAL MILLIONAIRE'S ROW

Allegheny City had a population of just under 30,000 in 1860. At the top of the decade, several important changes were taking place with regard to infrastructure, transportation and once again, land boundaries. The city decided to spend close to $400,000 to expand its water system. Water would soon be available to more sections of Allegheny, but still be decades away from the point where it would be afforded cart-blanche to all citizens.

The lower section of "the old Franklin Road," between the center of Allegheny City and the river, was now beginning to simultaneously be referred to as Federal Street. Around this time, the recently extended passenger railway could then traverse down Federal Street and cross the river to Pittsburgh.

The city was fiscally having some problems, as the Pennsylvania Railroad defaulted in meeting its bond obligations. For several years, the railroad had been going through reorganization, and the city would struggle in its general business relationship and financial dealings with the company.

Township boundaries just north of Allegheny City were changing at this time. McClure Township was carved out of the southern sections of Reserve and Ross Townships. Technically, then, the area just above the *City Line*, where McNaugher and McClintock lived, was part of McClure, even though the land was sparsely populated there and it was considered to be Allegheny, as in the original out lot designations.

It would be the month of December of 1860 that would bring the reality of the Civil War to Allegheny City. Alleghenians would witness quite a revolt from the citizens across the river to news that 700 tons of ammunition was being requested of Pittsburgh, for shipment to the port of New Orleans. These arms were sitting in the arsenal in Pittsburgh's east end, along the Allegheny River. Threats of violent resistance were vehemently expressed, should the arms be released for river transport. Both Pittsburgh and

Allegheny City, though surely holding some hidden sympathizers to Southern cause, were decidedly pro-Union.

The request of arms, to essentially Confederate territory, was stayed, and the citizens of all of Allegheny County realized that they needed to more fully consider the potential consequence of imminent war upon their region. By April of 1861, Union troops had already begun their passage east to west, and vice versa, via the railroad and the rivers about Allegheny City and Pittsburgh. Citizens of both, especially women, began to organize to feed and otherwise minister to troops passing through. As well, the Western Pennsylvania Hospital, a private early hospital of Allegheny City, would soon begin to tend to some of the wounded that were brought to the city.

President Lincoln stopped briefly in Allegheny, as he passed through on the railroad, en route to his inauguration in February 1861. His train was delayed due to a heavy rain, but upon arrival at the Pittsburgh & Fort Wayne Station, cannons boomed from Seminary Hill and Boyd's Hill in downtown Pittsburgh. He briefly met with the mayor, county officials, and a crowd of Alleghenians, outside the railroad depot near Stockton, then went across to Pittsburgh's Monongahela House on Smithfield Street, downtown, where he was to deliver a speech. He instead spoke the next morning, and strongly downplayed the war.

But then, around summer of 1863, the image of battle closer to home hit home for Allegheny City residents. John Hunt Morgan, renegade Confederate general, crossed north of the Ohio River into that nearby state, looting and terrorizing businesses along with his cavalry. This raider and his comrades caused true alarm for the first and only time during the war, for this region. Enough alarm for southwestern Pennsylvanians to consider garrisons spread about for protection.

They did just that, across Pittsburgh and especially in Allegheny City, where an approach from Ohio would have been far more likely, since the hilltop range on the south side of the Ohio River below the Point prevented ease of access directly into Pittsburgh. Factories and mills—which had already begun to tailor to the war effort in manufacturing armory, saddles, wagons, barrels and the like—shut down their normal operations temporarily in June, in order to mobilize (and pay) their workers to instead construct military defense. By the end of the month, almost 12,000 men, supervised by various government engineers, were completing the building of 32 defensive installations around the city, most of them simply earthworks behind which to watch for invaders—all at the very time that those few decisive days in Gettysburg would eliminate, en masse, any further northern-fought threat.

But Morgan and his raiders were still to be contended with, and Allegheny City was preparing. Of the 32 installations, the most important ones were those on the western side of the city, including an area of Manchester not far from the Allegheny River. Hilltop fortification was especially important and Fort McKeever, largest and most official of the defenses, would thus be constructed on a peak of an area of land north of the *City Line*. It could be gotten to west of the Perrysville Plank Road, a ways north of McNaugher's property and just south of northern land holdings of a man by the name of Samuel Watson. Here, at Fort McKeever, any movement of troops coming from the west could be monitored.

Within Allegheny City, there was a particular defense spot, albeit much smaller and without major structure, at the southern sloping end of McClintock's property, just above McBrier's land. As in the days when the natives had excellent vantage on this spot (of goings-on at both the rivers' confluence and down the Ohio), the garrison on this spot would provide a watch that could now be kept on Allegheny City below, and even on the Point of Pittsburgh as well.

Washington McClintock would likely have donated the garrison land for use by the city during the Civil War; his generosity for civic-minded pursuits would be evident for other purpose, as well, this decade. Too, his oldest son Oliver was a corporal in the 15th Pennsylvania Emergency Militia, involved in the "hasty construction of defenses for [the Pittsburgh region.]"

(THE PITTSBURGH RECORD)

Ohio state militia would cut off all escape routes for Morgan's cavalry by the end of July 1863, and his capture would be near Lisbon, not far over the Pennsylvania state line. Had he made it out of Ohio, Morgan would have been heading into New Brighton and other towns north of the Ohio River, and then directly toward Allegheny City. But the vantage points provided in hilly Pennsylvania were surely known to be superior to flat Ohio, thus a move eastward would have been foolish anyway. Nevertheless, Morgan's capture ensured that none of the military installations in southwestern Pennsylvania, most far more primitive than Fort McKeever, would ever have to become active.

Both the states of Ohio and Pennsylvania treated Morgan and his raiders as outlaws. He and 30 of his troops would be jailed in Columbus, Ohio, and another 118 of his raiders would be sent for incarceration at Allegheny City's Penitentiary. As their threat to the Union diminished, many of those men even began to be treated civilly, being let out for Sunday service in particular. One officer apparently struck up a friendship with a young woman of Allegheny City. Though he and the others would be transferred to Fort Delaware one year later, he maintained correspondence with her and upon release, would eventually marry her.

So Allegheny's West Commons played a minor role in the Civil War as temporal point of incarceration for some Confederates. But in the same year of their release, 1864, the Commons land would take on more war duty. A massive Sanitary Fair, for the cause of the War, was commenced, with extensive temporary structures built on the site of the old Town House and extending onto the West Commons, south of the Penitentiary. (The Town House was being demolished, just as a new City Hall was going up on nearby locale on the Diamond.)

Upon completion that June, thousands attended from Allegheny City and beyond. They would be contributing to the War fund by giving money for attendance at the Fair's Floral Hall, Ladies Bazaar, Exhibition Hall and Mechanic's Hall, among others. As well, visitors spent on "all that could be eaten, worn, sold, or [they] were curious to look at." The appetite for more underground entertainment had already been satisfied, ongoing, with the spectacles down on the banks; now, the more genteel of Allegheny City had also found their social and recreational communal outlet, albeit temporary.

Allegheny City and the City of Pittsburgh had cooperated on matters both essential to their security, and revealing of their humanitarianism and civility during the war. But the rest of the 1860s would have Allegheny as little-spoken about rival to the city at the Point, especially in matters of its houses. Because Allegheny's industry was surpassing that of Pittsburgh's in sheer number and prestige, the accumulated wealth of industry leaders was very evident in the magnificent structures they were able to build and call their homes. These were scattered about Allegheny, but the majority would be on Ridge Avenue on the city's southwestern end. Manchester also was home to wealthy industry leaders, in addition to the industry itself, closer to the river's edge.

The mansions lining Ridge over the next several decades to come would be the first display of such congregated immense wealth in an urban area in southwestern Pennsylvania. Though Pittsburgh's Fifth Avenue, in her east end of the city, would in coming decades earn the title *Millionaire's Row* for its grand homes of wealthy industry barons, it was Ridge Avenue in Allegheny City that was the *original Millionaire's Row*. Even many of the wealthy and influential who made their fortunes in business and industry in Pittsburgh would, just after the Civil War, make residence just across the river in what was seen as the very classy Allegheny City. The mansions would be single-family (but oft extended family), with servant quarters. Libraries and music rooms would certainly be included, as would grand staircases with oak panels, elegant crystal chandeliers, huge foyers, and parlors decorated to the maximum, with sliding pocket doors, stained and leaded glass, plaster friezes and the like.

One such structure in the area, the Killbuck mansion, with the old Chief buried under a mulberry bush in the yard, became at this time home to a Robert McKnight and young bride. (After Reverend Hopkins sold it in 1840, the home was owned for a time by a man named Kennedy.) Mrs. Elizabeth McKnight's maiden name was Denny, and she was the granddaughter of James O'Hara. The wealthy families of the time all intermarried, maintaining their privilege and power.

The McKnights would hold elegant parties over the decades to come, with distinguished visiting dignitaries, including President Ulysses S. Grant, who would come in 1869 to attend the dedication of a monument in the West Commons area. He called upon the McKnights and sat in front of their grand parlor fireplace, with its decorative brown, olive, and green tiles.

Large hillside or hilltop homes became popular, beyond Thomas Bell's *Ben Villa* and McClintock's estate—such as the stone structure Robert Henderson built on Nunnery Hill in the late 1860s, with accumulated wealth as owner of the Union Marble Works. He bought the land of William Hamilton (just east of *Ben Villa*), and built his house on 8 1/2 acres, next to the quarries and neighbor John Huckestein's successful brickyard.

Henderson Street would be the named western approach to Henderson's land holdings. On his land, as well, would be a cottage, a carriage house, a separate stable, and other buildings. His mansion was known for its pink and white Italian marble mantels. Also informed by *Ben Villa*, another cottage, one of humbler means and owned separately, was constructed about this time on the rough hillside as well.

The middle class of Allegheny City could be found, in the 1860s, occupying certainly simpler single-family homes, some with live-in servant stairs and quarters, scattered all about Allegheny City. But though simpler than the mansions and villas, the structures ran a variety that included Italianate and Second Empire style, among others. True attention to decoration within house structures was standard building practice at this time. Some of the more ornate middle-class structures, such as those found in the developed western section of the Mexican War Street tract, were nevertheless row houses—beautifully designed, though attached and land-poor.

The working and lower classes predominated in eastern Allegheny City—perhaps due to the canal tenements earlier permanently identifying that area, though certainly not completely. Nor certainly could the lowest working classes not also be found about other areas of the city. The area north of Ohio Street and east of the Commons, though, would in particular have homes of much humbler means en masse, and with many tenants as occupants, as opposed to owner-occupants or owner occupants with no boarders.

After the Civil War, Mary Schenley had her attorneys lease parts of what had been originally her grandfather's *High Rough Land* plot to developers, for constructing working-class housing and even commercial buildings. She was particularly noted as being resistant to paying for street construction in that area. Prior to Allegheny City stepping in with major infrastructure projects as a municipality, the early days as a Borough were marked by individual landowners actually doing for themselves, constructing and maintaining lanes and wooden sidewalks to their homes. Though a change for the better with the new city stepping in to assume responsibility, many old-timers resisted work on any areas adjoining their property, even if a street needed to be made.

Allegheny City come the 1860s was now full of ethnic diversity beyond that of its original settlers. Racial diversity was harder to come by. The Allegheny City Directory of 1865 would be the last to indicate race, and at that time, African Americans were almost invisible as counted populous. The work of Charles Avery in educating former slaves took place in the Fourth Ward, south of Ohio Street. Here, certainly, if could not be marked their residence, would be a welcome point of gathering for African Americans working as hired servants all about Allegheny.

Just after the Civil War, an influx of not only the wealthy, but also those considered middle-class, would come over from Pittsburgh. Many would set up residence in Manchester and the Mexican War Streets. The course of action would be for any smaller, older homes in those areas to be demolished and slightly larger ones built by developers on the various land plots available, albeit limited in dimension. Thus, areas that long before used to have structures for only lower-class workers of the land, such as the eastern Mexican War Streets, now were being revived by new structures built for doctors, lawyers and other professionals. This would be the first great example of gentrification to take place in Allegheny City.

Women in Allegheny City, like elsewhere in the country, were still afforded little real power at the time. Real estate would oft be listed in a wife's name, especially in cases where the property was just a rental property, but this was a technicality only. Aside from women of wealth like Mary Schenley, or other daughters of inheritance, like famed Allegheny City-born artist Mary Cassatt, being female in american society at this time was a fairly defined and regimented role, with institutions of learning even denying access still.

Allegheny City was no different; few women were *able* to hold real power except for the power that comes with massive wealth and prestige. Women for the most part held active roles in the household and society, but rarely elsewhere. There were indeed some women business owners; many times it was due to maintenance after the death of a husband, however. One woman merchant, Mrs. J. Arnold, who had been living in Allegheny City since 1834, was operating a business at 98 Federal Street in the 1860s. Occupying a three-story brick building there, she was a purveyor of "Book, Stationery, Toys and Fancy Goods" for adults and children alike.

A listing of business taxes collected in 1860, that survives in archival material, includes revenue from a foundry, innkeeper, grocer, lamp manufacturer, flour merchant, variety store, bakery, tinner, beer hall, blacksmith, confectionery, coal merchant, cooper, dry good merchant, plumber and gas fitter, livery stable, and tobacconist, among others.

The whole of the 1860s continued to see new businesses start up and thrive in the center of town. The Henry Wheeler Company, at 39 West Diamond Street, was established, and would continue to flourish for well over a century. As well, on the southwest corner of the Diamond was the Bepler Hotel, started in 1866. It would be a large three-story brick structure, with a stable accommodating 115 horses. Lodging was $1/day at the time to transients.

Likely the most important business to be established by the end of the decade, however, was a store that would for long time after be synonymous with the downtown of Allegheny City. Boggs and Buhl Department Store was started in 1869 by two enterprising men who would see to the clothing and household needs of Allegheny residents rich and poor. (There appears to be no relation to James Boggs, second white settler of the area, and Martha Boggs Robinson's first husband.)

Other businesses and industry thrived as well. The Eureka Planing Mill and store was a sash and door factory that would find their business services requested by just about every contractor and homeowner in the area. It would be founded in 1868. They were on North Avenue between East and Middle Streets. Allegheny City Mills was a flour mill started by John Voegtly, and the Pearl Steam Mills was owned by Kennedy and Bros., at the corner of Lacock, near the old Canal. Herr's Island further saw mills and even oil refineries set up shop at this time.

The First National Bank of Allegheny was chartered in the 1860s. Allegheny National Bank also was established around this time, and by the end of the decade, Workingman's Bank would open.

The condition of the Town House (built not during Town, but Borough era in 1833) was addressed at the top of the decade, before the Sanitary Fair plans were set in motion. Allegheny City Select and Common Councils apparently made plans, originally, to repair and extend the old building, but then four years later would have these specifications be applied to a new building on a nearby site: "The old gable is to be torn down.... All walls colored red on the plan are to be built, with the best quality, well-burnt, hand made bricks.... The first floor [stairs] and all corridors are to be Southern yellow pine. All other lumber is to be white pine...all perfectly sound and seasoned.... Water Closets are to be fitted up, with partitions...." As well, there were specifications on the iron work, plastering and gas fittings. The new City Hall would be built by 1864, designed by Charles Antoine Colomb Gengembre, a noted French architect who resided in Allegheny.

That same year, as the Town House was also being demolished and in its place the Sanitary Fair structures going up, the old Market House, too, would be replaced. Up went a one-story brick structure with attractive curved roof lines.

The first fire alarm boxes would be installed in Allegheny City of the

1860s, the first steam-operated fire engine was purchased, and upgrading of roads continued to occur. The Councils in particular deliberated over and approved the straightening of River Avenue in the fourth ward. Something council members had also been discussing at length in recent years, house numbering for mail delivery and as an address system, would get off to a slow but definite start. And the Pennsylvania Canal in Allegheny City finally came to its end before the decade was half over, when water would be drained and the harbor back-filled with large stones.

With the Canal's replacement, the railroad, had come related new industries: The Standard Car Heating and Ventilating Company, and the Westinghouse Air Brake Company. The Pittsburgh Locomotive and Car Works was also established; they were builders of locomotive engines. Located on Beaver Avenue in what was still Manchester Borough in 1865, it would flourish over the next several decades, especially under Superintendent D.A. Wightman. (SMITHSONIAN)

Allegheny had its share of financial trouble to begin the decade, due to the railroad bonds issue. What cotton mills were still there after the earlier riots also closed their doors, as supply from the south dried up as the war had raged on. The opening of new business and industry after the war was especially important, due to these reasons. The country as a whole, and still Allegheny City to an extent, would experience a difficult time after the War, with bank foreclosures being common, strikes, and unemployment. Industry, and especially the workers powering it, were changing, but Allegheny was doing quite well, still.

For social and recreational purpose, Alleghenians had started coming together in a newfound way as a community—both at the Sanitary Fair, which drew record numbers, and on the river bank, as the more adventurous would make a point of catching the edgier entertainments. Going out for relaxation and entertainment purpose, sometimes paired with community humanitarian concern, became popular. Literary societies, and art and musical groups which began forming once the city was in its youth, satisfied the taste of others.

No longer was recreation reserved only for the privileged who did not have to work a farm or operate a storefront. New community bonds in social halls, often formed around ethnic lines, were also established, including one for the german residents of Deutschtown, in eastern Allegheny, named the Caecelia Maennerchor.

As a larger community, Alleghenians were indeed doing more together. Victorian Baseball, played for the first time in the city after the Civil War, became an instant recreational bond, a pleasant past-time to be had by all. (Baseball enthusiasm was present in Pittsburgh, as well, at the time.) Union Park and Recreation Park, located in the western part of the city near the Manchester line, were the first locations for the game.

All of the described activities, that essentially had Alleghenians out in the community for fun and recreation, helped pave the way for a determination of what to do about the Commons land—since it was no longer feasible to consider it for grazing purposes, but nor could it be abandoned as the once-unique gem of the community that it had been.

With changes likely coming to the future of the Commons, though nothing had yet been decided upon, Allegheny's Councils felt it best, in 1861, to plan on moving the *Burying Ground*, which sat at the eastern foot of Seminary Hill. They asked Mount Union Cemetery to consider re-interring Allegheny Town's first souls. Mount Union agreed, and for a listed fee of $1, as well as $575, they did all the labor involved. Allegheny City paid them to dig up the graves and "cover the boxes," as well as for the carriage involved in transport and the ground space at their hillside cemetery just up Pasture Lane.

About a year or so later, *Mount Union Cemetery* would merge with its neighbor cemetery, Hill Dale, becoming Union Dale. They would get a state charter by the end of the decade, ensuring the protection of the seventy-five beautiful, hilly acres sloping toward the north, south and west. Also adjacent to the new merged cemetery, at that point, would be Highwood Cemetery just adjacent on the north, which would stay distinct from Union Dale.

The southern portion of Pasture Lane, just west of the Commons and especially well-traveled, no longer seemed a suitable name for the main road leading to Ridge Avenue's mansions. The city thus decided to honor John Irwin, who so made a name in that very area. Pasture Lane would be renamed Irwin Avenue, south of the intersection of North Avenue, by the year 1867.

Also after the Civil War's end, in 1865, did Allegheny expand again. This time, it did so as a city increasing its territory, rather than needing to achieve any higher municipal standing. As such, the Borough of Manchester was officially annexed to the City of Allegheny.

Manchester and Allegheny were close allies, considering that from Allegheny's conception, Manchester lots were actually Allegheny Town out lots. Those who lived in Manchester thought of themselves as Alleghenians anyway. And as would also be the case with all Allegheny City annexations of land that was joined with them originally, the annexed wanted to be joined back.

In this case, Manchester wanted the further prestige that came with an official designation as one of Allegheny's neighborhoods, as opposed to being a mere Borough. And this was despite the fact that Manchester, on its own, had quite a lot of prestige and sheer accumulated wealth. Nevertheless, it knew its prestige would increase in other ways if paired with Allegheny. With city status also came full privileges of gas lighting, water services and the like for all citizens (at least as much as was available to citizens in Allegheny at this time).

Allegheny City, of course, would find profitable the increased tax revenue, and the knowledge of realizing that even their most accomplished neighbors saw themselves as one of their own. The annexation was thus friendly, and "Old 'Chester,'" as it was lovingly referred to by all, would retain its name, as simply one of Allegheny City's growing neighborhoods.

At the same time, the 'Old City Line,' as it was now called, would in this area also expand below, or southwestward, of Manchester, all the way to the river. This land area, previously undesignated, would become the new Fifth Ward of Allegheny City, and what had been Manchester Borough, the Sixth Ward.

As well, the northern *City Line* (and the one most oft invoked as Allegheny's main border) expanded a bit northward by 1867. It was one area, in particular, however, that had the most hilly woods and vast northern countryside left unsettled. So at this time, the old Second and Third Ward boundaries were simply stretched incrementally northward again, to incorporate the added land. Their boundary lines were now as far north as where a line could be drawn from the place where Island Lane (further up Pasture Lane on the west) could go across to the northern boundary to where Duquesne Borough began. (Thus including McClintock and McNaugher as official Allegheny citizens.)

This same year that the Second and Third Wards would be extended northward, the Allegheny Observatory, which had such humble beginnings just nine years earlier, formally began an affiliation with the Western University of Pennsylvania. (It was still located in downtown Pittsburgh.) William Thaw, major benefactor of Observatory activities with his wealth from railroad business, had recently provided the means for the start of a partial endowment for the Observatory, and had been expressing the desire to have the University (of which he was a Trustee) oversee the Observatory. A "Dr. G. Woods" also urged all original contributors, who lent the land for the Observatory, to turn over the title to the university, cementing the connection even further.

So the hilltop Observatory land would not only become officially part of Allegheny City's Second Ward in the late 1860s—it also was now considered owned by the University. The Observatory Board was authorized to "execute to the Western University of Pennsylvania the necessary dues in fees for the real estate of the Allegheny Observatory for the consideration of stipulation and engagements in proper legal form that said University will maintain the Observatory in good order and condition...."

Not everyone involved with the Observatory liked the arrangement. It "met with opposition from a few stockholders, who [continued to] express their opinion that the interests of the Observatory were sacrificed by the transfer. But the great majority of the stockholders concurred in it." The newly appointed director the year its formal partnership began, 1867, would be a scientist by the name of Samuel Pierpont Langley.

Land on the east side of the city, meanwhile, up to but not including Duquesne Borough, was also now pulled into the eastern section of Allegheny. It was a large land area, incorporating part of the community of Mount Troy, the mount above the Butler 'Pike. Picking up from where it had left off in annexing Manchester, this eastern land would be Allegheny's Seventh Ward.

Then just one year later, the Eighth Ward would be created through the annexation of Duquesne Borough, which included Herr's Island.

The 'Old City Line,' on east, west and north fronts (and though really not so old at all), was used nostalgically to refer to those boundaries being thought up at the end of the Borough era, just before the official turn to city status.

Allegheny City was at the same time, in the late 1860s, exerting not-unwelcome influence in private matters of business with extreme civic importance. The then-called Federal Street and Pleasant Valley Passenger Railway would be incorporated by the city, and given the right to go wherever it wanted. One line actually traveled from the center of town all the way north to McClure Township via Pasture Lane. With all the recent annexations and extensions of Allegheny territory by this time, that township, and others northern, were themselves looking to officiate as city territory what had started as "Allegheny" land anyway, under Redick's survey.

On other matters of land, a beautiful deed survives from April 12, 1867, in archives of the City of Allegheny, showing the Councils' decision to move the Poor Farm:

> [Regarding] that ground situate in [what by then had become] Shaler Township. between the Mayor and the Directors of the Poor of the City of Allegheny.... An Act Authorizing the sale of the Allegheny City Poor Farm, and to purchase another farm for the same purpose... with a new, larger, double-tract of land within the state... with the buildings, improvements, woods, ways, waters, water courses, rights, liberties, privileges, hereditaments and appurtenances whatsoever thereunto belonging.

Allegheny City still would have more than its share of social service institutions for the indigent right within city boundaries by the late 1860s. The Orphan's Home, on the corner of Ridge Avenue that bordered the Commons, had become refuge to those orphaned by ravages of the Civil War. As well, there was an Orphan's Home on Troy Hill, the name that the Mount Troy community would slowly begin to go by once brought into the city. And there was the Home of the Friendless, the Little Sisters of the Poor, and others.

The latter half of the 1860s would end up being some of the most significant years to shape Allegheny's history. There were the dramatic changes to the 'Old City Line;' the University affiliation, endowment and new director for the Observatory; and finally movement toward doing something beneficial with the Commons.

The land upon which the City of Allegheny sat, around 1867, was no longer a pastoral town setting, and surely long beyond lush wilderness. For any of those left of General Robinson's generation, who might have been around just before the last century's turn, the landscape had definitely changed. (Rare it must have been, however, to hear of boyhood memories of the land at Allegheny Town's inception). In fashioning their country-like, but decidedly urban, dwelling place, Alleghenians over many decades had remade the spot of the *Reserved Tract opposite Pittsburg*. They had tried to bring along the pastoral qualities that had made up their little frontier town and rural community, but some of their land, in particular, hadn't made it through the transformation to city unscathed. Some of the land especially visibly suffered.

The Commons had really started to look degraded by mid-decade, as former slights on the land were still evident, and now the impediment of the railroad made the area look truly uninviting to the Allegheny citizen. Allegheny Councils were ready to act. They approved the appointment of trustees to a committee that would raise funds for the Commons improvement. The need was sorely apparent, to definitively do something about the eyesore for all city residents, and certainly the wealthy, those living closest, on its west side.

Allegheny City legislators were very aware that a decade earlier, New York City had held a competition over plans for their central land space. They also knew that the first 'Park for the People' had been established in London in 1840. Such parks as these two, and also one in France after 1850, were models for council to contemplate. It was understood, however, that for *sanitary* purpose, if not cultural and aesthetic, the Commons needed to be addressed. They had begun to realize that the citizens of a city needed clean air and land space amidst the bustle and smog and stench of commerce and industrialization.

One year before the Committee was formed, Allegheny City reached out to citizens to get ideas on what to do about the situation. They "offered a premium of $100 for the best plan offered for the improvement of the Common ground," according to archival material. And just one year after the committee's formation, in 1868, Allegheny City would finally have a plan. All of the Commons ground would become a public park, under the newly-titled *Common Ground Improvement Act*.

An appointed commission working under this Act would take their lead from Victorian reformers in England and New York. Finally the Commons would again stand for *collective* use. Park planners would be looking toward creating a pastoral space conducive to social and recreational activities, amidst, and despite the city's successful industrialization.

As was the intent of Central Park in New York, so would be the aim of the commission in Allegheny. In fact, the term *rus in urb* was used to define the desired effect, "country in the city." Open lawn areas, fountains, a pond, elaborate shrubbery and trees and flowers, music pavilions and sculpture—all were envisioned.

The City Engineer, Charles Davis, prepared a map and took bids for the park development. Five firms representative of work in Washington D.C., Boston and New York (including the engineer, and the designer of Central Park) were chosen to compete.

Central Park's engineer, William H. Grant, of Mitchell and Grant, was selected. His and the commission's intent, purposely artistic, was to *create a scene* with the land, but to be free of intricacy—simplicity and authenticity was the goal.

The park in its early development plan would be described a century later by architectural historian Walter Kidney— "an ensemble of partly straight, partly winding, mainly symmetrical paths for quiet strolling and sitting, punctuated by fountains and eventually statues and monuments."

The West Common, as it had the most land space but also most infringements over the years, would be particularly singled out as an area where attention could be devoted to development of several sought-after features—a pond, a bandstand for music, and a later floral conservatory. There would be excavation north of the railroad for an irregular-shaped pond and two natural-looking hillocks with the earth, joined by a rustic bridge over the railroad. A rockery around the pond was also desired.

Indeed, the presence of a railroad through the land now determined to be a park was a consideration to be dealt with. Though to a certain degree charming, it nevertheless brought up undeniable concerns about boundary, safety, and commotion—that which one aims to avoid in going into a park from an urban area. Plans in the beginning had the "grading and turfing of slopes by the railroad to within three feet of the rails, and neat, compact graveling of the road bed, with flowers and shrubbery planted within view of it...." (The railroad still simply crossed the flat of the land, only to be further elevated east of the depot on Federal Street.) As well, there were to be "deep ditches at the crossings by Irwin Avenue [formerly Pasture Lane] and

Webster Street [later] (Sherman Avenue) to exclude stray cattle and pigs."

Soon, plans would call for an entire wall to separate the line of the railroad. The problem of the railroad's entrance onto a space that was intended to be safe and pastoral would not be better solved until 1912, when the railroad tracks would actually be sunken, and an iron fence put up around both sides. Then, its presence would be less hazardous,its sound less grating, and the railroad finally would be accepted as a quaint addition to the park.

Because the commission was so impressed by views provided by inclined areas of parks visited in Philadelphia and New York, they had the designer look at the Seminary Hill land (most of the land recently available again to the City, and part of the original Commons.) Development plans proceeded, with a circular hilltop drive and plans for a monument there. Two years into this development, the city decided to purchase the full rest of the hilltop, as well, and to ensure a "desirable approach to the summit," which apparently could only be had by way of Irwin Avenue. Also to be dealt with was the fact that clay pits and brick kilns littered the very steep and craggy eastern side of the hill. Below these, at Merchant Street, and just about where the *Burying Ground* had been excavated at the beginning of the decade, was the expanse of a coal yard near the passing railroad.

The commission plans also called for "paving of all the roads encircling the park with gravel or macadam (asphalt), rather than cobblestones...." And the design of the park would deliberately have any fountains, elaborate plantings, and monuments to be easily visible from outside the park.

Grant originally called for the vacating of Stockton Avenue, and the transforming of the small Commons land area there, and more, as part of the park, directly adjacent to property lines and railroad depot. This was obviously seen as necessary to maintain the continuity of the park with relation to the original Commons being a full rectangle around the town. The little south part of the Commons would stay as a small strip of the park, but Stockton Avenue would remain.

Construction of the park actually started in 1868, but would not be fully completed until 1876. Even before the start of 1870, though, much work already had been accomplished. All citizens of Allegheny—the neighboring wealthy of Ridge Avenue and Manchester, McClintock's children coming down from their hilltop above, the middle class of the Mexican War Streets,

Figure 29 (opposite). North Commons, 1868

the working classes of Deutschtown, and passersby to and from Allegheny City, alike—witnessed a land whose history they knew to be once forested, made into pasture, then corrupted, becoming transformed again, into something lovely that all could equally enjoy.

Those traveling on foot, by rail, by trolley and carriage, could all see in 1868 the makings of the curved walks, the lake and rockery formation, the installation of fountains. And the beginnings of so many plantings of shrubs, flowering plants and trees, the latter hearkening any old-timers back to when Mad Anthony Wayne's forces so scalped a great portion of the West Commons of any trees still left standing.

Beyond the first real communal push in the late 1790s, to turn Redick's paper survey into the collective reality of Allegheny Town, this was perhaps the second greatest, immense effort by all. Legislators worked toward, and citizens supported, this great effort to have a true renaissance in their city, on the very land area that wrapped around their town, always to be for the provision of the people, and at their very core.

By December of 1869, the lake was filled, and though the landscaped rockery and other features were not yet complete around it, Alleghenians of several different generations converged on the West Commons for ice skating and boating. Cast iron water pipes were laid, for twenty-eight water hydrants about the park. There were two drinking fountains, as well—one more simple, installed in the public square west of Federal, and one more ornamental for the East Commons, designed by Allegheny artist Isaac Broome. The latter was a "terra cotta sculpture of a partially nude boy, four feet high, draped and supported by a tree stump, holding a basin with both hands, in which is placed a bubbling cup, all resting on a sandstone base." It was commissioned by the artist for $400, and though nothing further is written about its inspiration, it quite possibly came from fond memories of "Barefoot Square," or any of the other primitive watering holes about Allegheny.

Two more main fountains were also started—one on the East Commons, in its northeast corner near North Avenue and Cedar (the street running northward at the Commons boundary), and one on the southwest corner of the West Commons, almost as a gateway to Ridge Avenue from Irwin. Both were elaborate. The first had a large Grecian vase with a 70-feet high water jet. The second, in the West Common, was more heavily ornamented, with a cast iron centerpiece (a base in the form of a Greek cross). On top of this was a pedestal supporting a basin. "Surrounding the base were four winged sea

horses, in half relief, with jets thrown from the mouths. The pedestal incorporated four terminal female figures (Neriades), and the basin was beaded
and fluted with an ornamental border. The central jet in the upper basin
consisted of a water lily and the basin rim was punctuated with ornamental
heads from which the water flowed."

One other fountain would be tied in with the Humboldt Monument,
on the North Commons across from the middle of the Mexican War Streets.
It was a bust of Baron Alexander von Humboldt, with circular fountain, and
it was by the Masonic Fraternities of the Pittsburgh District. Humboldt was
"a German scientist, explorer and author noted for his liberal views and
humanitarianism." Its dedication was attended by President Ulysses S. Grant,
who also planted a tree on the Commons, nearby (as well as later visiting
with the McKnights).

Two other monuments were planned at the time. One would be the
Hampton Battery Monument, honoring Civil War captain Robert Hampton,
that would be placed on the East Commons, "at the intersection of Ohio
Street," where the commission felt "we have an admirable position for some
art object. In fact, the conformation and location of the grounds require *some
conspicuous and central figure* there."

The other monument would be the most significant. It was the Soldiers
Monument, a huge stone tower with a balcony, and its resting place would be
atop Seminary Hill (soon to be referred to as Monument Hill). Its presence,
sitting on that bluff which since early time had witnessed so much catharsis
in the region, would be visible to Alleghenians and Pittsburghers, alike,
from afar.

Benches and gas lighting would also be planned for installation about
the park. During the construction in the decade-long work, a "cheap wooden
fence" was put up along the periphery, to be replaced later by ornamental iron.

By 1868, the *City Line* had changed yet again, the northeasterly boundaries ever increasing. The Spring Garden Valley, below, southward, the hilly
area above Butcher's Run, as well as all of the East Street area of that lower,
southern valley, would now be pulled into the city. The area around the
latter valley was also termed Woodville, in addition to overlapping areas of
Swiss Hole and Deutschtown. Curiously, the hills of Spring Garden would

form a separate borough here, Spring Garden Borough—the very section of the Reserved Tract outlined in yellow as a separate section on an early map (for some reason a parcel in the full Reserved tract that was specially-delineated by some ownership discrepancy of long ago. (*see Figure 6*)

Simon Drum was now Mayor, and he lived on the Perrysville Plank Road, just past the gated drive of Washington McClintock, and across the street from the land holdings of William Thaw. Joseph McBrier, nearby landowner along the hillside where the Civil War garrison had been located (an area just recently incorporated into the city) had taken a break from hauling locust posts to devote time to being President of the Select Council and Chairman of the Water Committee. McBrier was also Chairman of the Water Committee.

Close by, just off the Plank Road and up the hill that brought one to the Observatory's peak, was land owned first by Peter Bates and his wife, and then sold in 1863 to William Clayton. He was a Pittsburgh liquor dealer and real estate investor, and actually had not done anything with the land yet, as he was living just below, a resident in one of the structures dotting the curve upward of the Perrysville Plank Road. The Observatory was still the only building on the high land.

The Allegheny Observatory, in 1869, broke ground nationally by establishing "electrical time," maintained by star observations. Systematic, regular signals were distributed to the railroad, as well as to the city. The electrical impulses were telegraphed to a clock in Allegheny and Pittsburgh City Halls, automatically synchronizing pendulums. This Allegheny Time System would then be adopted by the United States Naval Observatory.

Professor Langley, the new Director, was conducting aeronautical experimentation as well at the time "By means of a whirling table on which were mounted planes tilted at various angles and carried at various speeds," he first observed "the lifting power of air," and contemplated the feasibility of sustained flight. (Over twenty years later, he would take this with him as secretary of the Smithsonian Institution, and only later be properly credited as the 'Father of Aviation.')

In just two years under Langley, in 1869, the Observatory had made an international name for itself, with the "Allegheny System" of timekeeping. All as it sat, serenely, by itself, on the central peak overlooking Allegheny City, part of the *High, Rough Land* "not fit for inhabitants of the moon," as Redick had descriptively also included in his survey eighty-two years prior.

In addition to these lofty pursuits, Allegheny City's infrastructure was beginning to be attended to as 1880 approached. New sewer lines were beginning to be laid about the city, to replace primitive and inefficient stone ones. Waste from individual outhouses and cisterns contaminating the land was indeed a growing problem. Cholera was beginning to show up as a health menace. Beginning with the previous decade, there had been great concern over the overall maintenance and specific cleaning of individual resident privies across the whole city.

In particular, an important sewer line was laid in the bed of the old Canal near the east side of the city. This would service Deutschtown, the eastern area of the *Rough, High Ground* by the quarries, and the adjoining residential neighborhood by Howard Street. Waste was particularly a problem here, with the slope down to Butcher's Run, and the valley adjoining East Street, which made its cut northward away from the city.

The water-works was expanded in 1867, to better supply more city residents, and free mail delivery was started. That, with the new numbering of houses that had begun with a postal system, eliminated both the recent-years' chaos of trying to find the right house by description only, and the need to go to the post office to ask for mail by family name. The elimination of the latter, it has been posited, was "the last remaining vestige of the once rural character of the community."

By 1868, the Street Committee would move to "take possession of that part of the Allegheny and Perrysville Plank Road within the [new] city limits and have the same put in repair and the toll gates removed." (The first toll gate, and toll booth, for the road had sat where the Franklin Road turned back upon itself and went up the ridge, the formal beginning of the Plank Road.)

Dealings with the Railroad, as well, were showing up in plenty of Council Minutes at the end of the decade. The railroad was beneficial for the city, but it also brought legislators grief. Since the corporation was powerful, and the Act allowing it through the city was written ambiguously, Councils had a hard time reigning in discretion over boundary lines, and the timetable for construction of retaining walls. But to their credit, the Councils never relented in their determination to get the best possible compliance by the railroad for the citizens of Allegheny.

In Allegheny Select Council Chambers, January 9, 1867, the single biggest issue to come before the legislators was rearing its ugly head once again.

The Board of Trade of Pittsburgh has prepared a bill to be presented

to the Legislature asking for the consolidation of all the cities and Boroughs embred in a radius of five miles.... The matter [should be submitted] to a vote of the people...within the limits of the contemplated consolidated city.... It is believed that the citizens of Pittsburgh are much more anxious to have the measure consummated than the city of Allegheny....

Again in March of 1867, Council discussed the matter. Simply yet emphatically put, Allegheny City legislators noted, "Write to Harrisburg. We are opposed."

In April, the Mayor John Morrison would write the Council President and the letter was shared in Council chambers. The mayor began, in his correspondence, by stating that he, himself, had recently received a letter from "the highly esteemed townsman, General Robinson." Allegheny City's 'first citizen' and mayor was congratulating current Mayor Morrison on "the successful resistance made to the project of consolidation." Morrison then eloquently states,

> [General Robinson] shows a more zealous active interest in this matter than any other person young or old.... [He has] more than eighty years been of our soil, the first native-born of Anglo Saxon stock among all the millions now between the rivers Ohio, Allegheny and the Lakes... on what was then a hunting ground and wilderness.... We find that he has stronger claims to our attention and respect than it is possible for any other man to show—born before the separate existence of the County, older than the Charter of either City, he has witnessed our growth and seen such changes among us as can be comprehended only by the Pioneers of the American West.
>
> Identified with the interests of our city from the very start, always prominent in every progressive movement and standing high in the community for integrity and talent, he now stands up stoutly to maintain our corporate existence, our chartered privileges, and the name which is bourne alike by mountain, river, county and our city.

chapter eight:

DIVISION OF ESTATES & THE
EXPOSITION GROUND

The first thirty years of Allegheny City had been marked by economic and industrial growth and stability, rapidly expanding boundaries, and tremendous new scientific achievement. The population had skyrocketed again; at the beginning of 1870 it would be about 60,000, double what it was a decade earlier.

With the creation of the new wards in 1867, it became obvious that new streets would have to be created as well. The old lanes had to accommodate by widening in some cases, where it was possible. Some less prominent were almost gone, their vestige being alleys between roads that were starting to stretch across the city. Changes were coming about as to the look of the city, especially northward.

The 1870s could be classified as the time when streets were created, graded and paved en masse for the flourishing city of Allegheny. Though top priority was to work on this infrastructure in sections that were previously undeveloped, it would also be the first time that many of the outlying estates of Allegheny City's early years would be divided up. Entirely new streets, not at all based on Redick's grid, would thus be carved out of land expanse previously attributed to single wealthy families.

By this time, those wealthy Alleghenians that had been living on these country-like estates or farms on the hilltops, or the flats of Manchester, had either gone through a generation in the family, or to a lesser extant, had started to venture further out into the countryside beyond the *City Line.* Their children would often stay in Allegheny, but either move off their father's land to other parts of the city, or live on a smaller section while the rest was divided, developed, and rented out or sold as further income-source.

The wealthy in the more urban section of Ridge Avenue were largely unaffected except to begin consideration of the country, themselves, for summer homes. Butler, far northeast of Allegheny City, was one destination, as especially was the land down the Ohio River.

Because land governorship was still in some ways controlled by the Commonwealth of Pennsylvania, Allegheny City had to address its larger expansion issues with the state. This included formation of streets.

An Act Relative to Streets in Allegheny City was filed with the Senate, of the Legislature of Pennsylvania, dated March 9, 1870. That Act, given power by both the Commonwealth's Senate and House of Representatives, stated, "That the Select and Common Councils of the city of Allegheny are hereby authorized and empowered when they deem the same necessary to lay out and open new streets, lanes and alleys in said city, and to widen, straighten and extend any streets, lanes or alleys of said city, and to levy and collect the value of property thus taken, or the damages done to property thereby an assessment of the properties benefited by any such improvement...."

The Act would then set forth extensive parameters by which the city had to properly survey lots, post notice to residents of adjoining property, hold public hearings on citizen concerns, etc. These guidelines, widely reported upon in Allegheny newspapers, would not be lost on citizens, and a new era of rightful property holder involvement in possession and redirection of land would be ushered in, as it would in most American cities come this time.

Some of the first changes happened at Pasture Lane. Once the area from Washington Avenue to Island Avenue was considered within *City Line*, Pasture Lane started changing. It began with the name, as the Irwin Avenue reference would now extend north of North Avenue, as far as Taggart Street. Pasture Lane at this point was not following the straight line given it by Redick, as it had gently curved to the left to accommodate the land that had been gently ascending. So at this point, Pasture Lane would not continue with the new title of Irwin, because it took citizens past Pleasant Valley, the cemeteries, and beyond into countryside.

Because the lane would arrive at the newly formed community of New Brighton, it would begin to be called at this point the New Brighton Road, and Pasture Lane (so reminiscent to citizens of more provincial times) would disappear from the community lexicon. McClure Avenue would be another street, opened by the end of the decade, in this northern area near New Brighton.

Only where the dirt lane did continue in an earlier straight fashion, near the start of Taggart Street, would Pasture Lane continue to be used by those few citizens that ventured back into that still-dense wooded valley below, northward, of McClintock's holdings. This was land was now owned by Charles Taggart.

The improvement of Troy Hill Road was discussed in Councils in the early 1870s. This was the main road slowly ascending, parallel to the Allegheny River, into the community once known more popularly as Mount Troy, the hill on the eastern side of Allegheny City.

In 1872, Councils considered the first of many measures related to improvements to the area near where the Franklin Road turned into the Perrysville Plank Road.

As the Franklin Road had proceeded northward, just past the Mexican War Streets to the west, a tiny lane-sized portion of the road tried to maintain its due northerly direction, along the lines of Redick's survey (External Ally), until it directly hit the hill's abutment and stopped (just below and north of Henderson Street). This tiny dirt lane was referred to as the Franklin Alley, to distinguish it from the Old Franklin Road, or Federal Street, which had curved to the left just at Henderson Street, then straightened out again (now on a further west longitude than Franklin Alley).

Because this hill abutment had always been too steep to traverse, and remained untouched, an ideal situation was created for the Observatory, which sat just above and westerly, on the hilltop tier above the Perrysville Plank Road. Despite being visible from far below in the city, it sat in an area relatively isolated and private, suiting its studious purpose in the early years.

Allegheny City Councils were looking at the needed improvement, though, of Federal Street/Old Franklin Road, from the city center to the Perrysville Plank Road (in what they termed in the Minutes as "the North End district"). And the intention with this motion was to set in gear the plans to actually extend Federal Street beyond where the Plank Road began—to go due northerly, almost, and shoot all the way up the steep ascent. Engineers would be working on this for many years, but it was a beginning. It stemmed from the desire to head to the land north of the Second Ward without having to go up and around the tier of the Plank Road, which natives long ago recognized as the only efficient means to traverse the hill.

By 1873, the heirs of William Clayton, who owned that high land next to the Observatory, sold several lots for $3,800 total to Henry Berger. Still a relatively young man of twenty-eight, it would be Berger who would finally have a structure built there—a house sitting on the far southwestern corner, overlooking the final large bend on the Plank Road before it leveled off and passed McClintock's and Drum's residences. He had the house completed by 1875 on what was then already called 1 Clayton Avenue. It had "unusual wood siding," as if to almost "look like stone" from a distance. The house with its distinctive roof peaks, like its neighbor Observatory, was most viewed only from afar, as it sat on a perch below which was essentially another—the ridge of the Plank Road.

Berger would live there with his new wife Maria, having previously lived in Manchester and also Allegheny's First Ward. Along with his son, he conducted business in Pittsburgh, owning the New Mammoth Furniture Depot. But he had other interests as well, and it would be no coincidence that he would pick land next to the Observatory to build a home.

The Second Ward (or what was essentially the extended Second Ward since 1867) figures prominently in the 1870s for a variety of reasons. Certainly, what would take place with the Washington McClintock residence is a great example of what happened this decade with the division of some outlying estates.

McClintock would die in 1870 and his 96 year-old father one year later. His heirs decided to divide up some of the hilltop land holding. Allegheny City would then come to own, in the 1870s, the great amount of land to the west, or the sloping back portion of the McClintock land. It began to develop it by outlining, and then doing grading for, new streets. Structures would not be put up until a decade later.

Eliza McClintock and her older children still lived in their large house at the top of the hill. They, like other landowners of Allegheny City at this time, would indeed be positively affected by the improvement of streets and other infrastructure about the new wards. Buena Vista Street, from General Robinson's land holdings below in the Mexican War Streets, would at this time be extended upward to connect the Second Ward below, north of the West Commons, with the upper Second Ward.

The extension of Buena Vista Street would ironically have Robinson's chosen name for the tract indeed live up to its name. The road would be a straight shot upward, and it was a likely template for the Federal Street extension about to be attempted. Though not envisioned (or ever used) as a major avenue up the hill, and though not quite as steep all at once, or as long, as the proposed Federal Street extension, Buena Vista nevertheless was a challenge to lay. But in doing so, man had made a new entry to the northern hilly section of the Reserved Tract, previously only feasible along the Indian trail ridge.

Cobblestones were used to pave the hilly extension of Buena Vista from the Mexican War Streets. The street, very wide actually, climbed and then curved rightward along the hillside above, which was actually the sloping off of the great ridge, supporting the bottom side of the Perrysville Plank Road. After its curve, carriage riders were in for a view of an even steeper climb than the first portion. The street would take them out of the original, or lower Second Ward. It would be a steep, long ascent, as they passed on their left the wooded property of James McBrier, still council president in the early 1870s, then the old earthwork garrison, and eventually McClintock's and Drum's homes coming into view at the summit, where Buena Vista intersected with the Plank Road. A right from here would take travelers to the entrance road to the Observatory, or back down the Plank Road. A left, to the farms and countryside that stretched along the Plank Road's many curves to and fro northward.

In November 1874, $1125 was "paid back to the Allegheny City Treasurer/Controller from the McClintock heirs, in account of extra damages" for essentially the creation of Buena Vista Street extension. The McClintocks, just like other Allegheny City property holders of wealthy and of modest means, would have been offered damages by the city for improvements that nevertheless infringed upon private property or limited, temporarily, means of access, etc. But in this case, "the amount of damages due the estate of Washington McClintock, deceased," for the improvement to Buena Vista, was essentially deemed by the family as "not needed... after deducting the benefits accessed there on." This original receipt found in archives of the city, was signed by "W.L. McClintock, Executor of the estate of the W. McClintock Deed."

The McClintocks, whose patriarch had modeled generosity and citizen goodwill during the Civil War and afterward, were honestly evaluating that their property values monetarily were helped by having another access to their land.

The extended Second, and a lot of the extended Third Ward, sitting high atop their hills, were definitely more middle-to-upper class than portions of the low-lying city. If for no other reason, this was due to the barely-accessible land unless one had private carriage. Once Buena Vista, soon-to-come Federal Street, and other back accesses to the northern hills would be opened up (as well as a means of transport provided to a general public up and along the Plank Road) would those areas be able to develop. Access to groceries and doctors were in walking distance in neighborhoods below, in particular the Mexican War Streets. Even the more well-to-do that resided on the hills had

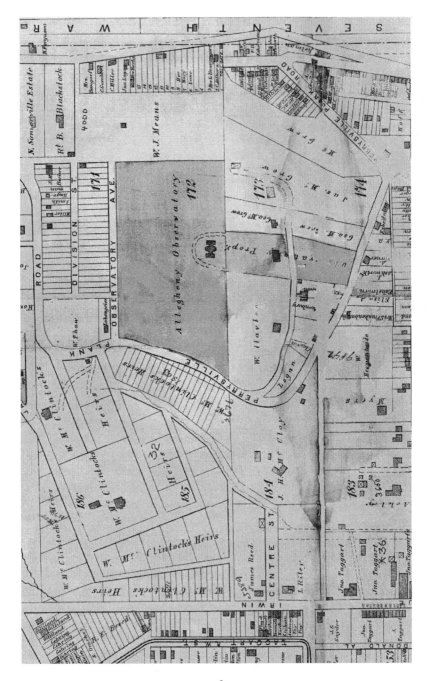

to come down into the city, on buggy or carriage, to attend to errands and business.

In addition to property owners being awarded damages for city development, they would also be assessed new taxes and fees for improvements to adjoining areas. James McBrier would be assessed $262.80 for 180 ft. ($1.46/ft.) of grading of the land and street access near his home in 1874. Washington McClintock's estate would be assessed $890.60 for 610 ft.

Other property about the city would be purchased in the same manner as the McClintock holdings. Though it would take place all about the city, Allegheny City's interest at this time was especially in stretching into the hilly and wooded northern farmland.

Manchester during the 1870s was doing as fine as ever, now as simply a neighborhood of Allegheny City. The main streets included Grant (named for Ulysses) and Allegheny, both of which originated south by Ridge Avenue, and which ran to the newly-named Pennsylvania Avenue (replacing Ohio Lane). Pennsylvania by Irwin Avenue was close to the railroad yard, but further west, heading toward the Ohio River, beautiful structures serving as homes, and home offices, had been built.

One successful businessman of the time was R.G. Vandevort, whose law firm was listed as located at "100 Pennsylvania Avenue, Allegheny Pa." Less prestigious, perhaps, was the business of Peter Blatt, who manufactured Coaches, Wagons, Buggies and Trucks at 34-36 Allegheny Ave. The top of the building housing his business proudly carried his name, and Victorian decoration, just at roof line.

The land north of the railroad yard, and west of Irwin Avenue and Pleasant Valley, would start to be developed later in the decade. California Avenue, (Redick's *Island Lane*) lay below, southward, the hilly land of the cemetery. The cemetery keeper's home sat atop the hill, and was accessed by new roads leading up to the elegant brick and mint-green gabled structure. It had corbelled parapets and stylish brackets in the eaves. Other homes were built descending down the hill, some of them in elegant row design, and some echoing the first grand home of the area, atop the hill.

Though residences sat on the hill slope to the north, the area on the southern side of California Avenue, especially further west, had a commercial flavor, as did areas in Manchester. Past the industrial sections that so made

Figure 30 (opposite). Allegheny Observatory, 1872

the area prosper, citizens could travel southwestward, toward the Ohio River, where they would come upon Beaver Avenues' burgeoning commercial district.

Plumbing would be the latest modernity of the 1870s to come to some of the masses, as opposed to the wealthy, special cases, of the earlier decade. Certainly, not all households would receive it. Due to lack of accessibility, still, to new water and sewer mains, plumbing often came in jurisdictional groupings, with certain streets done at a certain time, and others later. And income disparities would still keep certain houses on various streets without plumbing after the convenience would come to the neighborhood. As well, in many cases, there was a refusal to yet move toward the modern way.

Irwin Avenue, in particular, even its section somewhat north of North Avenue, would have access to plumbing as early as 1874. This was likely due to its flat location adjacent to Manchester, where the earlier requests of several wealthy families had brought mains to that area. Plumbing for Allegheny City households would not really catch on, however, until the 1880s, when more neighborhoods gained access, with new mains connecting them to the water-works, and as more people could afford and became acclimated to the idea of spending money to have indoor water availability, if not still an outdoor privy due to cost.

But it was those outdoor privies, among other things, that were causing major problems in Allegheny and Pittsburgh. Allegheny City established a new Board of Health in 1871, mainly to address the smallpox epidemic of the time. The Director of the Board of Health, R. Stansbury Sutton, addressed Mayor Callow in correspondence dated June, 1871. He wrote of the epidemic "at every point of the compass," but being especially prevalent "in Manchester, in various wards of the old city in Deutschtown...in Pittsburgh at various points...and Birmingham (south of the Monongahela) and even on Mount Washington (Coal Hill). The number of cases is not I think very large, but the seeds of this dreadful and loathsome disease are wide spread in the community and the question arises what is the best method of annihilating the enemy."

Sutton then called for two methods he deemed appropriate: "1st Destroy the material upon which it feeds by vaccination. 2nd Isolation of every case, by preventing ingress and egress as far as possible at every house where a case exists." Free vaccinations were to be given to every one who was unable to pay, and a physician was to be assigned to every ward, with the aim of vaccinating all citizens within a few weeks' time.

For isolation purpose, a further letter to the Mayor, dated two months later, delineates that the city should, for every household effected, "run a chain across the alley or street if practicable on either side of the house. A Placard with 'Small Pox' in large letters has often proved a perfect guard...." Of the cases "unable to provide for themselves," Director Sutton states, "the only thing can be done is to provide a temporary Small Pox hospital or use tents as was done during the late war."

The director also depicts other matters of public health at the time. "Drainage matter is very prolific of typhoid fever. The decomposing slush from slaughter houses is a fruitful source of scarlet fever, and low wet marshes, of ague and remittent fever. To cover this entire question [how to prevent further spread of disease?] would tire your patience but in this city— Privies, Pig pens, Sewers and drains comprise the worst sources of the diseases which you are able to limit."

The city listened to the Board of Health Director, and the 1870s would be the decade that better sanitary measures for the city began to be enacted. It started with the required infrastructure to sustain proper sanitation. Across the city, different sections of different wards would be worked on, with the Mexican War Streets area one of the first, since that land north of the Commons seemed long plagued by this issue. Eventually, the whole city would have sewers built about it.

In 1873, there was a great financial panic in Pittsburgh. Interestingly, that same year, Allegheny City Councils had to again address the nagging concern that Pittsburgh was still interested in annexation:

> Enter[ing] upon our 34th year of corporate existence...during which period [Allegheny City] has risen in importance, politically and financially, and today ranks as the third city in the Commonwealth, in population and wealth, and in the character of her improvements... she is without a rival.
>
> Second to none are her public parks, sewerage system, fire alarm and police system, and water and gas facilities. No city has made more worth, and provision for her worthy poor....

Important to note is Allegheny's municipal ranking here, at so young a point in her history as a city. Philadelphia, of course, held the top ranking, with number two and three, Pittsburgh and Allegheny City. This ranking would not change throughout the decades to come, with sister cities at the river's confluence in southwestern Pennsylvania being the second and third largest cities of Pennsylvania.

After the above declaration on council floor, the Minutes then note that Council built up resoundingly to a "cheer of 'No'" again, in response to Pittsburgh's scheme of consolidation.

Councils mid-decade applied themselves to further infrastructure for the city. A new pumping station would be added to the city's water works system. It would be the Howard Pumping Station in the area near the quarries and Henderson's land. Something had to be done to traverse the East Street and Madison Avenue valleys to get water up the next series of hills by the upper Second and Third Wards.

A working class neighborhood around the new pumping station began to develop, part of Mary Schenley's intention with her plots. This area became known as Toboggan or Rising Main, named for the steep slopes usually gotten to by city-constructed stairs, but that nevertheless made for winter fun for Allegheny's children. Rising Main was the main avenue ascending upward from the southeast.

That area along Butcher's Run, east of East Street and Madison Avenue, and at the foot of Spring Hill and Troy Hill, was prone to water problems of all kinds. Waterspouts burst more than once and flooded at least portions of what was called Spring Garden Valley. In 1874, in particular, it was noted that "water poured down in impetuous torrents, bringing up the little runs in a short time into small rivers...." As well, there was a disastrous flood that over-took part of the low-lying areas of the city in the summer of that year, and Spring Garden Valley was especially devastated.

By the latter part of the decade, citizens were wise to the rights being afforded them as homeowners, and this would make a difference in how one woman responded to water damage in that area. On Dec. 31,1877, a Mrs. C. Simmendinger made a claim with the city "for damages alleged to have been sustained by her property on Spring Garden Avenue...on account of water being discharged from Troy Hill, on and over her property." (The water tower was just above her land.) Allegheny City, "being desirous of making an amicable settlement with her," decided to pay her for past damages as well.

But knowing all too well that the area was far from shored up when it came to potential water leakages, the city even decided to enact any future damage payments to be "fully compensated at $150" per occurrence, apparently.

A new fire house, the Friendship Engine House, would be erected in the Second Ward in 1877 for a base cost of $1420. Its location would be the corner of Arch and Jackson Street, in the Mexican War Streets section. (This firehouse exists to the present day, serving as artist studios, and is one of the oldest in the Pittsburgh surrounding region.)

Allegheny was playing catch-up to accommodate for all the 'new' land to be covered of late. But it was not through yet with its expansions. Impatient to get its original territory officially back, Allegheny City completed its desired annexations in the latter 1870s, of the full rest of the territory that were out lots of Allegheny Town. Called the Ninth, Tenth, Eleventh and Twelfth Wards, these land areas would be north of the Second and Third Wards, and assigned numeral, respectively, from west to east.

Beyond infrastructure, Allegheny City had other concerns as it grew so large in size. With its many wards, it only had fifteen school buildings. (In addition to these, there were twenty-six private schools. seminaries and academies.) Thus it would begin to establish schoolhouses to support the children beginning to live in the new wards.

A small Second Ward Schoolhouse would sit not far from Simon Drum's property, on a street recently carved out of the McClintock estate. And having bought other land previously from Jonathan Gallagher, the city also erected Milroy School—so named as it sat at the corner of the Perrysville Plank Road and a street named after a property owner Milroy. This still-dirt road was a spectacle beyond that of Buena Vista, in that it sharply descended, with equally sharp curves, down into the East Street Valley. It likely was sufficient for horse-travel, only.

In the 1870s, what was left of Killbuck Island was still sparking controversy. 1873 saw the state of Pennsylvania upheld Zenas Neels' heirs' sale of 1849 (to John Parke, William Reed and others), but the city did not want to give up the property. Allegheny City had witnessed that, for twenty-four years, Parke and fellow owners had not done anything with the extremely low-lying site mainly now attached to the north shore. But the city had,

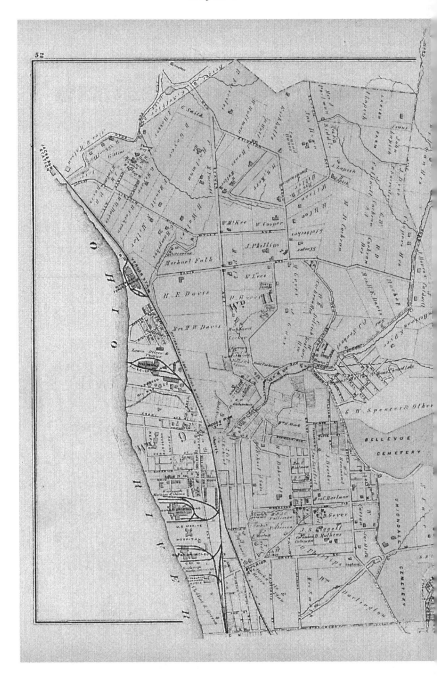

Figure 31. Northern Wards, 1876   154

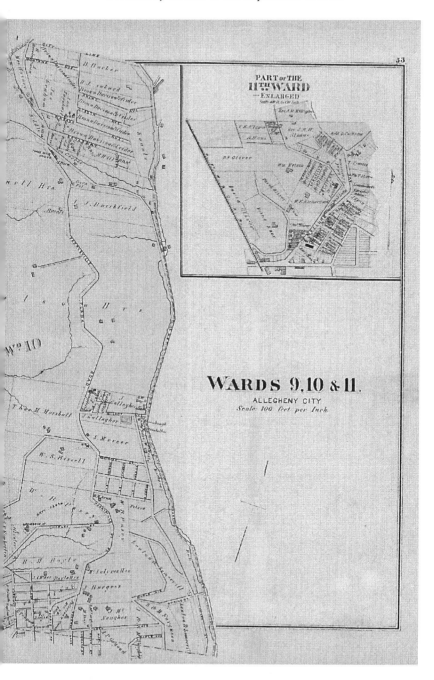

PART OF THE
11TH WARD
—ENLARGED—

WARDS 9, 10 & 11.
ALLEGHENY CITY
Scale: 100 feet per Inch.

at least, allowed the traveling shows and carnivals to encamp there, what seemed the perfect spot on the bank below the city center. At times of low water, the land there was even called the "stony beach" by Alleghenians.

The Supreme Court of Pennsylvania had to get involved one year later, since Parke and his comrades contested Allegheny City's claim. Parke won, but the city did not feel it to be justified because of the land boundaries described in the award.

As explained in an article of 1961 entitled "Killbuck and Killbuck Island," by Margaret Bothwell,

> "There was evidence for [Allegheny City] that previously to 1832, there was a small channel at the head of the island, which ran down between that and the main shore, thus forming the island; it was about 100 feet from Bank Lane; the main shore was a perpendicular bluff [Seminary Hill]; the water would be at the base of the bluff about half the year; in dry times the water would not run there. Bank Lane was on top of the bluff; along some places it was so narrow that a horse could not travel; a man could walk along it; there was a path and a fence some places...."

The article continued, describing the unusual land that changed throughout the course of any given year, and over the decades. Essentially, when there was as little as five feet of water in the river, the island would be submerged. And thus the area of the "island" varied anywhere from 3 to 15 acres, depending on the time of measurement.

The judge ruled that, even though shown on Redick's map as gracing the bank, the island was not actually part of the Reserved Tract. (Alleghenians would have a different opinion, however.) More pertinent to the lawsuit, though, was that the channel between the island and Allegheny City became so filled with water as to be useless, and that Mr. Parke and his associates probably had claim to more than the island itself, in fact what was now the surrounding low land.

Then while the case was further tied up in court, in 1874, several Allegheny *County* leaders decided it was time to have "a permanent exposition of the arts, sciences and industries of Western Pennsylvania." Parke and associates surprisingly submitted the idea that the island, or the tract of low land beneath the bluff of now-Monument Hill, would be a suitable locale.

(He got that notion from the success of the circuses the city was allowing through.) Though his aim may have been honorably citizen-minded, Parke was likely also hoping to profit from his proposition, and hang onto that low strip of land that was really worth more than the sunken island at this point.

County authorities, liking the idea, decided to lease the land but, in a strange twist, leased it from the proclaimed current owner, the City of Allegheny. The County surely thought the City would eventually win its suit, because they indeed obtained the land from Allegheny City, for the Tradesmen's Industrial Institute. It would be fifteen years at free rent. (The city likely saw their own claim, though they believed in it, being ambiguous enough that the judge may *not* award, and so decided to throw the rent in free.) No one, it seems, had the last say but the land itself.

Architect Edward Butz designed a grand, long building for the Institute, and it would be erected the following year, on that part of the low land that was not directly on the back channel or the part of the 'island' that was being washed under. It sat at the corners of Shore and Cherry Streets, and ran the length of Monument Hill above it. The first exhibition, held in the fall of 1875, was pre-advertised:

First Grand Exhibition
Competition Open To The World
Tradesmen's Industrial Institute Of Pittsburgh, PA.
Premiums Valued At $50,000
Nothing Excluded

Every department will be filled with the most interesting
Inventions and arts of the age.
Music by First Class Bands will be in attendance from
10:00 A.M. until 10:00 P.M. during the entire exposition.
Unparalleled Attractions in Every Department
All Kinds Of Live Stock And Farmers' Products
Reduced Fares On All Railroads

With just the first announcement, and Allegheny City being the renowned locale, the land including what was left of Killbuck Island became now the premier space for exhibitions, showcases and soon-to-come sporting events for all of the southwestern Pennsylvania region.

Much like the Civil War Fair, and similar to the atmosphere in the Allegheny Market House, the building would house a Machinery and Floral Hall, a Dining Pavilion and a Main Exhibition Building. With the more bawdy spectacles of yesteryear off the land, the building's beautiful wood-floored galleries held all manner of events, decorated for each to the max, with colorful bunting and tinseled display booths. Visitors would roam the halls, chewing hard candy and holding bags of peanuts, stopping in booths to have the novelty of their photos taken, and attend recitals in the auditorium.

Nearby in Manchester, during fair weather, the first professional baseball team for the entire region, was playing ball. Their name was the *Alleghenies*. They were organized in 1876, right after the National Baseball League had been founded.

It was a good thing that Alleghenians had lighthearted recreational activities those last summers of the 1870s, because there was intensity surrounding industry and the labor market. The summer of 1877 saw the great railroad riots in Pittsburgh. Alleghenians paid close attention as violence erupted. The militia killed and wounded many, just across the Allegheny River at Twenty-eighth Street. Within a course of three days, the Union Depot there would be burned by the rioters, as everyone in the region was transfixed by this horrible labor struggle.

Two days after issuance of the *Act Relative to Streets in Allegheny City*, at the top of the decade, the Commonwealth Assembly had issued a Supplement, making official and proper what the Park Commission had begun work on. It was an extension, "authorizing and providing powers and means for the conversion of the common grounds of the city of Allegheny into public parks," necessary for the final dissolution of the theological seminary's hold of some of the land atop what was now becoming Monument Hill.

This would make way for the Park Commission to finalize their plans for the hill. A sculpture was commissioned, by Pittsburgher Peter Reniers, to rest atop the hill, commemorating the 4,000 Civil War soldiers from Allegheny County. By 1871, the massive 70 ft. high work of Massilon stone, inscribed

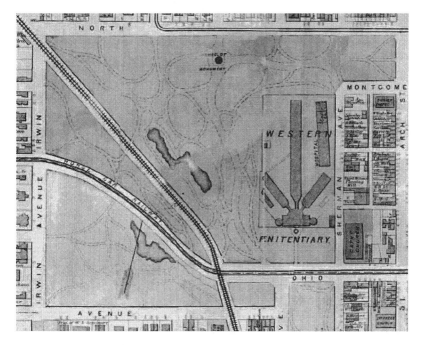

Figure 32. West Commons & Lake Elizabeth, 1870s

with dedication to soldiers, and topped with the Goddesses of Fate and Fortune, sat triumphantly atop the land. Instead of separate belvedere at eastern edge of hill, as originally proposed, the monument itself would have a circular stone stairway leading up to a 40 ft. high balcony, as the centerpiece overlook.

In a report of the Park Commission, it was stated, that "crossing Ridge Street from gate at the southwestern angle, we enter upon a roadway at end of Irwin Avenue leading to top of Seminary Hill. A small circular drive here is all that is practicable, and is only suggested in view of the wish of many strangers to enjoy with as little fatigue as possible its incomparable view."

Though many Alleghenians and others indeed would trek to the top for the view on the storied bluff, the Civil War Soldiers Monument, itself, would be the main recipient of the vista—extending across to Pittsburgh and Birmingham south of the Monongahela. And its long and majestic line upward could indeed be seen afar from many points in Pittsburgh.

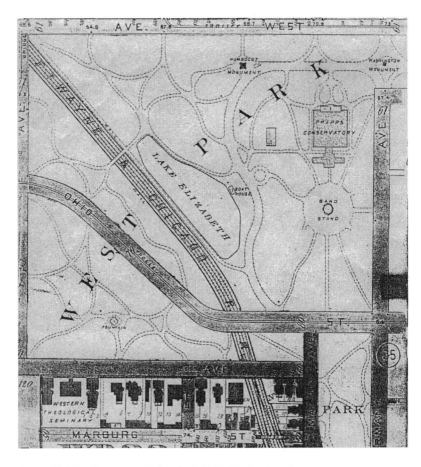

Figure 33. West Commons & Lake Elizabeth, 1870s. Another view

On the East Common, the same year, the Hampton Battery Monument
would be commemorated. As well, a unique little sculpture was added to the
park. An iron deer sits close to the pass of the railroad, on the southern end,
and is surely remembered by every child to ever visit the West Commons
from that point on—having been picked up and placed upon its back, or
simply having walked over and stroked the creature. Different theories
abound, but it is most believed that the sculpture was presented by council-
man James Orr, who had promised the mayor a trophy head upon return
from a hunting trip, but instead offered the deer.

Benches, some cast iron with oiled wood seats, were added in the early 1870s, and a greenhouse would be built in 1873. The wall enclosing the railroad would be completed and finished with an iron railing atop by mid-decade. Even some stone watch-houses were designed and built at the time.

After the Park Commission had been formed, city council had gone to work issuing park bonds—beautifully reproducing one of the fountains on paper—and they ascribed a budget. The next several years would have Select and Common Council minutes filled with references to park vouchers and bills, and many Allegheny City businesses got in the act of bidding on various aspects of work needed in the development.

Park lighting would be controversial in the early years. By the beginning of the decade, lamp posts had been erected, upon high masts. Apparently, the masts were so high as to provide light to the tree tops but not to the path below. (The same lighting was used at the time for streets throughout Allegheny.) Citizens complained, and finally the poles would be replaced and the Allegheny City Electric Power Plant, a new entity, would spend instead on incandescent and direct current lamps.

By the year 1876, the work of the Park Commission of Allegheny City was completed, and it turned over Allegheny Commons to the city. And this year also would be another remarkable one in the confluence of men and ideas surrounding the Observatory.

At this time, yet another lover of astronomy and self-made man—in this case, self-made working class man—came into the sphere of individuals gathering on the upper Second Ward, Allegheny's original Observatory Hill.

John Brashear had been a worker in the iron mill industry of Pittsburgh, in one factory of many that lined the Monongahela River. But he made optical lenses and telescopes as a hobby. "After many discouraging failures through three years of effort," he was finally able to successfully complete a 5 inch lens, and it was then that he made a visit to Professor Langley in Allegheny City. (Brashear was living and experimenting in his home across the Monongahela River, in Birmingham.)

Langley was impressed with the expertise and enthusiasm of Brashear, realizing that he had found "near at hand a man who could do for him optical work just as good as could be turned out anywhere in the world." Langley introduced Brashear to William Thaw, and Thaw immediately became Brashear's patron. No longer needing to work in the mill, Brashear—first

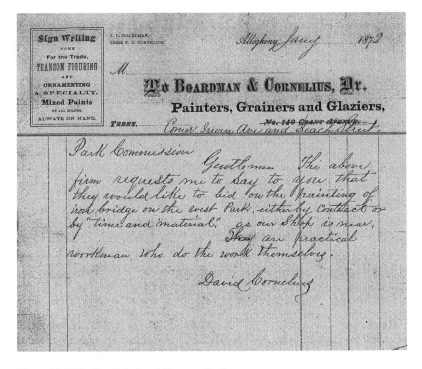

Figure 34. 1870s Sign Painting & Transom Business

from his little shop across the river—started cranking out optical instruments, to be sent all over the world. Soon, the world would come calling for him in Allegheny City.

chapter nine:

PLUMBING & INCLINED PLANES

In September of 1881, *The Pittsburgh Dispatch* advertised

First Races in the World!
On a Half Mile Track, by Electric Light!!
At The Exposition To-Night! Grand Fireworks!

But the Exposition would not have a very long life in Allegheny City. During a Grand Army of the Republic veterans' celebration in the fall of 1883, just eight years after its opening, sparks from a different fireworks display caused a massive fire, destroying the buildings. It would then be rebuilt two years later just across the river, up from the Point along the bank of the Allegheny, in Pittsburgh.

On the site of "the old Expo" building in Allegheny City, the Pittsburgh Baseball Club built a ballpark—Exposition Park. The Alleghenies, who had been playing nearby at Recreation Park, would soon start playing their games there.

The Western University of Pennsylvania, which had tried so hard to plant themselves on Commons ground sixty years earlier, made an announcement, in 1882, of its new intention to move from downtown Pittsburgh to Allegheny City. (Some move was necessary, since the land the school was sitting on, at the corner of Ross and Diamond Streets, downtown, was sold to Allegheny County for a temporary courthouse location.) Recalling talk from 1819, of the state charter that supposedly guaranteed the University land in Allegheny, the University tried once again to relocate to the Commons area.

Allegheny City, which had done such a good job, in the last fifteen years, attending to the Commons and creating the Victorian park, dropped their vigilance and acquiesced. Allegheny City Councils passed a bill granting the University the place on the Commons about to be vacated by the Penitentiary.

The citizens of Allegheny would not have anything of it, however.
To their credit and not the legislators, they wanted no private institution,
even if it was the prestigious school, sitting on land that had just been
cleaned up and made into public park. Allegheny City council chambers
heard one unified voice—"This land should return to the people, and no
more buildings should be erected on Allegheny Commons."

So another plan was suggested, and it was accepted. The University
would rent out rooms in the Presbyterian Theological Seminary until the
University could build new buildings. The spot they targeted to do that
would be the hilltop land adjacent to the Observatory, which they owned,
due to the alliance with the Observatory. It was understood by all that it
would take close to a decade to complete

In the meantime, students came from all over the region to attend classes
in the rented University rooms. Two-thirds of the students actually were from
Allegheny, but for the other third, "newspaper announcements
of the opening in the seminary rooms contained directions for reaching the
buildings from East Liberty, Lawrenceville, Braddock, the South Side and
downtown Pittsburgh." They read, "students coming via the Pittsburgh and
Lake Erie Railways can reach the University by the Point Bridges (toll-free)
in 25 minutes walking. Students from the Union Depot can [reach the
buildings] in 20–25 minutes, walking or taking the Pleasant Valley Street
Cars.... Students from the B & O. R.R. Depot [will have] a 30 min. walk."

Despite having to be renters in a temporary space, the University saw
leaving downtown Pittsurgh as desirable, with its smoke and noise and
tightly congested quarters. (Pittsburgh and the surrounding region, including
Allegheny, was fast becoming a smoky region, with all of the coke furnaces
fueling the iron mills. Downtown Pittsburgh was as industrial as it was
business/commercial at the time.) The seminary buildings were small, too;
in fact, "the bulk of the library books had to be boxed up and stored in the
Observatory building...under Professor Langley's care." But the school looked
with anticipation toward the end of the decade when it could be on a proper
campus of its own.

A hospital campus, too, was in the works in the early 1880s. With a
population approaching 80,000, the need for establishing a public hospital
for the city was discussed under Mayor Lewis Peterson, Jr. A charter was
approved and signed in the fall of 1882, and a few years later, the Hamilton
and Watson homes on East Stockton Avenue, between Federal and Sandusky

Streets, were purchased for the purpose of creating Allegheny General Hospital.

The hospital opened in 1886, but not in time to offer emergency assistance in the wake of another great flood to come to the region two years earlier. The hospital had fifty beds in thirty rooms, and a nurses' training school would be established two years later. By the end of the decade, a nearby building on Sandusky Street was annexed to the hospital, and the first horse-drawn ambulance was received as a gift. (The first horse-drawn police wagons had come to Allegheny mid-decade.)

City government records that detailed such calamities as the 1884 flood and the progress of a hospital opening were all handwritten, still the norm in the mid-1880s. Everything recorded was written in ink, in fancy script (though not as flowery as of a century earlier), and then bound together in groupings from the various departments, for posterity's sake. At the same time for the state, Pennsylvania Legislative Acts became far more readable since early typed documents began to be used, sporadically found in archival material dating to this time.

In a report on the Public Building at Allegheny, PA, made in the State House of Representatives in the 1880s, it was reported that the city was successful, but that a larger post office was needed, and that the accommodations in housing and public building were inadequate. Allegheny City would certainly agree that a new post office was required, but the other findings were unusual, because no reports of such glaring shortages surface in Allegheny City records. Nor does evidence necessarily suggest the like, though the city was certainly playing a little catch-up to the territory gained in the new wards. But the stage was being set for the state to reflect upon and give significant recommendation to the whole of the Southwestern Pennsylvania region.

A long line of wharfage sat at the banks of the Allegheny and Ohio Rivers in the 1880s, continuing to conduct all manners of successful business. Rolling mills and factories dotted the banks, and businesses flourished on the Diamond in the city center, as well as in the surrounding areas.

On what started to be termed "East Ohio Street," that portion of Ohio east of the Commons, many businesses were housed in the quaint, long row of commercial buildings (which sported all styles of Victorian architecture). Close to the end by the East Street Valley would be businesses, with residences above, by H. Anshutz, Voegtly & Kopp, and Leonard Wagner—all on the southern side of the road, between Ohio and Avery Streets. Gaus & Loeffler sat across Ohio. The German Savings Bank was one of the furthest lots on the southern side.

Further down East Ohio, at the foot of the Troy Hill Road, and the corner of Chestnut Street, sat Eggers Drug store. Greeting those driving across the new Mechanic's Street Bridge from Pittsburgh would be another newly-constructed German Social Hall, the Teutonia Maennerchor.

The area in Deutschtown that was north of East Ohio Street and south of North Avenue was in its heyday in the 1880s and 90s. Though lower-class housing had been prevalent in the early years as a city, many thriving businesses would come to be located here, including the Farmers and Drovers Hotel at Suismon & Middle streets, owned by William and Minnie Seker. Even after her husband's death, Minnie Seker continued to operate the Hotel, as well as rent out property in the Mexican War Streets.

The Farmers and Drovers Hotel had adjoining large stable, used by the traveling farmers who stopped and stayed there. Temporary lodging could be had, as well as boarding (room and meals) for longer stays. Another hotel nearby was the Bowmont.

The working class that was predominant in this section of Allegheny City, and many of the houses here were built in the 1840s. Though not too different from structures for the middle class, in that they were still built of solid construction that in some cases employed, outwardly, similar Victorian features in roof or window outline, they nevertheless were often much more plain inside. Wood and slate for staircase and fireplace would be present—the manner of heating homes still came from gas stoves set into the fireplaces—but embellishments were lacking.

What would likely be termed the upper middle class of Allegheny City often included a variety of individual families that were able to own several plots of land, with rental properties, throughout the various wards of Allegheny City. Included would be David Hostetter, who owned land by the developing California Avenue at this time. Grading and paving of that street would begin to take place in 1885, and improvements would continue through the 1890s. Other streets in this area were Peach Alley (it seems peach trees had been introduced there and on McClintock's hilltop, above) and

Kirkpatrick Street. As well, John Kerr owned several plots in the Mexican War Streets.

Eccles Robinson was a land owner with large tracts near Fulton and Manhattan Streets, in an area newly referred to as Chateau, by the Ohio River in the newer Fifth Ward. Like several other names that come up consistently in records of this time period, William R. Buente and his wife Rosina owned many lots spread across Allegheny. Theirs would be in the same area as Hostetter, lots at the foot of Quarry Street near Howard and Madison, on the old Water Lane (now called Western Avenue), on Fulton, and on one of the new streets outlined in the 1870s on the back of McClintock's land.

The McClintock estate would look different in the 1880s. The gated drive, which took individuals from the Perrysville Plank Road on back to the home of Washington McClintock, became McClintock Street. The McClintock house apparently still sat at the end, but the rest of the street leading up to the grand home would be developed this decade, along with the streets that had been outlined in back and alongside the hill. Some neighbors, too, had changed. Simon Drum would be gone, but Robert Smith's estate now sat nearby.

The housing stock that would be developed for these new streets of the Second Ward, like so many developed at this time for other Allegheny neighborhoods, would later be described (from a WPA housing survey of the 1930s) as "working class, nothing extraordinary, fair workmanship," in an "older neighborhood of the city." But the homes were essentially middle-class. Slightly fancier ones sat on McClintock Street than those on surrounding Overlook, Ridgewood, Garrison (named for the land it sat upon) and other streets. They, in turn, were fancier than true working-class housing stock about Allegheny without any accouterments.

Though Allegheny's middle and perhaps lower-middle class houses did not have the leaded or stained glass, the chandeliers and libraries, or the plaster friezes of the mansions and grander homes of the wealthy and upper middle class, they nevertheless had what was considered standard then, but embellishment today. Tin lined the inner window sills, as well as being *the* material for the roof. Parlor walls had sliding pocket doors that showcased the best of faux-work by artisans of the time, emulating finer wood grain than that used. Sitting on posts of locust, not even chopped down from the land but having cement poured around their bottom to make the basement floors, these houses would go up with stone foundation and wood frame.

Mantels of slate that appeared as marble, or at least granite, were in evidence in parlor, dining, and bed rooms across Allegheny, also showing the expertise of the faux-working artisans. Yellow pine floors with not-so-narrow planking made the floors, and there were gorgeous wooden staircases stained to look like cherry. Attic rooms had simple wood mantels, and basements had painted wood staircases, as well as Dutch doors for the farm animals—goats and chickens—which were kept about the hillside homes of Allegheny, where you could get away with more than if you lived by the Diamond.

These middle-class houses of Allegheny would go up on tightly adjacent plots, but not as attached row houses, perhaps creating the biggest distinction between the lower and lower-middle classes. The structures were close together with narrow alleys between them, but there would be small patches of land in front and back as coveted yard space. Long and narrow, with windows mainly on the front and back, these types of homes typified Allegheny in the second half of the 1800s.

The Perrysville Plank Road, which was starting to be called Perrysville Avenue in the 1880s, was finally getting developed as well. It would have very grand houses built for individual wealthy families, set around the twists and turns of the old Indian trail. A little ways northward, the homes on the eastern side of Perrysville sat high up from the avenue, with elegant, stepped entrance and verandah porches. It was an area that came to be referred to as "Judge's Row," home to many of Allegheny County's judicial elite.

Other residents of this new 10th Ward were generally upper middle class. Some were involved in Allegheny City politics, like James Hunter. In the early 1870s he had been Allegheny City's Wharf master, and then later served as President of the Common Council for fourteen years. In the 1880s, he would have a house built at the corner of Perrysville Avenue and Riverview Street, which ran westward once beyond the property of two influential landowners there, a man by the name of Marshall and Samuel Watson. Right at street level, along Perrysville Avenue, were found the stable houses of the politicians and successful businessmen now living in the area.

In 1886, Perrysville Avenue got perhaps its most famous homeowner. William Thaw would sponsor John Brashear's move to Allegheny City, in order to have him close to the Observatory. He posed the offer to the world-renowned lens maker, and Brashear accepted. On land that had belonged to Thaw, and that was directly across Perrysville Avenue from the entrance to McClintock Street, a beautiful mansard home was built for Brashear at 1954

Perrysville Avenue. Shortly thereafter, a factory building was completed behind the house.

There were undoubtedly many excited neighbors, especially those living in the few fancier Victorian homes across Perrysville on McClintock Street, and gracing the curves of Perrysville going northward. Many of the neighbors' houses were Queen Anne in design—multi-angled, with inward and outward detail. The one built for Brashear, though grand, was not over-the-top for the neighborhood.

Perhaps the most excited neighbor, however, would be Henry Berger, who by this time had retired and was pursuing his love of astronomy. As an amateur, but next-door neighbor to the Observatory, he surely felt that he had the most exciting place to live if so interested. Now life in the neighborhood was about to get even more interesting, with the arrival of Brashear and the University's official opening in just a few short years.

In January 1887, the D.W.C. Carroll & Company erected a new water tank on Spring Hill, under the direction of the Superintendent of the Water Works, Alexander Bennie.

The mid-1880s marked the end of the era when new houses were built without indoor plumbing fixtures. Plumbing would become available, by the end of the decade, to Alleghenians who could afford to have their housing or business structure so equipped. With the service lines now becoming available to all wards, the only obstruction to outfitting one's structure with a water closet or bath was the cost of the tub or toilet, and the cost of the service usage, based upon the chosen amenity.

"Receiving plumbing" would mean different things to different households. Among a multitude of saved items in archives of Allegheny City are Housing Surveys and "Ferrule Books," of the Public Works Records, from the mid-to-latter 1880s. A ferrule was the pipe fitting, over pipes which at this time would have been of terra cotta. The records show the classification of the various amenities chosen by different households, and how the timeframe of availability was now standard for the rich and poor alike.

In one of those fancier new houses, with eight rooms, constructed on McClintock Street, an initial service connection would be made for "1 bath, 2 water closets, and 2 washstands." On Washington Street, in Manchester, a 4-room house had the service connection made, but "no baths, no water closets" were installed.

Down the hill on Monterey, in the Mexican War Streets, a typical house's "water facility charge" would be $28; a larger house on North Avenue was listed as being charged $35.

On Western Avenue lived C.C. Scaife, Esquire, of one of the more prominent families in southwestern Pennsylvania. He had what was listed as an "old house" (likely Borough era) outfitted with plumbing at this time. One of his equally affluent neighbors on Ridge Street, owning a 7-room house, would get "1 bath, 3 water closets and 2 wash stands."

A 12-room mansion at the corner of Western and Allegheny Avenue would receive "2 baths, 2 water closets, 3 wash stands and 1 'street washer,'" along with its first connection in 1888. The same year, an 18-room house owned by A.E.W. Painter, on Irwin Avenue bordering the Commons, got an "update" to a previous connection. It included receiving "8 baths, 8 water closets, 3 street washers, and 12 wash stands." Apparently there had "not been enough," as the record indicated, with the first service to the home. Sam Arthur and William Rowbottom (the latter whose business was by the intersection where the railroad cut Irwin and North Avenues diagonally) were both plumbers doing quite a lot of business at the time, as evidenced by the ferrule records.

The Boggs mansion on North Avenue, across from the West Commons, was the "town home" of Russell Boggs, of Boggs and Buhl department store fame. ("Town home" was the popular reference to those wealthy who had decided to maintain residence in the city, but also reside in "country homes" further north and west of Allegheny.) Plumbing had surely been installed in the Boggs' mansion at the earliest availability. But in the second half of the 1880s, the department store merchant decided to add his carriage house, behind the main home, to the list of those structures needing to be outfitted for water fixtures.

H. W. Stephenson, nearby, at the corner of North Avenue and Buena Vista, also updated his 10-room. house by 1899. Neighbor John Zanibec had a more humble abode, "a 7-rm. house at the head of Buena Vista Street," in which he had plumbing installed around this time.

Most of the Mexican War Streets, in fact, were fully developed by 1870. In some instances, where much older and smaller structures succumbed to age, new development would continue on certain plots until 1900. One such

Figure 35. John Brashear's house & factory

newer house would go up on Palo Alto in 1888. Just as it featured new plumbing as a selling point, an older house at 37 Monterey was modernized for the first time.

Any structures that had gone up in the mid-1880s, from the major estate subdivisions of the 1870s, were built just before the new modernity of plumbing. This would be the case for the houses constructed on the back and side streets carved out of McClintock's hilly property. Built in 1885, with the first homeowners in almost immediately, these homes missed just by a year the influx of plumbing that would make it standard to at least have a couple fixtures fitted in a newly-constructed home.

Most of these 'newer,' but pre-1886 homes around Allegheny City would upgrade a couple years later, getting various stages of desired and affordable plumbing, and with the added cost of the amenity going directly to the homeowner. At least the most simple plumbing features would be added to a majority of, but not all, homes by the end of the decade.

The deeds for the lots on Overlook Street, and for the surrounding others conceived in the 1870s, named the land as "part of the McClintock plan of estate." 1886 shows up as the year, in ferrule records, when prolific plumbing activity would occur on this hillside. Most of the new streets appeared to have owner-residents, but some of the homes were occupied by tenants.

At 41 and 39 Overlook Street was a "double house" or duplex, with four rooms. One of its owners, Mr. McGinley, was charged $7 in May of 1886, the month when most of the street appears to have been done. (The ferrule records, though vast, are by no means clear or consistent. At times pricing per room of house is given in lieu of chosen amenities; at other times, there is just a listing of the amenities.) The owner of the other half of the duplex was "Mrs. R. C. Buente," at 39 Overlook, one of the many properties she and her husband owned around the city. Mrs. Buente was also charged $7 for her "four rooms." (Both sides of the structure had attics, not assessed, since attic stories, despite livable rooms, were apparently not counted in house surveys.)

A "Mr. Williams" was the name of Buente's tenant. He would have been next-door neighbor to L. F. Stitzell, a consulting engineer who did some work from time-to-time for Allegheny City, living at 37 Overlook Street. His house was listed as having 6 rooms, but he apparently chose "no baths or water closets," despite a likely service connection (in that it was listed in the 1886 record), and despite the fact that he was an engineer!

To Stitzell's immediate east was apparently a friend, one who likely helped Stitzell in his employment, at times, as a private contractor by the city. This man was Water Works Superintendent Alex Bennie, living at 35 Overlook Street with his wife Annie. Their house is listed as having six rooms, and the ferrule record is rare in its being fully complete with both amenities chosen and the cost of such. Bennie's structure was listed as having "one bath, two water closets and one p. basin" for $19.25.

Like other homeowners in similar houses across Allegheny, the one basin for the house, as well as one of the water closets, was in the basement of the home. This was very typical for the time, but especially so for those who lived in hilltop homes like Bennie's. Sandstone foundations were built right into the line of the hillside, and basements served for animal tending (the keeping of goats and chickens), as well as for the household's hygienic needs. Bennie was also able to afford a bath tub and toilet on the second floor of the home, in the space originally occupied by a dry-sink.

Further down short little Overlook Street, closer to the end of Garrison Street, was another double house with 6 rooms each. It would receive the service connection only, and the plumber who completed this job was

Reinecke Urlson & Company. Fred Tate would be the plumber for the home of businessman Fred Thurber, which with five rooms, opted for just one wash stand. (Apparently backyard privies were still acceptable for many.)

Another very small cottage-type house, owned by Paul Blasy, was listed with just three rooms. Its privy area was not so much in the backyard, but in an adjoining structure to the house—a little room without any heat abutting the basement, furthest from the living areas above. This house, like so many others, would continue to have this primitive site as its only bathroom, albeit with later modern facilities and heat, continuing into the twenty-first century, never being fashioned with an upstairs bath.

Apparently by the end of 1886, other residents on Overlook who had not opted for plumbing earlier in the spring would have a change of heart, as was happening all across the city, with the modern amenity being the envy of neighbors. A Mrs. Dempsey, in a 5-room house, was listed as receiving her first service connection in December. Another relative latecomer to plumbing would be a house that likely was one of the first built in this street's development—a 6-room structure slightly more elaborate in design than the other long and narrow houses. Owned by J.S. Davis at the time, and anchoring the end of the street that connected to Garrison, modest amenities were put in this home. It was just above the wooded area once owned by James McBrier, and that was now Terrace Avenue heading down to a Second Ward school house on Irwin Avenue.

Terrace Avenue was part of a development along the midsection of Buena Vista's extension up the hillside. It went westward down the side of Buena Vista, to Irwin. New homes along this street—which would completely disappear in the next century after a modern school would take the place of the old Second Ward school building—were built about 1885, and also received plumbing similarly. A six-room home at No. 4 Terrace Avenue paid $12 for "one bath" fixture to be put in.

Some of the homes, of course, on Buena Vista, were a bit more extravagant and older than others. One 7-room structure at 171 Buena Vista received "not its first" service connection in 1886, with one bath and one water closet added. J. Lehman, at 103 Buena Vista Street, brought his 10-room. house up-to-date in plumbing by the approach of the 1890s, as well.

"John A. Brashear's house on Perrysville" was noted as receiving plumbing in 1886, likely just before he moved in. Archival records show, though, that a larger, "3/4 inch ferrule [was installed] on Sat. at 3:00, April 17, 1886."

The neighborhood of the extended Second Ward (known back then as Observatory Hill) was haven, before Brashear's arrival, of McClintock, McBrier, McNaugher and Drum. They were wealthy businessmen and prestigious public servants. Close to 1890, Brashear's neighbors were middle-class businessmen, city government department heads and workers, and real estate developers. There also would be the Observatory, and soon the Western University of Pennsylvania, which was in the final stages of preparing to open. The University, listed as "3 Perrysville Avenue" in the public works records, would pay $125, $14 and $16 for water facilities in its various buildings.

Plumbing would be added to the railroad watchtower on Irwin Street, near Washington Avenue, as well as to select homes in the section nearby Washington and leading northward to New Brighton. The cemetery structures, as well as nearby marble works, would thus have gotten plumbing at this time as well.

In 1887, houses that had just gone up along Taggart Street were able to be sold to a first buyer with plumbing. Modernization had finally caught up to new development in the city. Before similar middle-class and more humble houses came to this valley this year, it was just a few landowners that held large parcels of land. One was a man by the name of Gallagher, whose residence sat in the other valley northeast of Taggart Street, that ran right along the northern base of McClintock's hill. In his lifetime, one of the skinny side streets developed as leading out of McClintock's divided hillside would be named in his honor. Joseph Wheeler would live nearby Gallagher on Ridgewood Street. Both were known businessmen in Allegheny City around 1890.

Interestingly, these northern valleys which were the far-reaches of the Second Ward and beginnings of the Tenth Ward, despite being developed after the hilltop above, would receive sewer facilities sooner than their hilltop neighbors—as was also the case with other valleys and flat areas around Allegheny City. The exceptions would be the wealthy areas where sewer facilities could be provided. For example, the McCreary family, on the start of another hill of that area, would get sewer lines to their sprawling farmhouse in this back wooded area in 1884, despite it being upon a hill. Those living on the developed area around Overlook Street would not have sewers installed until fifteen years later, in 1899.

Sometimes enterprising property owners would take matters into their own hands, as did an A. Arnsthal, who owned property in the early 1880s on a section of Buena Vista Street. He constructed a private sewer for his residence. Perhaps he somehow linked it in with the old Penitentiary sewer on the Commons, which had caused so much earlier grief earlier in the century to homeowners in that area!

When the other northern areas, rich and poor, were getting their plumbing, around 1890, the Ashworth Estate on Federal Street, as well as the John R. Watson Estate in the new Tenth and Eleventh Wards, received theirs. A section of that northern ward, lying just south of Samuel Watson's property, was owned by Thomas M. Marshall, Senior. He lived in a 12-room. structure on what was already termed Marshall Avenue in the 1880s—an avenue that would be graded about this time, "along the Reserve Line." This street started high up on the hill at Perrysville, and would go gradually downhill past old Fort McKeever, and close to the bottom, the cemeteries as they made their upward sprawl. Travelers on this road could see far past the Ohio River ahead and below, to the great rolling hills heading away from Pittsburgh and Allegheny City.

Troy Hill residents generally got plumbing in 1887. An old house at its foot, possibly Canal-era, at 226 Ohio Street, was outfitted with plumbing in 1889. One year before, an entirely new structure with 'modern plumbing' would go up at 351 East Ohio Street, for Martin Ley. Neighboring 340 Ohio Street was a 13-room. structure, a residence and business owned by the Groetzinger family, who had been in Allegheny City now since early times.

George Ober, of the Eberhardt & Ober Brewery, also at the foot of Troy Hill, wrote a very nice letter to Allegheny City Councils in 1888, stating that the proposed plan to put a new sewer through that area would be just fine, and not an impedance to his business. It is not known what his neighbors thought of the city's plan. At 499 Ohio Street would be a Molt House owned by Julius Giuselhart, and below the Water-Works was the Reibel Estate, and an Eighth Ward School House.

Spring Hill's plumbing would follow suit, coming in 1888, as would all the rest of the northern wards. Also according to archive records, some occupants of houses in Manchester, along a portion of Western Avenue that was still going by *Water Lane* (those that had not opted for plumbing earlier when available) caught up to their neighbors during this time.

At 52 North Diamond, mixed among the businesses, another "old house," as noted, would be updated with plumbing in 1888. There was a nearby motel at this time, at 121 Ohio Street, belonging to John Dolde, but there was no mention of plumbing installed in the 1880s. At 42 Ohio Street, H. Anderson owned a 12-room. structure likely for residence and business (as most were), and he would take the opportunity to outfit it, before 1890, with "1 bath, 2 water closets, a street washer, and 2 wash stands."

Lewis Irwin owned a more modest house than his ancestors, near the location of the old Rope Walk, in the 1880s. Still with 8 rooms, he modernized with the addition of "1 bath, 2 water closets, 1 street washer, and 2 wash stands." Another relative, Mrs. Henry Irwin, at nearby 314 Western Avenue, had a 10-room. house, and in 1888 would have simply a laundry tub installed.

Mathilda Denny owned property close to the corner of North and Irwin Avenues, actually two 10-room. houses, where the railroad cut through on the diagonal. But the adjacent plot just north, on the southwest corner spot, was the Webb Tool Company, and the start of an industrial and commercial section that would stretch across North Avenue. The tip of this land plot, however, was a tiny triangle likely occupied with shrubbery or flowers, to compliment the West Commons Park across the street. It is not exactly known when this small portion got cut away from the rest of the land parcel, but it survives like that to this day, with a right turn from North Avenue, southward onto Irwin, easily possible with the cut-away street "right of way."

Just across the Commons, past what would be called Lake Elizabeth, the Penitentiary would be demolished in 1886. (A new facility for housing inmates was being constructed up the Ohio River in the flat area of the Ninth Ward, right by the river.) Just a year later on the site of the old Penitentiary, Henry Phipps (who also made a fortune in the region's steel industry) talked both Allegheny legislators and citizens into allowing him to bequeath a Conservatory, the first in southwestern Pennsylvania, showcasing foliage from around the world. In so doing, it was seen as living up to at least the renewed purpose for the Commons land, as a pastoral place to be enjoyed by all in the community.

On his estate holdings at the corner of Ohio and Arch Street, near the edge of the Diamond very close to the new Conservatory, was an old hotel operated by George Riddle. From another prominent family of Allegheny City, he also ran two stores in the late 1880s, at 28 and 30 Ohio Street. They all, along with a barroom and house operated by William Semple, Esquire, at the corner of N. Diamond and Federal Street, received plumbing service connections at the end of the decade.

At the foot of Nunnery Hill, across Federal and between Fountain and Fairmount Streets, Robert Henderson owned a lot of land. Sometime in the mid-1880s, he apparently sold some of the property. As described in archival material, improvements were made by the city during the early part of the decade on "certain encroachments for stone walls and slopes, to support the street, upon the property then of Robert Henderson, now belonging to Mary, wife of Samuel Watson, [as well as that of] Caroline Henderson and Robert L. Henderson."

At the spot of the northeast corner of Federal and Fairmount Streets, by late 1887, was a building that housed one of Allegheny City's three inclines. It was called the Nunnery Hill Inclined Plane, and was built by engineer Samuel Diescher. It ran on wooden trestle westward along the northern side of Henderson Street (surely one of the reasons why the slope needed reinforcement earlier). Then it curved, unusually—its distinctive quality unlike the other two inclines. From there it went northward, around where Sandusky Street sat below. It would end up at the top near Clyde Street, opposite the Twelfth Ward School. This incline would provide transportation down the hill to all the working-class residents who now lived in the quarry area.

Allegheny City's second incline was located on Troy Hill, and was actually up and running a year before the Nunnery Hill one, in 1887. Its base was just east of the entrance to the bridge to Herr's Island, at the foot of the hill, and just west of the old Brunner Hotel, a building still standing today. It ran up a sharply steeper ascent than Allegheny's other inclines, coming out at the intersection of Lowrie Street (the main avenue in this neighborhood of the Thirteenth Ward) and the old Ley and Froman Streets—just across from the No. 11 Fire Engine House. The other way down Troy Hill, besides Troy Hill Road sloping gradually up the base near the breweries, was Ravine Street, or "Pig Hill," which ran almost vertically straight down, plummeting onto the entrance to Herr's Island Bridge. Pigs would be scooted down this chute of a road onto Herr's Island's early butcheries (and later slaughterhouses).

Wicklines Lane would also connect the activity on Herr's Island, via Troy Hill, to the Spring Garden butcheries to the north and west.

The third incline would open up the area developed out of McClintock's land, by connecting it to the valley below where Irwin Avenue was near its terminus. The area, by the newly-opened up land once belonging to Taggart, would lie directly below the back hillside of those streets opened up behind the McClintock property—in particular, the last of the subdivided land, Yale Street. The hillside, though wooded, was steep sandstone cliff.

In an attempt to link the two new neighborhoods and provide another means to scale the extended Second Ward heights, the Ridgewood Incline Company built a structure on lower Taggart. It was so-named because the upper terminus of the incline brought passengers right to the lower end of Ridgewood, just around the bend from where Stitzell, Bennie and others had just moved in three years earlier. It was also conceived to provide transport, from different direction, up the hill and soon home to the University.

The cars would travel on rails that actually started on Taggart, below Irwin, and then went up and over that road—in this respect making it unique to the other two inclines. Here, once-flat and grand Irwin Avenue (Pasture Lane) humped up to go over the stubborn land at the foot of a massive sandstone outcropping, one that still drips water from the vestige of a spring in the area. The incline would pass over this spectacle, as if an amusement park ride, and would terminate at the crest, where Yale Street intersects Ridgewood. (The top of Ridgewood Street, just before its intersection with Perrysville and where the Drum residence used to be, would still hold the smaller Second Ward school building at this time.)

The incline seemingly opened in 1888, but the city and the company operating it were still working things out with regard to infrastructure. A "Change of Grade" notice was posted in 1889 regarding, in particular, Yale Street, but "involving," as was posted, "the Ridgewood Avenue Inclined Railway."

The Ridgewood Incline was planned for as early as November 1886, when a 5/8 in. plumbing ferrule was installed in the building below, containing what would be the boiler for the machinery. The proximity of water, unfortunately, still could not stop the very premature demise of this incline. It only survived about one year, as a fire in the year 1889 destroyed the trestle base. Adding to its storied history, the rest of the incline would then be dismantled and go up one year later on a similar hill close by.

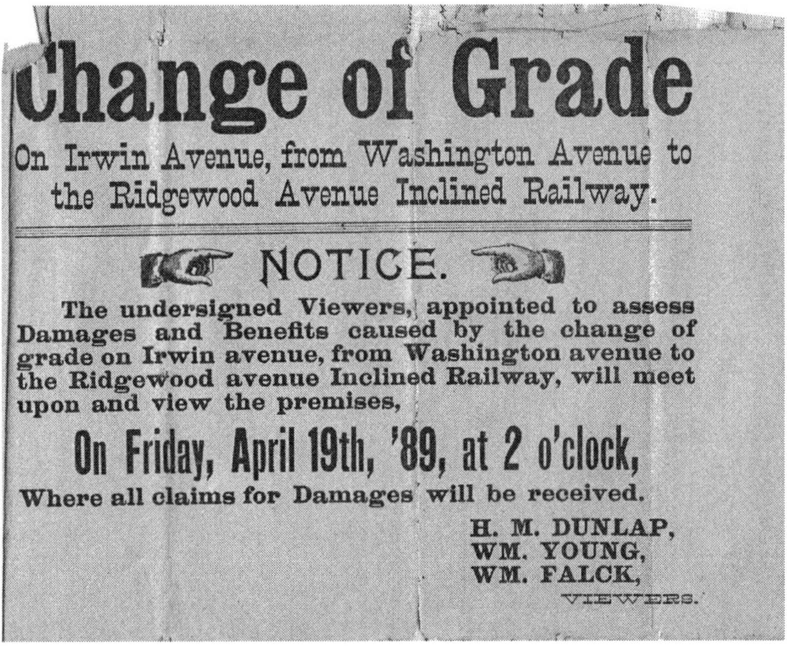

Change of Grade

On Irwin Avenue, from Washington Avenue to the Ridgewood Avenue Inclined Railway.

NOTICE.

The undersigned Viewers, appointed to assess Damages and Benefits caused by the change of grade on Irwin avenue, from Washington avenue to the Ridgewood avenue Inclined Railway, will meet upon and view the premises,

On Friday, April 19th, '89, at 2 o'clock,

Where all claims for Damages will be received.

H. M. DUNLAP,
WM. YOUNG,
WM. FALCK,
VIEWERS.

Figure 36. Change of Grade notice, 1889

Just about 600 feet north, where Irwin Avenue stopped, as it hit the other hilltop cradling this valley, the resurrected incline would travel the other northern hill leading to the McCreary farm. ("Irwin" actually would continue, in the form of a series of very steep steps like so many others about Allegheny City and Pittsburgh, and then become a road again at the top of this hill. Its name was even carried out past the other large valley. As such, the name Irwin, or originally Pasture Lane, began at Monument Hill and went all the way northward to very near where Fort McKeever had been.)

Starting from below Sarah Street, near Taggart, the incline would go up to Catherine Street, where intersected by the Irwin steps. Supposedly, three rows of houses were built on the little plateau on the edge of the hill, all just to provide customers for the incline. Unlike the old top destination, albeit still to a residential street, this other hill brought people to a new ward, an isolated residential section a bit off the beaten path of the main avenue, Perrysville. Residents of the new neighborhood certainly benefitted, though.

It would be called Clifton Park. Clifton was the likely owner of an even grander farm house than McCreary's that once sat in that area. A little grocery store operated by a Mike Lewis would be found in the neighborhood, as the residents found themselves far enough removed north of the city.

The resurrected incline would have a fairly short life, as well, lasting only until about 1906. That year, one of the cars got loose and smashed into a yellow-brick house on Strauss Street, below.

In December 1886, Allegheny City further dealt with the issue of the "summit of Federal Street" up to the new wards. A public notice was posted about town—at the city hall, on street posts and bridge posts, just as the Ridgewood Incline and other notices would have been. As well, the *Pittsburgh Evening Chronicle* was a regional newspaper that began to carry all the "Bids Accepted" postings.

It proclaimed that "petitioners to the county allege that the purpose of opening and extension of the said street is wholly useless....." They were referring, though, to Federal Lane, that primitively-left section of the street before the needed curve at the hills' first sandstone abutment. Should it be this lane that was to have been extended (and not the area of Federal bypassing the abutment, near the start of Perrysville), the residents would have been right. There was no going through, easily, that extremely craggy abutment. But the terminology was probably misleading, as surely city planners would begin to see that the best way up the hill would be an extension from the wider avenue of Federal Street, instead of Federal Lane.

The city made its case that the street could now "be easily [ascended] with little expense or inconvenience to property owners." Apparently, such owners in the area were not against the idea of having an ascent up the hill, but they, too, either misleadingly or wrongly thought out, were calling for something "narrower and crooked-er," according to records, than the city was proposing. And any street ascending the hill, here, would rightfully need to be of substantial width.

Property owner James Graham "very respectfully" signs a letter to Allegheny Common and Select Councils, outlining that the cuts that would need to be made to the hill were too deep, and states, "I need not urge that the street can never be made a good driving road, without entreating upon the abutting property owners, and at expense that would amount to confiscation of their property."

The city would move forward, however, and the summit of Federal Street would be reached, with excavation of the hill finally tackled. A steep road would be graded and paved over the next five years. Federal Street Extension would thus connect at the top with Perrysville Avenue, as it wrapped around from the curves away from the University's property, once again, like at the bottom. As in the handle of a cup, Federal Street now hit Perrysville in two places.

Finally the "straight shot" upward to reach the land in northern Allegheny had been made, after all those years when earliest travelers had to go up and around the curved tier of the Venango Trail. This would further ensure that residents of the Tenth, Twelfth and Fourteenth Wards would be able to participate fully as Allegheny citizens.

The extension of this main road, once drawn simply as *External Ally*, would also open up an area north of Nunnery Hill, connecting to land owned by a woman named Jane Pusey. Both McNaugher's land and McIntyre's was nearby, and streets in this area would be named for both of these men, as well as one for Lafayette, the general who so long ago visited Allegheny Town.

For the most part, closing in on 1890, the land wrapping itself around the northern curves of Perrysville was either an emblem of the developed residential wealth of "Judge's Row," or was still farm tracts and orchards. Developments like Clifton Park and other side-streets took off from this time on, however.

In 1886, the newspaper *Alleghenian* discussed the Western University's coming to Observatory Hill, as part of an op-ed also about "the noble red man's" historic place held in the city's history. Namely, the effectiveness of the Ridgewood Incline, still then under construction, was addressed—regarding getting students to the locale of the new campus under construction.

> Now that the scheme of an inclined railway to Observatory Hill seems to be in a fair way of reaching accomplishment, there is talk, as was to be expected, that the Western University may be located on the eleven acres of ground belonging to it, which surround the Observatory. The propriety of removing to this site has been frequently talked over by

the trustees of the University, but the great objection hitherto has been
the inaccessibility of the location. With a good incline up the hill,
charging what would be a constant advertisement of the claims of
moderate fares, this difficulty would be obviated, and the site would
become a very desirable one.... The claims of the institution to the
patronage of the people, and the spacious grounds would give ample
opportunity.... Of course the scheme for an inclined plane is not yet
actually certain of accomplishment, no decisive steps have been taken
with regard to changing the location of the University to the hill,
but if one project comes to pass, it is altogether likely that the other
will also."

During the 1880s, while students attended classes in the rented seminary
rooms, the University was able to contain its dismay about its current status.
But they were indeed a bit torn as to exactly which direction to go. Trustees
eventually felt that, "it seemed best...to build on ground the University
already owned and to stay in Allegheny," rather than pursue a search for
suitable land elsewhere. Stalled no longer, the University officially began
building plans for the hilltop land parcel in the late 1880s.

A further modernization to transportation in 1888 (and likely a necessary one, considering the imminent demise of the Ridgewood Incline) also
helped the cause of the University. There would be the construction of the
first *electric* street railways, or trolley cars. Traveling up Federal to Perrysville
Avenue, at least as far as to Wilson Avenue (just past Simon Drum's old property), the Observatory Hill Passenger Railway was much heralded. Because
the grade sloped upward, even though gradual, the line had trouble. Or
perhaps it was because it was gradual, and thus so long sustained, problems
were encountered. The trolley line even had to be suspended temporarily.
Things would get adjusted after a couple years, and the trolley would be back
in business by the University's opening.

Professor Langley had been offered, in 1887, the position of Secretary
of the Smithsonian Institution. He accepted, but would stay to teach at the
University and continue to fully oversee the Observatory. His great friend and
Observatory benefactor, William Thaw, would die in 1889, just two years
after Langley's celebrated achievement and one year before the University's
official opening on the hilltop land that Thaw helped arrange.

Before the 1890s would be ushered in, two former Alleghenians made news. One was the Mary Schenley, land owner in Allegheny, who gave the City of Pittsburgh three hundred acres for a park. The other was Andrew Carnegie, who as a young businessman made a name for himself in Pittsburgh's steel industry. Carnegie was associated with negative news in the mid 1880s, however, due to intense labor problems. (May of 1888 finally saw the Edgar Thompson Works steel mill strike settled, after long and arduous proceedings.)

But in 1889, Carnegie announced his intent to build and give to the region a series of libraries and music halls. His first announced gift was to the City of Allegheny, but it would be not the first one actually completed by contractors. That honor would go to Braddock, one of the centers of his steel making activities. Looking to repair his negative image of late, the Library and Hall opened in that eastern neighborhood of Pittsburgh would also include facilities for nearby mill workers to have a bathhouse and rest area.

Changes had also been coming to the city's antiquated street numbering system. Following Philadelphia's lead, it was reported in the Alleghenian that, "slowly the city is getting to the point when it will have legible names and numbers on its streets and houses. The Street Committee on Thursday evening ordered printed ordinances changing the names of streets running from the river front, beginning with Preble Avenue...."

As plumbing took hold in the city, Alexander Graham Bell's invention became the next novelty. Allegheny City offices would be furnished with telephones free of charge. The eight fire engine houses had already been installed with theirs since the top of the decade. Telephones for residents would still be several years away, except for the wealthy few.

In 1889, the same year that Alleghenians and Pittsburghers alike reacted in horror to the great flood in nearby Johnstown, claiming close to 2,300 lives, there was happier news regarding one more utility—electricity. While R. T. Pearson was Mayor, a "Resolution to Advertise for Proposals for Electric Lighting in the city of Allegheny" was called for in the councils. There would soon be the sale of an electric light plant to the city, a further call for bids to light city buildings, and electric lighting was made available for a general public soon thereafter.

chapter ten:
AMUSEMENTS & THE UNIVERSITY

A llegheny was a proud city of fifty years in 1890. A Semi-Centennial
Celebration & Jubilee would be celebrated by all on July 17, 1890.
It had been just over one hundred years since the land had been made the
Reserved Tract and Allegheny Town was conceived.

Population was at 118,000, having grown quite a bit again throughout
the previous decade. Finally a new post office for the city, to support this
number of residents, was completed, built on the public space in the far
northwest of the Diamond. The building was designed in 1894 by William
Martin Aiken, architect for the U.S. Treasury Department, and was in the
Italian Renaissance style with a beautiful gleaming dome, an emblem of the
advance of the city.

The Market Ledger for the times shows the following merchants
most often selling their wares at the public market house: Oscar Gallagher
of Gallagher Brothers, George Beilstein, Christian Breining, C. Gerlach,
Thomas Kimberlin, Mrs. Jane Brady, Jacob Greiner, Mrs. Fornoff, Jacob
Oesterle, Jacob Heck, Louis Seiple, George J. Vogel & Bros., and Joseph Best.
Rents for the Market House stalls would be collected quarterly, it was noted.
The Garden Stand was often occupied by D. Leech, Margaret Hartman, Geo.
R. Leety, C. Vogel, A. Hackel, Margaret Peterman, Riley Ewing, J.B. Wallace,
and E.C. Ludwig.

Records of vehicle registration also first appear in archives from the
1890s on. Issuances would take the form of horse wagon plates, buggy plates,
horse carriage plates, toll plates, and timber wheel plates.

By the end of the decade, Armour & Co. meatpackers, on Anderson
Street, would have six one-horse wagons in operation. The Allegheny
Exposition Company at Federal Street, no doubt connected with coordinat-
ing the traveling shows still coming to the north bank area, had eight two-
horse carriages. By the early years of the new century, Boggs and Buhl
Department Store would register twenty-three buggies. Though there appears
no listing for the H.J. Heinz Company, its colorful pickle buggies could be

seen about Allegheny City. Heinz, in the Eighth Ward, came to Allegheny City in 1889, after its founding in nearby Sharpsburg. Its factory along the Allegheny River, along with its success, soon became synonymous with Allegheny City.

Business and industry in and surrounding Allegheny City continued to extremely prosper. News in 1891, in addition to another regional flood, was of an an oil boom in West View, just north of the city line and south of the borough of Perrysville. But as industry and commerce continued to thrive, along with that came the voice of labor, speaking ever louder to the plight of the workers who were behind the productivity and making men like Carnegie, associate Henry Clay Frick, and others ever richer. Labor strife would dominate regional news in the first two years of the decade.

In April of 1891, coke workers held a strike at the Morewood mines of the H.C. Frick Company, and Samuel Gompers visited the Pittsburgh region and rallied confidence in the eight-hour work day. Most significantly, though would be the Homestead Steel Strike, against Frick and essentially Carnegie, who was living in a castle in Scotland by this time. Pinkerton Guards were ordered to Homestead to control the strikers. They came down the Monongahela River, and great violence erupted, more than southwestern Pennsylvania had ever previously seen. The steel industry would never be the same.

A mere year before these culminating events, which cast Carnegie and Frick in the worst possible light, was the time that the Carnegie Library and Music Hall had started to actually be constructed in Allegheny City.

$730 would go to Rose and Fisher for shelving for the Library. They also provided the storm doors. A.J. Lacock, at 39 S. Diamond Street, provided the galvanized iron for the roof over the clock. Samuel Hasting produced the oak strips for the flooring. And carpeting was provided by H.B. Snaman, of 136 Federal Street. Renvers and Flechsig upholstered the chairs, and Margaret Ulpegkail made the curtains. R.J. Stephenson & Company of 912 Federal St. did the plumbing.

James Wilson was the name of the artisan doing the paneling and fresco work of the lecture room, art room, rotunda, hall, vestibule and all library departments. James Watson provided the bronze radiators and iron railing. Rhein & Fortenbacher, of 530 E. Ohio St., would work on fine-tuning the skylight. Fire Insurance was provided by the A.H. Trimble Fire Insurance Company. Once opened, the Crystal Ice Company would provide ice for

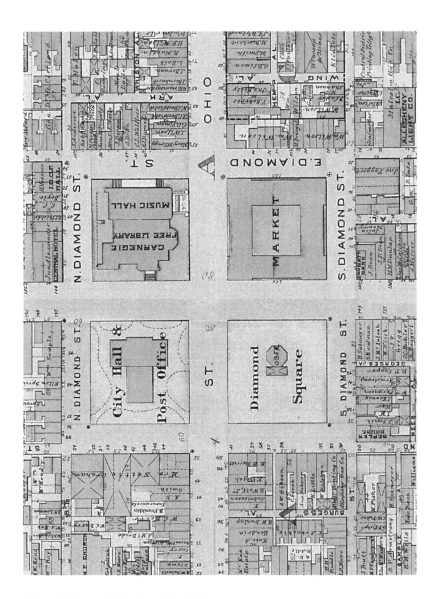

Figure 37. Center of Allegheny City, 1890

events, Boggs and Buhl any needed cheesecloth, and S. Ogelvie sponges and brushes. Fred H. James would tune the organ weekly.

Andrew Carnegie wanted to honor the memory of Colonel James Anderson of Manchester, who gave the young Carnegie free access to his personal library decades prior. In gratitude, Carnegie bestowed this gift, the first so bestowed (and second opened) of more than 2,500 to come in the English-speaking world. (Carnegie's biggest library, music hall and museum complex was planned for the middle of the decade, to be built on some of the donated park land of Mary Schenley, in Pittsburgh's East End.)

The Carnegie Library and Music Hall stood northeast on the Diamond, across from the Market House. By 1897, the new Post Office would sit nearby, on the northwest corner. Both buildings would be still squarely on the reserved public spaces of the original town center. When the Library and Music Hall opened, United States President Harrison would be on hand for the commemoration. The Library would have a massive clock tower that, as recognized as the gleaming Post Office dome to soon appear nearby it, would come to symbolize Allegheny City fifty years in.

Carnegie Music Hall would start to host events, even as the city also continued to have traveling entertainment visit the north shore area. As well, many social groups and clubs were holding events on their own. The city would collect a small fee for all. Archive material from the mid-1890s show a listing of "Amusement Licenses" handed out to and for the following:

> a camping club, hunting and fishing club, rod and gun club, a masonic hall, the McNally Baseball Club, a nonpareil club, German-Austrian Beneficial Association, Lafayette Lodge, St. Cicely Melhado Kroabischian Band, Ford Paw Circus, George Lacock's Allegheny Cyclers, Croation Society, Bicycle Road Race, Charity Ball for Charles Schumaker, Bohemian American Orchestra, and the Theatrical Mechanic's Association.

Many of the "acts" had addresses listed as the Exposition Grounds, those that were traveling and just making a stop in Allegheny. The Barnum & Bailey Circus performed many times throughout the record-keeping, usually paying a $1000 fee each time. The Wenceslaus Society of Allegheny, who met at Turner Hall, and the Allegheny Jacksonia Club, who met at Cecilia Hall, paid a fraction of that.

Citizens throwing private parties sometimes paid $5, as did Florian Kastner of 63 Spring St. for "Entertainment" at Halvetia Hall. There was the Harry Beltzhoover Charity Ball, the Radiant Society, the Hessie Singing Society, Crescent Camping Club, and the Disrael Society. The Puritan Athletic Club, Superior Athletic Club, and the Order of Railroad Telegraphers. Iron Moulders, the Schuabisch Singing Society, and the Druden Smorgasbord. Even a Phonograph Exhibit and Silver Plate Show.

A Boxing Exhibition would come to the New Turner Hall, and Boxing at Rear 66 Irwin Avenue. There was a Woods Run Escort Club, the Swiss Time Society, Austin Gushurst's Lecture and Gambling Institute, and the Bavarian Ladies Society.

The Buffalo Bill Wild West Show would come to "Exposition Park" in August of 1897, and the same month the Jolly Young Bachelors were at Kenyon Hall. The United Mine Workers met, just as did the Hessian Sick Relief Association and the Pol Litewskichh Society. There would be snake exhibitions, sparring exhibitions, and performances by the Perry Social Orchestra. The Stone Masons International Union met, and the Abe Lincoln Club and Lily of the West Club hosted in-house meetings. Others performed at the various halls and society gatherings. One of the many Bicycle races was listed as occurring from "Ohio Avenue to Preble to McClure to Woods Run to Perrysville."

The Carnegie Music Hall had a separate list all its own, with rents certainly higher than the small amusement license fees elsewhere. Renting out the space in 1894 would be Amherst College, the Western University Glee Club, the Allegheny Musical Association, the Duquesne Conservatory of Music, the Warren Colored Church, Cornell Glee Club, and the State Teachers Association. Their budgets were higher, their performances surely very good, but their names, it seems, a little less showy.

The majority of events at the Carnegie Music Hall, however, were organ recitals—making good use of a great pipe organ in a lovely space. The resident organist was a gentleman by the name of C.P. Koch. His organ recitals, on off nights from the rentals, had the hall filled almost nightly. Superintendent of the Hall would be H.H. Buente. Allegheny citizens were all for the culture. "A number of our prominent citizens have subscribed sums of money with which to pay for additional talent."

In addition to all of the activity already taking place, adjacent to the Exposition Park was a horseracing track, where the wealthy and middle-class of the area would be entertained while taking stake of the runners. As well, the wealthy from Ridge Avenue and Manchester were known to spend recreational time by going down to the track on off days to run their horses.

The 1896 budget for the Department of Charities for Allegheny City has colorful facts stored away in the archives, as well. A *Listing of Groceries* included choice yellow sugar, barley, dried fruits, oolong tea, soda crackers, and ivory soap, as well as camphor, arnica and morphine among many items. Boggs and Buhl would also supply materials of all sorts to the Department.

An Allegheny Visiting Nurses Association was formed this decade, and there was an Allegheny Free Dispensary, where for lower-income citizens, prescriptions could be filled, meals and transportation furnished, and funeral assistance obtained.

Soon, in the early 1900s, a new Bureau of Health would be organized. It would include inspection of meat, milk and plumbing, as well as take steps toward garbage removal for the city. The First Annual Report to come out for what was at this time called the *City Home, Asylum and Farm*, located in Claremont, Pa., described how many that were sent there stayed their lifetime, and, as noted, that there were many coffins periodically sent for those that died while in residence.

The new century would also see referrals given to the Anti-Cruelty Society of Allegheny. Four of the perhaps fifty listed cases, a small number, had proceedings begin where individuals would be then deported back to their native countries.

The most celebrated opening of the 1890s in Allegheny, in fact right at the top of the new decade, was that of the Western University of Pennsylvania, finally on its own hilltop campus. The school would now be cited, in deference to the 1819 charter, as "the first chartered school of higher education west of the Allegheny Mountains and north of the Ohio River."

The beginning of classes was January 6, 1890. The School of Engineering was the main course of study for most of the students. The next year, however, would bring an affiliation with the Western Pennsylvania Medical College, for students interested in public health.

In June of that first year, just six months in, Chancellor Goff would leave his post. He reported, before so doing, that the school's enrollment was at an all-time high, with engineering and chemistry now holding the bulk of the students' interest. Sadly, Goff would pass away in the fall, and the University in just two years had lost two leaders, with Goff and William Thaw.

> Mourned throughout the community, it was a sad beginning for the new University. The faculty and students had moved into the new buildings believing that the hardest days of the University were over. The community still showed appreciation for the loyalty and courage of the faculty, and faith in the honestness of purpose that had survived the financial difficulties of Ross and Diamond [Streets] and the inconvenience of retrenchments in the rented rooms on North Avenue.
> The simple days of the college were over. From 1890 the school went still further on its way toward the destiny that had been the hope of the men who, in 1787, founded the log Academy at the outpost in the wilderness—further toward realization of the plans of the men who, in 1819, petitioned the legislature to charter a Western University for Pennsylvania.   (STARRETT)

Several buildings had been erected on the hilltop; one had an impressive balcony looking out onto the yard of the campus. It was a very intimate campus atmosphere. The University students knew Professors Brashear and Langley well. (Brashear was given an honorary degree.)

It is documented that, from the beginning of the time on Observatory Hill, students would walk across the lawn with one or both, going back and forth from the engineering studies department to Brashear's factory. "Part of their education came from visits to the shop where 'Uncle John' and William R. Ludewig worked at the grinding of mighty lenses. Once when Dr. Brashear was grinding a sixty-inch reflector for the Lick Observatory, when he was drilling through the center to mount it, the lens exploded and tore a hole through the brick wall of the laboratory. Dr. Brashear... dismissed the University classes so that the boys could see the force of an exploding piece of glass; then he started to work grinding another lens."

Many former students of Langley's would, for decades, remark on his infamous "whirling table" and "contrivances with wings made of tin and cork and rubber..." what he called 'mechanical birds.' Langley published Experiments in Aerodynamics, after years of work at the Observatory, with the help of students and colleagues in the first two years of the school being on the hilltop. On the land behind the Observatory building, on the 'whirling table,' he would also, with the assistance of Brashear's assistant Ludewig, "place the mechanical birds and actual birds, to study the action of air upon them and their balancing power at different velocities."

John Brashear would often invite all students "to come across the campus," for example, "to see the large and powerful spectroscope that was being erected for the Royal University of Dublin." And Langley started a tradition in the first summer of opening up the Observatory to a general public interested in viewing the heavens.

The intellectual and social atmosphere surrounding the school in its new location was extremely stimulating, with professors very down-to-earth and attuned to student interest. There was a time when "students wired the University buildings, as an engineering project, with Edison carbon lamps." The University would have many clubs—Glee, Mandolin and Banjo, and the like, as well as a university newspaper, *The Courant*.

The school was known for other characters beyond Brashear and Langley. A Professor Phillips apparently rode to class, up and down Perrysville Avenue, on an unclipped pony, gaining him the nickname "Professor Wooly-Horse."

It seems Brashear, with his reputation, was very instrumental in getting even more students into the engineering studies department. He, who had only a common school education, yet was now known worldwide as a scientist and astronomer. Starting in the 1890s, in addition to teaching, he would be on the University's Board of Directors. "When the great observatories for astronomical research throughout the world wanted a lens, accurate to the one-millionth of a degree, they sent for it to the workshop of John Brashear in Allegheny City."

The mutual activities of Brashear and Langley would end after two years together, when Langley would leave both the Observatory and University campus in 1891. Brashear would carry on the spirit of both, though, continuing to mentor students above and beyond the call of the classroom.

Langley's successor would be James Keeler. At the same time, the new Chancellor of the University would be William Jacob Holland, who was born in Jamaica, had traveled in South America, studied Moravian, and was educated in language, art, literature, theology and education.

By the year 1892, Director Keeler had started thinking about a new site for the Observatory, on higher ground, because pollution from Allegheny and Pittsburgh both were starting to adversely affect the viewing conditions.

In 1895, the scouts for the new site found what they were looking for—a new locale in what would be Riverview Park, north on Perrysville, and to the west of the avenue. It was secured for that purpose due to a great effort by John Brashear. He arranged for David C. Park, founder of Crucible Steel, to donate the plot of land. But the new Observatory would still be well over ten years in the making.

The year 1895 would also mark when women were finally allowed to attend the University, and when the School of Law would be founded. By 1897, the Western University of Pennsylvania would celebrate 110 years of existence, from 1787 when it was founded as the Pittsburg Academy. At the anniversary, Dr. Holland spoke:

> We have no ivy-wreathed buildings—but we have great teachers. In Allegheny, on the top of Observatory Hill, we have a chemical laboratory, and Engineering School, and the Allegheny Observatory. Our medical department is at the West Penn Hospital; our law department is in the downtown triangle near the courthouse at Fifth and Diamond; our pharmacy division is on a bluff overlooking the Monongahela River; our School of Dental Surgery is in one of the most congested sections of the triangle.
>
> We have no old weathered buildings and no tree-shadowed campus, but we have places that are doing good work. We have the kind of teaching, the kind of research, and the kind of service to meet the needs of the people of Western Pennsylvania and to justify this celebration. There is no university in the United States at the present time that is doing any better work and with so small an endowment.... We celebrate the past and we look forward to the future.

For the celebration, the students held a parade through Allegheny and Pittsburgh, "with a chemistry float that exploded in front of the courthouse without injuring anybody; an engineering float loaded with machinery, castings and engineering tools, propelled by a steam engine that gave out in the middle of the Sixth Street Bridge and was hauled away by a team of horses; and a large float on which stood a number of students dressed in costumes representing the various stage's of Pittsburgh's history, from the days of the Indians and the early settlers down through the nineteenth century."

Keeler left the Observatory in 1898, and John Brashear was appointed temporary Director until Frank Wadsworth came aboard one year later.

Then in 1901, he would again be called to distinguished temporary duty as Acting Chancellor to the University. In between, a cornerstone for the new Observatory would be laid in Riverview Park, in October 1900, and Brashear would speak. He referred to the building about to go up as becoming the "new temple of the skies."

The new Observatory went up slowly, in stages, as the fundraising effort needed was far beyond originally planned. Many of Allegheny's, and even Pittsburgh's wealthy contributed. Included would be Westinghouse, Carnegie, George Theiss, Andrew Mellon and Henry Clay Frick. But perhaps none like the contributions of two sisters who were prominently known in Allegheny City.

Jane McGrew Smith and Mathilda Hudson Smith lived on North Avenue, and they looked very favorably upon the Observatory's internationally-known activities. (They had also been tremendous supporters of the University going to the hilltop campus, as well, with one extremely generous gift, in particular, to the geology department.) Their contributions for causes intellectual and social in nature form a long list, but their keenest interest seemed to be in getting the new Observatory up and running. They donated funds for scientific instrumentation, for the building fund, and then for one very special gift.

An art glass figure window, designed and crafted by artist Mary Elizabeth Tillinghast, would arrive in 1903 and be installed in the building during the stage of its construction. It depicted *Urania*, the Greek muse of astronomy. John Brashear would thank the 'Misses Smith'—"Of all the friends of the Institution you are the most active...."

Construction continued, as did fundraising efforts, solicited by the Observatory Committee, which also included the wealthy and influential Lucien Scaife. In 1905, the addition of a crypt underneath the north dome was requested of the architect, with plans to there rest the ashes of former director James Keeler, who had passed away in 1900.

By 1906, the telescope from the old observatory and the new Keeler Memorial Telescope were installed. Even though the full facility would not be finished until 1912, the public at this time was allowed to visit and use the old viewing instrument. A continuation of Langley's idea, this would open windows for all of the community to the wonders of the heavens.

The building construction went into its final phase in 1906, while scientists resumed their research now on the celebrated new telescope.

Many of the wealthy in Allegheny, by the mid-1890s, at least had country homes, or were beginning to completely move out of the city. There was a real desire to get away from the industrialization and commerce of the town. A few of the affluent families would go north to the countryside of Butler, and others still to Bellevue, but the majority now went further down the Ohio River, to the communities of Emsworth and Sewickley. The Buhls stayed in Allegheny City, but would have a summer home now in Sewickley.

Heirs to much of the great wealth that was built during the early industrialization of the preceding decades still lived in the great city, however. Daughter Kate McKnight still lived in the grand hillside home atop Western Avenue, on whose lawn, under a mulberry bush, was buried Chief Killbuck. A women's "Monday Class," a lecture series and discussion group, met at this mansion before the turn of the century, and later became known as the Twentieth Century Club.

Newspapers of the time included the morning paper in Allegheny, the *Commercial Gazette*, and Alexander Moore's *Leader*, which billed itself as "Absolutely Independent in Everything."

Contractors working with the city in 1897 included the Sicilian Asphalt Company on Beaver Avenue in Manchester, who did much of the curbing and walkways around the Pleasant Valley area. They also did the repaving on the portion of Irwin Avenue from Western to North. Around 1901, the Wadsworth Stone and Paving Company would resurface and build new walks in the park. Duncan & Porter was a cement and pipe company used; their business was on Anderson Street.

Despite the successes of business and industry, there would be a small economic slump from 1893–94. But a great building boom was beginning to take place, and would lift the city from short-lived economic concern. By 1904, the city was easily purchasing 125 enclosed arc lamps to modernize its Bureau of Lighting.

New structures would soon go up all over Allegheny, including the first air conditioned theatre, the Palace, built on the lower end of Federal Street near the 6th Street Bridge and Robinson's old property. A man named Sam Little was the contractor. He apparently connected a flue to an ice house next-door, and blew cold air in with one of the new Westinghouse Electric motors powering a fan. Like so many other pre-twentieth century structures, the building had a short life, being destroyed by fire after only one year. Various other "Fire Causes," as listed in municipal reports of the time were "clothes drying too close to heat source; chimney fires; brush fires and burning rubbish; children playing with matches and candles; oil can explosions; sparks from engines; wood stoves; lamp explosions; smoking in bed; and crossed wires."

Municipal reports also listed sentences within Allegheny's criminal justice system: "Sending someone to the Workhouse for six months; to the Huntingdon Reformatory; to the Polk Feeble-Minded School; to the jail in Allegheny City;" and an assortment of fines were levied.

Police in Allegheny City arrested citizens for "drunkenness; violations of city ordinances; vagrancy; trespassing; streetwalking; gambling; exposing the person; keeping a disorderly house; fast driving; disorderly conduct; impersonating an officer; and stealing flowers and ribbons at the cemeteries." There were also more substantial crimes than ever before listed in archival records—a few recorded rapes; assault and battery; a lot of larceny charges; and even a couple murders.

The municipal record from the year 1902 also includes extensive listings of more minor, but heartfelt, matters. No matter where in the city they resided, wealthy or not, the dog license registers showed that Alleghenians obviously loved their pet companions. Undoubtedly, they walked them in the Commons and, in a few short years, in Riverview Park.

At 721 Irwin Avenue, Mr. Darlington, Jr. paid 50 cents per each license for his seven dogs—Cap, Fox, Sport, Toby, Monk, Christopher Jr., and Fritz. Brewer and also benefactor Henry Ober, at 1314 E. Ohio St., had a beloved male speckled spaniel, Sam. Two white male pointers were owned by W. Hesperheide, who owned quite a bit of property at Federal Street near Perrysville. He also was master of Prince Leon and Leon #2.

Mrs. Holliday, at 1 Overlook Street, owned Frank, a gray and black male Yorkshire terrier. Her neighbor at the other end of the street, the consultant engineer for the city, L.F. Stitzell, owned Dipple. Sport lived at 40 Norman Street, just around the corner. Alex Robinson of 813 Federal Street affectionately kept his black-and-tan Trix, and Scotch. The Denny's, at 811 Ridge were kept company by Paddy, Peter and Flotty.

The City Department of Charity spent $58,000 for the needy within the first five years of the 1900s; about the same time, the collection of garbage would be noted in council as the most important civic and health issue to deal with. As well, a new ordinance would pass, requiring property owners to take care of their sidewalks.

During the construction boom, mid-1890s, a new high school building was built for Allegheny's youth. It would sit on Sherman, just south of the North Commons and to the east of the Conservatory. Jubilee Day was an annual event for the younger children at the end of the school year, unique to Allegheny City in the latter part of the nineteenth century. It was essentially an end-of-school celebration and picnic. As reported by the main Pittsburgh newspaper, the *Press*, in 1893:

Allegheny School Children Enjoyed Their Jubilee

The Annual Jubilee day of the Allegheny schools was observed yesterday afternoon by school children in the Allegheny parks in the most approved fashion. At 3:00 the grounds were covered with crowds of grown people burdened with wraps and luncheon baskets, many of them pushing baby-carriages and others carrying in their arms wee children.

The crowds concentrated themselves about the band stand.... The children marched in procession from their different ward schools at the head of each line being a brass band. Entering the grounds through one of the main entrances of the park, they marched to the bandstand, there passing the mayor and his associates.

The Second Ward school was the first to enter West Park, and pass before the reviewing stand, the Third Ward followed.... The other wards followed in numerical succession and were led into the division of the park allotted to them. It took the 12,000 children in line a full hour to pass, after which the thousands of visitors who crowded about the stand and along the line of March, scattered through the parks. Each child carried a flag in his hand, which he waved heartily as he marched.... after all had passed in review [they] were free to leave the ranks and amuse themselves to their hearts' content.

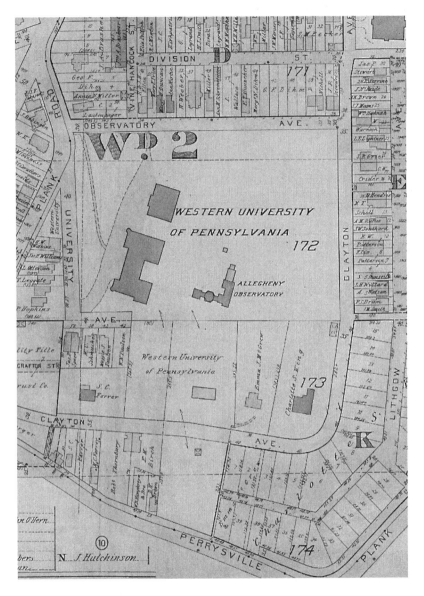

Figure 38. Western University of Pennsylvania

Figure 39 (opposite). View of Center of Allegheny City, 1900

Figure 40 (pages 200 and 201). 1899 map of the City of Allegheny

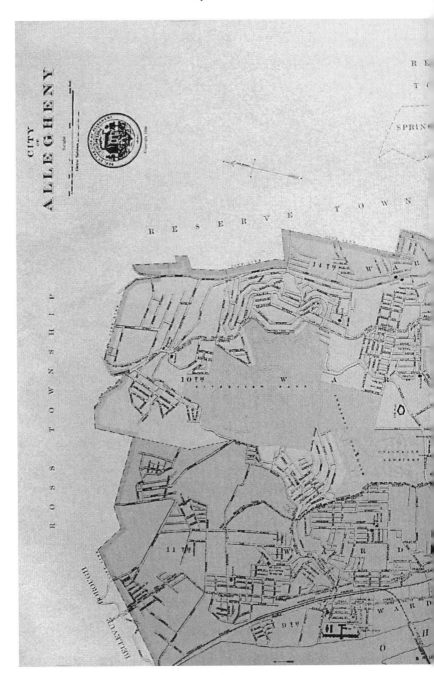

chapter eleven:
INFRASTRUCTURE &
THE NORTHERN WARDS

In the 1890s and earliest part of the new century, sewer lines would be laid in all of Allegheny City. Extensive maps of some of the areas still exist, such as one entitled *Plan Showing the Property Drained by West Common Sewer*. Obviously not ashamed of the city department in which he worked, the clerk who was recording the sewer records wrote them in a flowery scrawl that compares to surviving records from the time of the Revolution.

Streets would see curbing and sidewalking put in for the first time, and the changeover from terra cotta to lead ferrules took place under the city's Bureau of Water. Little did engineers across the country know that this, along with the lead used in paint of the time, would be a deadly choice that would be overturned far later in the new century.

By the year 1906, new water mains would be finished for the northern wards. Councils also heard that, "to meet the demand for water from the higher elevations of the 14th Ward... require[s] the erection of new tanks on the highest available part, as the tanks on Lafayette can not supply this demand."

Ligonier Block, named for the area in the nearby Laurel Highlands (and more commonly called "cobblestones") and Vitrified Brick were used for street paving here early on. Come 1902, the Northside Coal and Sand Company provided some of the grading and curbing services to the city, as did the Kreps Coal and Sand Company. By 1906, there had also been much success with asphalt on the streets. There was a recommendation in Councils of laying sheet asphalt especially on streets where the grade did not exceed 4%.

The Department of Public Works would later report on progress made in the earlier street projects of the decade:

> 10 years ago, Lafayette Avenue was paved with vitriolic brick,
> having a grade of 12.5–15%, against the protestation of Mr. Charles

Ehlers, Sr. and Mr. Robert Swan, City Engineer.

Residents were for it. The pavement today is in excellent condition and is a smooth pavement, but can not be used for vehicles at all in winter, and only at considerable risk in summer.

An ordinance was introduced to repave this street with cobble stone, the only material that could be used to make the street available for vehicle traffic.... 4 ft. of vitrified paving will be left next to the curb for gutters.... Cobblestone... would result in a great saving to the city in the cost of road repairs.

Planning for the widening of Brighton Road took place in 1894. Brighton began at that area of Irwin that had jogged westerly around the area of John Taggart's property, right past California Avenue (and previously referred to as the 'New Brighton Road' in sections). *Brighton Road Improvement Bonds* would be issued in 1901, to further the work.

In the Eleventh Ward, the widening of nearby California Avenue, from John Eckart's Plan of Lots, would take place. In order to do so, the city in 1896 bought some property from George Heideger, Sr. California Avenue had previously been opened and widened from Strawberry Lane to Jack's Run.

With the University now atop the hill, Allegheny City Councils also approved amending the widening of Perrysville Avenue in 1893. Their initial focus was on that area of Perrysville right near the top of Buena Vista and University Street, heading in and upward toward the University.

But one of the most intense public works project that the city ever encountered was to come on its heels—"Re-widening and Establishing the Grade of Perrysville" all along the street's ascent. Public Notices were posted and the Councils heard from just about every resident who lived along the street, all in order to properly "assess the benefits and damages caused" by the proposed action. All owners of property along Perrysville Avenue were given individual notice of the engineering plans, as well. Archive records show various comments recorded by citizens at the hearings. It was noted on one day that the Select Council's page, who was Earl McClintock, introduced the following:

Conrad Helm, Hugh McCune, Robert Duncan, and J.S. Ashworth are owners of property along the line of Perrysville Avenue, and their houses extend from 1 to 2 ft. over the established line of said avenue,

and in fixing the damages no allowance was made for the removal
of said houses by the Board of Viewers. We, your Board of Viewers
thereby recommend that the city of Allegheny, by ordinances duly
posted and approved, give permission to said parties to keep their said
houses on the present locations until such time as they may rebuild,
at which time they shall be compelled to build with reference to said
established line.

Individual statements to the official record are then noted. Jacob Born
claimed a loss of $50/month through the loss of his stable and other prop-
erty. He wanted "$5,000 above all benefits whether [adjoining] alley is left
open or not." Some property owners at the bottom of the hill "claim frontage
according to the original plan of [Samuel] Watson's." The Watson Land &
Improvement Company, too, would voice that they wanted "some remission
for work already performed."

Matthew Siddell wanted additional damages on account of the short
depth of his property. James Hunter wanted more damages on account of
the embankment on his property. Apparently, the latter would get disgusted
enough with imminent changes to his property that he would soon build,
instead, a fine home on the corner of Perrysville and Riverview Park Drive.

Someone stated that "more damages are wanted due to an old stone
sewer." And someone else commented, "Damages awarded were not sufficient
to pay for wall [on his property alone], which is necessary on account of
landslide." Similarly, John McGrew's heirs stated, "Unless the city would build
a wall, [they] want more damages."

But the need for a wall to hold that hillside up for everyone in Allegheny
City was becoming evident to everyone in the Councils. Besides these property owner admissions, engineers were weighing in, and the University was
attracting a large number of students up and around the avenue. What was
once simply a tiered, natural ridge of the steep hillside for the Indians to
make their way slowly upward, was now being traveled extensively and
excavated and trampled upon from above.

"William A. Anderson made comparisons with his neighbor's assessments," and "Oliver Maerkel objected to the system of assessment."
(Assessments, or tax valuations, were based on land, house, stable and
buggies owned.) They also noted that "R.W. Bissell sent a statement and
sketch of his property, showing a comparison of award, computed on a

system of his own. The grade fills in the front so high, that the house will have to be raised."

Mrs. Anna J. Scott, a rare woman property owner reporting "for herself alone" (without having to say that she is referencing her husband), claimed, "to have already spent $100 for grading her property front, and considers the $65 benefit adjustment unjust." And a neighbor of hers offered, "C. W. Schwarburg's house needs raising. Lower than Lacock's." Also, "Catherine Laubengeiger wanted more damages. Explained the case in german to Mr. Zinksand."

Some objected to the increased property assessments for fear of increased taxes. This prompted some truly original replies. "Peter Warrington claimed no title to the triangular piece of ground in front of him, had never entered into any agreement for the same and therefore considered his assessment excessive," but, nevertheless "claimed to be damaged above all benefits." William Miller admitted having no damage claim, but wanted a release from all benefits."

Some citizens, like Mary Johnston, acted in upstanding fashion, akin to the gratitude and citizenship McClintock had shown years prior. She "had her house fixed [already] to correspond to the new line. Satisfied with equal benefits and damages."

At the very start of the hill's climb, where Perrysville Avenue turns back upon itself to begin up the ridge, Frank and Eliza Eshelman had a unique concern, being the only landholders on the very bottom, eastern edge of the hill, and at the corner of the foot of the ridge. (As well, they were situated just where Federal Street Extension had blasted up the hill. Thus with the cleave of the hills opened extensively now, they had a man-made carving out of the cliff to their rear and east, as well.) Knowing of the academic activity far up on the peak above them (but focusing on the potential of physical, not intellectual movement), the Eshelmans decided to take some other precautions on their own, while the city was reconsidering this whole project.

The Eshelman's informed Council that they were "erecting and mounting a retaining wall along the front of their property, along the south line of Perrysville Avenue," also a slope downward to Federal Street, "in accord with plans and specifications prepared by the Department of Public Works, and in consideration of city keeping said wall and the sidewalk along the same, in good sufficient order and condition... and do hereby release the city from any claim for damages...."

Also something the Allegheny City Councils had to consider, during the several-year period that this was all being worked out, was a related development stirring controversy in that very area—"The opening, widening, and damage by grade of Perrysville to the east line of [Henry] Berger's property."

This would essentially be Clayton Avenue, the street above Perrysville and adjacent, westward, to the University property. Back in 1890, the city needed to lay water pipes to the school from University Street (which was one further up the hill from Clayton), and apparently some problems arose. "Whereas University Avenue, in the 2nd Ward, has been laid out as a private street, the title of the said avenue being with the University of Western Pennsylvania, and said University has never formally granted said street to the city of Allegheny.... and Whereas the citizens owning property abutting on the south and west side of said avenue have petitioned councils to authorize the laying of a water pipe.... The University says we may... so long as said avenue continues to be a private street."

Soon enough, Perrysville would receive the attention it needed, as well as the citizens' voices being quieted. Clayton as well, even though there would be another issue to surface in 1899.

Other retaining walls were going up in Allegheny City, too. One was built on the sloping area of Nunnery Hill near Howard Street saw one built. There the contractor decisively made drains in the wall to carry water through, as announced in the Councils. The city paid $500 to have the wall constructed for the residents of the area, and then had those residents attest that they "hereby release said City from all claims arising or accruing by reason of the slipping of the hill on which our houses are erected."

The city Water Works by the late 1890s would include a Montrose Pumping Station and a main pumping station lower, close to Herr's Island. Shortly thereafter, the Montrose Station would do the majority of the work. Allegheny was reaching a population of 130,000, compared to 320,000 in Pittsburgh, which had been steadily growing in land area.

Allegheny needed a water system that could keep up with its rising population. At the time, Allegheny considered the water systems in and around the Pittsburgh area, and consulted with their Bureau of Water. Pittsburgh's water works were focused, as Allegheny's, on the Allegheny River, but Pittsburgh's base of operations was upriver near Brilliant.

A few neighborhood areas completely disappeared, rather than were developed, in the 1890s. This was particularly true of the area south and east of the town square. The rail yards took over the area once known as *Hopeville*, that housed cotton mill workers. During the continued industrial expansion in the 1890s, the city also allowed building contractors to fill in the area around Exposition Park. Essentially, the backwater channel behind what little was left of Killbuck Island was filled in with earth, and stone, and even industrial refuse. Excavations for new manufactories provided filler material to finally pack in the swampy ground. It seems that by 1900, that land would be as completely affixed to the mainland as possible.

This served Exposition Park especially well. In the year 1903, the First World Series between the Pittsburgh Pirates and the Boston Americans was played there. (Unfortunately the Pirates lost this first noteworthy series, three games to five.) Exposition Park would be home to the Pirates until 1909.

The trolley on Perrysville and Federal Street was known to jump ahead on the tracks, when it ran downhill with students from the University. Supposedly, then, the "motorman swore ecstatically, and the student riders cheered." It was part of The Federal Street Company; there was also the Pittsburgh, Allegheny and Manchester Line, and the traction companies with their inclined planes.

The cornerstone for the new Allegheny Observatory had been laid in Riverview Park in 1900, and just a few years earlier, road improvements from Perrysville Avenue to Riverview Park Drive, the entrance to the park, took place. This would include the grading of the very steep Milroy Street, east of Perrysville and heading almost straight downward after its perilous turns, to the East Street Valley.

Beyond Riverview Park Drive, Perrysville Avenue would finally get attention from the city's Public Works Department. So far out was this new section of the city that it was sometimes even referred to by its older name, the "Old Franklin Road."

Back in 1891, John Berckbichler had taken out an insurance policy for $2,000 in selling the title for "lots situate[d] in the 10th Ward bounded and described: Beginning on the westerly side of Allegheny and the Perrysville Plank Road at the northerly line of lot 254 1/3' in a plan hereafter mentioned... then by line of Allegheny and Perrysville Plank Road north and northwesterly 332 1/3' to the southeast.... to Derry Street... in the Revised

Plan of Watson Place recorded in Plan Book Vol. 10, page 62."

This would be land included in what was to become Riverview Park for the city of Allegheny. When Mary Schenley donated land for a park in Pittsburgh's East End, the City of Allegheny realized that it, too, had land that would befit a similar park with numerous wooded trails. Though Allegheny was extremely proud of the Allegheny Commons, a Victorian park and the oldest park in Southwestern Pennsylvania, it desired to showcase its beautiful woodland of the Tenth Ward.

Riverview Park was named for the beautiful view from its heights of the Ohio River, off in the distance. It was spearheaded by William Kennedy, who became Allegheny City's Mayor in 1892. He was a well-known naturalist, and one of the city's wealthiest citizens at the time. Born in the city, on Western Avenue, and a student of the Western University, he was a partner in the Marshall, Kennedy and Company Mill. (In 1875, he had married Eliza McClintock, elder daughter of Washington and Eliza Sr.)

Two hundred acres of land was purchased from Samuel Watson's tract for $110,000. Known as Watson's Farms, it had previously been used as a dairy farm. The Himmelstein Dairy, also in the area, would have special privilege to graze their cattle in Riverview Park, once it opened.

John Walker, President of Carnegie Steel and resident of Western Avenue, chaired the fundraising committee for the park. Lawyer D.T. Watson, an heir to Samuel and a lawyer who lived on Ridge Avenue, also served on the Committee, as did steel magnate David Park, who lived just across North Avenue at the northeast corner of the Commons.

The city would pay $9500 as "Balance Due" to W.H. Denniston and Mary Schenley in the fall of 1894 "on account of the sale," by them, "to the city, of the McGuffy property, situate in the Tenth Ward, for park purposes." Plans were made for the Watson Presbyterian Church building, which sat at the corner of Riverview Park Drive and Perrysville Avenue, to be brought into the park and to serve as its picnic shelter. The structure was wooden and was placed on rollers to be moved to the park location.

A beautiful stone building would soon serve the church, gracing that same corner on Riverview and Perrysville Avenue. Next to this corner was a Watson Land & Improvement Company building, and across the street, next to the new home of James Hunter (later in the decade) was the Hebrew Orphanage and Home.

There would be two log cabins in the park—one much older and far more authentic than the other. What would later be tagged the *Watson Cabin* actually belonged originally to a Frenchman around 1814.

Long after the conflict between the French, English, and Natives, a lone French settler decided these woods were as good a place as any to stay and call home, as this area north of Allegheny Town remained frontier for some time. The cabin was on the hillside near another locust grove, and by the later Woods Run Avenue entrance to the park. Charcoal burns from that first inhabitant's early time there would be visible up until the twenty-first century. Later, the Schmidlein family rented it from Samuel Watson, who took ownership when the Frenchman left the area.

The second cabin was placed in the park after the Exposition of 1895 (held in Pittsburgh) was over. It was presented to Allegheny City, upon the Mayor's urging, by Marshall, Kennedy and Company, as it was a replica of their first flouring mill.

On June 26, 1895, an agreement was drawn up between Mayor Kennedy and Thomas M. Marshall, of the Tenth Ward:

> 11 acres, being Lot # 6 in the plan of E. Hewett, owned by Dr. Robert H. Gilliford and Mr. Charles Pfeifer [previous], and whereas Marshall secured an option in his own name for said property, for $12,250, which option, the said Marshall really secured for the benefit of Allegheny City.... to be paid out of the Parks Contingency Fund, assigned to the German National Bank with interest.

Riverview Park was created mainly in the late 1890s. 1895 had been the year that Brashear's scouts had found the top peak of the proposed park desirable for a new Observatory site. Riverview Park Drive would come straight back, off of Perrysville, to the bottom of that peak. Once finally completed, the Observatory domes would stare serenely down upon the park guests as they made their way close to the wooded trails to left and right.

The roads were unique in their spiraling downward from that central peak. Indeed, from this main entrance to the park, one stood on the park's highest land. From here, all roads traveled down and around the hillside.

The roads were laid out among the heavily-wooded hills by former City Engineer Robert Swan. A later merry-go-round and nature reserve would be built in the park around the time the Observatory was finally completed, but in 1896, plans for a zoo commenced under the direction of August Overbeck.

The park lands had much wildlife indigenous to the area, living among the many springs, and seen just off the numerous trails ringing the hillsides below the central peak.

Visitors to the zoo would find a bear pit, elk and zebra pens, twenty-eight bird cages, and duck ponds. A driver's station, where vehicles would be parked at the main entrance, sat near Perrysville Avenue. Many trails, with groves off to the sides, wended their way throughout the park, and horses could be rented for riding, guided by the dairy owner, Mr. Himmelstein. Maintenance on the trails was done by horseback, as well. Picnic areas, a Greenhouse, a Spring House, an archery range, a "gum drop-shaped pool"—all could be found within the park. In addition, a dam was constructed between two ponds for a skating area.

Snyder's Point was that southwestern most plateau of the park that overlooked, albeit from a distance, the Ohio River and rolling hills beyond, and, to a closer extent, the cemeteries sprawling upward from near the lower end of Marshall Avenue, to the park's south. (And likely connected to the same Snyder of Snyder's Hollow, the previous name of Pleasant Valley, along Brighton Road toward the city, below). A bath house was even to be found in the park at a later point, and a "Killbuck Pond."

In 1906, French drains would be constructed in Riverview Park to avoid slipping of the roads at different points. The park, shaped like a cone, had terraces underneath the roads that, like Perrysville and surely many others across Pittsburgh, would naturally lie at a side wards angle to the hill, instead of a forty-five degree angle.

The bear pits would be removed to a different location in the park after a short time—sometime before 1910—because the first location was not the best for the bears, who liked to sun themselves. They alone would face the setting sun in the park, as opposed to the rest of the zoo nestled between Perrysville Avenue and the central section of the park.

The Woods Run entrance to Riverview Park was on the lower western land of the very large Tenth Ward. In June 1898, Gustav Kauffman was contracted by the city "to construct and erect the superstructure of the Davis Avenue bridge across Woods Run in the Tenth and Eleventh Wards." The bridge entrance would serve as another popular entry to Riverview, not to mention being a necessity in general, better connecting the new neighborhoods of the Ninth and Eleventh Wards to the main part of the city.

In 1903, there was a calling in council chambers "for the Vacation of
Davis Avenue, formerly located from Hearnley & Gilliford's Plan of Lots
westerly to Davis Ave. as now located." As well, Woods Run connected
Perrysville Avenue north of Riverview (just at *city limits*, the terminology to
replace *City Line*) to the New Brighton Road (Brighton Road far north, still).
This whole area, for the longest time the 'back woods' of Allegheny, was
about to see the development that the rest of Allegheny saw earlier.

Nearby Jack's Run, too, would be widened and improved upon—in
places that would sustain such, that is. The road to the present day is still
rural in feel in certain areas, passing along ravine and through woodland that
so marked these northern reaches of the *Reserved Tract*.

Industry was a real powerhouse in Allegheny—in particular, in
Manchester. Clouds of smoke were unfortunately signs of that power,
hovering over the area, above Crucible Steel, the Rosedale Foundry and
Machine Works, and other industries. The foot of Liverpool Street, at the
Ohio River, was equally active, congested, and smoky. Isaac Reed's docks
were best known for marine machinery repair. The internationally respected
Ritchie Smith & Company was building steamboats. The bustling scene was
capped by any number and variety of houseboats that would begin to line
the shore for decades to come.

Fire hydrants would come to the city in 1895. Usage of the new devices
was not without mishaps, though. One comical incident relayed in archival
records recalls former mishaps from the water-works:

> 2-27-1895— A fire hydrant on Robinson Street was opened by a city
> employee opposite W.S. Wiggins residence. Mrs. Wiggins declared, 'All
> my carpets were destroyed when a certain part [of the hydrant] gave
> way through the whole force of water across the street into the house,
> flooding the first story of the same before the water could be shut off.'

The city decided to furnish new carpets for Mrs. Wiggins. But then
her neighbor, Mrs. Shannon, also stepped up for city-given carpets, as she
described (and surely showed proof) that "part of the water was thrown into
my parlor, destroying the carpet and flooding the hall...."

By 1897, archival material recording the ins and outs of Allegheny City life became far more legible, organized, clean, and finally typed. It would be noted that, by the end of the century, for those who wanted it, homes could be fitted for radiant gas heat.

Up to this time, Alleghenians warmed their homes and cooked their food via the many fireplaces outfitted in the structures, usually one per room. Coal would be delivered to the house and shoveled into a coal repository in that part of the foundation nearest the street (under what would often later be a porch area). Coal would then be brought up from basements, to be shoveled into the fireplaces.

When gas lighting became available, gas fixtures were put into the masonry of the fireplaces, with knobs that extended out and also down by the foot of the hearth, as a way to have a heat-generating source in the fireplace, as well as for gas stoves and lights. This started the move away from the mess of shoveling coal.

But the latest revolutionary mode written about in council chambers had to do with taking gas heating one step further—out of the fireplace. Radiators would slowly begin to be fitted throughout houses for owners who so could afford to modernize. The more prestigious hotels of the era wasted no time in upgrading. Federal Street at the turn of the century had two particularly notable ones close by the Chicago & Fort Wayne railroad depot, the Bracken Hotel and the Hotel Savoy.

Modernizations were moving fast now. Close to 1900, the Pennsylvania Light, Heat, and Power Company received a contract by the city to "construct and maintain an electric plant, and to string poles, or maintain underground wires." But electric lighting for homes and businesses would still be several years away.

With improvements to Allegheny Commons made by the creation of the park in the late 1860s, and with the great success of Lake Elizabeth as a public recreation spot, there had been increased pressure on Allegheny City legislators to rethink the railroad's presence through the park. The decision made long ago to allow the railroad access through the Commons would be too difficult logistically and financially to redirect the routes at this point, but a decision had been reached to depress the tracks, such that the sound and presence of the railroad would not be so intrusive upon the park ground. As well, there was suggestion that the tracks be elevated as they leave westward, by the large rail yard.

This met with satisfaction, for the most part, by both parties—the city and the railroad—but the feasibility of bringing it about did not happen without the wrangling that seemed to mark all of the railroad dealings with Allegheny City so far. There would be notations of the railroad negotiations being "messy" and "time-consuming."

Also by the twentieth century, there is evidence that the city had become aware of its responsibilities to protect and look after the health and welfare of its workers. In March 1903, William Hanna was an employee of Allegheny's Bureau of Highway & Sewers. He would receive $495 in workman's compensation after crushing his hand on the job, having "slipped, [with] a heavy box which [he] was... carrying from the basement of city hall...." In September of the same year, Nicholas Huckestein fell from an electric light pole, and was awarded $596.55 from the same city fund.

On June 17, 1905, citizen Henry Hemmerle, at the corner of Main and Chestnut Streets, had an accident. "On the said day my horse, having fallen into a sewer, thereby caus[ed] me to loose the contents of my wagon, and making it necessary... to hire another horse for two days."

Some accidents sprang from more civic activities. Amelia Sontag would be awarded $200 from Allegheny City for her daughter Amelia, "by reason of her being struck and injured by a skyrocket fired from Monument Hill on July 4, 1906."

About the beginning of 1900, councils had put forth a rather extensive Report for the city that, "among many things" the administration was currently dealing with, as its largest concerns, was

>...the elevation and depression of the tracks of the Pittsburgh Fort Wayne and Chicago Railroad Company through the City of Allegheny.
>
>One of the worst features of this change of elevation of tracks was the elevated crossing of the intersection of Washington Avenue, Allegheny Avenue and Sedgwick Street. The plans accompanying the original ordinance... show the new grade at above mentioned point... making it necessary to change the grade of all intersecting streets.
>
>To make these changes in the grades meant damages to all the properties affected, and to many of them total ruin. With the aid of City Solicitor, City Engineer and a number of competent house raisers, we arrived at the conclusion that $300,000 was a fair estimate of damages to private property.

Councils also decided to condemn some property just north of Washington Avenue such that an adequate approach to the bridge over the tracks could be built. "In this belief the [Public Works] Department has been upheld by the owners of the affected property [and] the Manchester Board of Trade.... The approaches will be built without disturbing the houses, the street or the water supply."

With regard to "the construction of retaining walls through the park," for the track depression in the Commons, the report noted:

> The railroad company had constructed walls on both sides of their right of way from Ridge Avenue to Ohio Street in such a manner as to render practically useless the portion of the park lying between said streets.
>
> It was the intention of the railroad company to construct the walls west of Ohio Street in the same manner. This the Director of Public Works refused to permit, but compelled the company to construct at an additional cost of $35,000 all walls to such height as to permit the use of all park property.

The same Report dealt with the ground recently made into Riverview Park, reported by the Commissioner overseeing this particular department:

> As to the Marshall Road, leading from Marshall Avenue to Riverview Park, I have allocated the purchase of 11 acres from Marshall heirs. According to an old agreement between the City of Allegheny and the Marshall heirs, this roadway was to be graded, paved and curbed at the cost of the city of Allegheny. Recognizing the fact that the city would be compelled to fill in this ground... I deemed it for the best interest of the city to buy these 11 acres... although mostly ravine, and thus have the opportunity to gradually fill this roadway as opportunity presented....
>
> We urged the passage of an ordinance preventing automobiles from entering Riverview Park on account of damage to life and limb, also the commencement of the construction of roadways and the building of Shelter House in this park.

Next talk is of other railroad problems—this time regarding Herr's Island. "The West Penn Railroad was compelled after much wrangling to erect the River Avenue approach to Herr's Island Bridge."

The report also states amusingly, "We have added a Children's Library to the Carnegie Library. The changes made in the management of Carnegie Library and the manner of conducting the Organ Recitals in the Carnegie Music Hall, it is asserted, were made for political purposes. Come and convince yourself that the assertion is false."

The Report continues,

> We have spent a great deal of money on steps and boardwalks in localities where necessary, rather than surrender the city liable to being mulcted into heavy damage suits, due to personal injuries which were likely to be sustained on old and worn steps and boardwalks.
>
> We have renewed and rebuilt the electric light plant under this department and are furnishing light to the city, and as compared with what the City of Pittsburgh pays is a revelation. Come and see your light plant."
>
> We have at present completed by solicitation the widening of Evergreen Road... and have urged that all main thoroughfares leading to the suburbs be made good, wide and substantial avenues, thereby making it inviting to our people and to strangers to come thereto and build houses.
>
> Through this department petitions were prepared, circulated and presented to the County Commissioners, asking them to free the bridges between the cities of Allegheny and Pittsburgh.

The Report also discussed changing the grades of Sandusky, Federal, Anderson, Chestnut and Grant Avenue, because of their being

> ...inundated annually by the rise in our rivers. The changes proposed would enable our citizens, at all times, to pass along these thoroughfares dry shod, and during high water the necessity of using skiffs, wagons, etc. as a means of conveyance would be done away with. Abutting on the line of these thoroughfares are some of the best and most available sites for business and warehouses in either city, and it is certain to be covered with first-class buildings in the near future.
>
> Troy Hill Reservoir was cleaned and some repairs made during

the last year. It is in fair condition at present.... the reservoir has only four hours' supply when full.... Tanks B and C were painted and are in good condition, with the exception of the trestle under Tank C, which is of wood and I would recommend that they be replaced with steel.

A detailing of various other department findings wrapped up the Report. Included near end would be a list given of the problems found about the city regarding property inspection and uncitizenly conduct: broken cellar doors; obstructions on sidewalks; dead and dangerous trees; holes in streets and alleys; low and dangerous chimneys; bonfires on streets and yards; signs on telegraph poles; sewers not connected; driving on sidewalks; soiling dirt from wagons; pool rooms without a license; spilling oil on asphalt streets; lots not properly drained; feeding horses on streets; blasting without a permit; distributing samples of medicine; and erecting sheds without permit.

In May of 1899, the following statement shows up in Council records:

Allegheny City is released from damage claims arising out of construction of a certain stone wall along Clayton Avenue, across the end of a certain unnamed street running from Clayton Avenue through our property, that the wall so constructed shall not be taken by us as a closing off of said unnamed and unopened street....

It is agreed that in erecting the masonry aforesaid that said wall shall not be constructed of such height on the easterly side of said unnamed street running along Clayton Avenue as had been originally contemplated, the reduction in height being the request of Henry Berger, in order that the masonry should be continued across the end of said unnamed street.

Henry Berger

Also, Mr. Berger attests before signing that property on both sides of unnamed street is his.

Henry Berger had mounting financial difficulties in the years since he retired and became involved in his amateur astronomy, despite inherited wealth. Sadly by the year 1900, he and his wife Maria would lose their house on the peak near the Observatory at a sheriff's sale, with a back debt of $6622.35.

The property would not be sold until 1907, however, with the involvement of the Fidelity Title and Trust Company. In the meantime, Henry and Maria were living in Oakland, in the East End of Pittsburgh, where they moved after being dispossessed of the very visible hilltop house he had built in Allegheny City.

Berger employed a lawyer, Nelson McVicar, whose practice was in downtown Pittsburgh. This statement appears in Allegheny City records of 1901:

> For value received, we Bergers transfer to Nelson McVicar of Borough of Tarentum, $3850 (less benefits assessed) for damages to property abutting on Perrysville Avenue, by reason of the grading and other improvements of said avenue. The money so received under this assignment to be used by McVicar in liquidating a mortgage from Berger to McVicar.

Tragically, Maria, would never recover from the shame and disappointment over the way her and her husband's life had progressed. So distraught over their money troubles, she committed suicide in 1903. Her body was pulled from the Ohio River.

chapter twelve:

THE CONSOLIDATION

The Mayor of Allegheny City in the late 1890s was James Wyman. There were the usual government departments, and some more unusual—the Bureau of Electricity, a City Veterinarian, Bureau of Assessment of Water Rents, and still a Bureau of Wharves and Landings, under Captain Henry Hauser, Wharf master.

Allegheny City and Pittsburgh had been sharing Annual Reports with each other for several years now, as was common for some nearby American cities to do. In Allegheny City archives would sit gracious cover letters introducing Annual Reports from Cincinnati, Detroit and Rochester, among others.

The year 1873 had been the last time Councils, on the record, discussed and heartily dismissed Pittsburgh's continued desire, over many decades, to annex Allegheny's land and consolidate into one city. Allegheny City legislators, over the ensuing years, then threw themselves headlong into the work at hand—developing new streets, expanding innovative transportation systems, introducing plumbing, sewerage, electricity and gas to citizens, and bringing new northern wards up to speed with the infrastructure boom in the city. Legislators and citizens were occupied with a University moving in, and were entertained by baseball, expositions and other amusements. But Allegheny City never lost sight of the fact that the city across the river—the one that in so many ways was their comrade, their friend—continued to eye their success with the desire to incorporate it as part of their own.

At first glance, the wealthiest and most influential of Allegheny City supported any behind-the-scene talk of municipal annexation, but the majority of these particular individuals had been living elsewhere for some time now. Carnegie and Phipps were two examples of men who no longer were residents of Allegheny City, but who nevertheless lent a well listened-to voice in determining its fate. H.J. Heinz, whose factory was very much a present-day reality in Allegheny (but who, too, had territorial interests now outside the city) was rare among those residents also in favor of annexation.

Without a doubt, however, the majority of Alleghenians, in catching any word from as far back as the 1830s, when annexation talk first surfaced, first laughed at the thought, then defended their loyalty to Allegheny unwaveringly. As shown in the impassioned reasoning of Mayor Morrison, recalling General Robinson's moving letter to Councils, Alleghenians were fiercely and understandably proud.

But there had been another force slowly at work within the city for pro-consolidation, even greater than any one wealthy and successful businessman's voice. It would be the University, and the men that had conglomerated around it, who would slowly, covertly at first, bring a chorus for consolidation to the forefront of Allegheny society. It would truly spell Allegheny City's demise.

During the 1890s, the trustees of the University consisted of some of the most enterprising that Allegheny City had ever seen, including Carnegie. Collectively, their views became the formal stance of the University, and 'the good of the University' is what ironically drove each of these men to forget about the good of a certain city.

The Western University of Pennsylvania, despite its heralding the banner that it was proudly linked with being north of the Allegheny River, was intrinsically linked to the ideas and motivations of the City of Pittsburgh come this time. And the views of the City of Pittsburgh, quite a known fact in the region, were backed by none other than the Commonwealth of Pennsylvania, as was hinted in an early Annual Report of the new century.

Important to note is that those who were on the Board of Trustees of the University, also, due to their power and influence, happened to be on the board of the new Carnegie Institute (Library, Music Hall and Museum) in the works in the East End of Pittsburgh. To further the cause of one institution, these trustees were also looking after the cause of the other—an indisputable fact of corporate existence, despite ethical conflict of interest.

From the beginning of the time that the plan for the Carnegie Institute, in particular, was going forward, in the early 1890s, and coinciding with the new thoughts on the Observatory needing to be dismantled and re-erected on a different site, the University became aligned with the stars that shined

"Pro-Consolidation." This was at the very time that the University was just settling into its Allegheny City hilltop home.

There is no doubt—and surely there was little doubt back then by Alleghenians—that the Observatory could be better served, after over thirty years on the original site, on a higher hilltop. Nor that shortly after the campus was completed, it became evident that the University might simply need more space than that provided by the storied peak above Allegheny's great ridge.

But the City of Pittsburgh had finally come to find a novel way of masking "Pro-Consolidation" with the City of Allegheny under the cloak of something else. They began a persuasive campaign, at the beginning of the new century, to link the 'University's good' with the 'good of the sister cities.'

It began slowly and demurely at first, but then was taken full-force to further justify Pittsburgh's reasoning behind wanting Allegheny. The University's official position would support the new rationale being leaked in intellectual and political circles, as its very trustees had stakes in Commonwealth government, the success of the Carnegie Institute, and City of Pittsburgh government.

What would happen is that the Western University of Pennsylvania's very existence in Allegheny City would be used as a pawn in the consolidation game proposed by the City of Pittsburgh. It was obvious to Pittsburghers as well as Alleghenians that consolidation would strikingly benefit Pittsburgh, and certainly not Allegheny. As documented in social records of the time, Allegheny City had been considered, since at least the 1860s, as having more "class" and social refinery (despite its inclusion of citizens at all ends of the spectrum of wealth), better homes, and greater consolidated commerce and industry than Pittsburgh. The latter's sheer size, only, put it over top Allegheny in population and amount of industrial wealth.

So the City of Pittsburgh, with its own citizens even savvy to political ploy, would only further suggest consolidation, come the end of the 1890s, under the guise of academic collaboration. Pittsburgh was especially careful to no longer stress what economic and political benefit it would reap in 'taking Allegheny,' but instead emphasized a more 'genteel' benefit for all parties concerned....

Pittsburgh conceived and introduced a notion in intellectual circles entitled *The Greater Pittsburgh*. The idea posited was that there was a better, more enlightened Pittsburgh being aimed for, rather than just an industrial and business power. The goal was to attain intellectual and cultural enlightenment, the "surpassing of material wealth," thus securing the region its place in the modern twentieth century. And the definition of 'Pittsburgh' boldly included all of the *region* that was surrounding Pittsburgh in southwestern Pennsylvania. Akin to the 'French father-figure' in Celoron's campaign (among others) who tried to persuade the Indians that their existence would be greatly improved with their mutual connection, Pittsburgh legislators were trying to cunningly win over Allegheny, who they saw as their subordinate. And forced under Pittsburgh's patronizing arm, in this betterment campaign, was Allegheny City—which had mastered enlightenment decades ago, at least according to popular social thought.

Behind a surely genuine and noble desire to increase the cultural value of the City of Pittsburgh was the less-genuine desire to increase it in size, scope, magnitude, power, and material wealth. The concept circulated only in intellectual and also political circles of both cities, at first, around the end of the 1890s. This would include the progressive, young University students. Then a mere year later, southwestern Pennsylvanians started to read and hear about the idea, as it was aggressively promoted.

Then another idea hit the presses and social circles—of Allegheny officially becoming part of Pittsburgh. Again. But the age-old scheme had a new name. The very campaign for that action, of Pittsburgh annexing Allegheny City, would now be cunningly called "The Greater Pittsburgh Act."

Who would be against, at first glance, a large area of southwestern Pennsylvania being considered socially enlightened? But to support cultural and intellectual enlightenment, and social growth in the region, one had to be for the consolidation of Pittsburgh and Allegheny City?

All Alleghenians, rich and poorer, certainly were aware of their fine reputation throughout the Commonwealth. Most would be perplexed and angry at what they were hearing bantered about from news reports and social circles. Pittsburgh's sheer size never matched Allegheny's 'greater' qualities, not only in proud Alleghenians minds, but also according to reports from outside the region. So Allegheny City residents wondered about how the Commonwealth was receiving this idea that Pittsburgh was positing.

Allegheny City had a long record of philanthropy and extreme pride in the history of its northern land. It possessed the only Commons land area outside of New England, and then the first park of the region, modeled on Victorian standard. The original "Millionaires Row" was on Ridge Avenue in Allegheny City, with residents that were the founders of the industry and business that then gave Pittsburgh its wealth. What the humble Allegheny Telescope Society started, later was to become a world-class Observatory. And Allegheny gave the University its first true home, which it had desired for some time. In Allegheny City, the school prospered and the students were happy on their hilltop land.

The only real and undisputed fact accepted by Alleghenians, come the turn of the century, was that the University needed more land, so that all of its departments could be unified on one campus. The City of Pittsburgh exploited this need.

Perhaps it was the apparent toast, by someone anonymous to the history books—but whose expression prompted a documented, significant, counter-toast nevertheless—that started the undue paralleling of the causes of Consolidation, the University's necessitated transplantation, and cultural enlightenment for southwestern Pennsylvania. Perhaps it planted the seed for Pittsburgh legislators, well in attendance that evening back in 1897, at the University's 110th celebration. Influential Pittsburgher Christopher Magee was noted as having responded that night, to a toast from someone else. Magee was so inspired by the first toast as to declare a counter-toast, "To the Greater City and the Greater University."

A growing sentiment on campus started around the time of this celebration, with students and alumni feeling the need to become concerned about the welfare of their University, but at the same time about the welfare of a particular city, and it was not Allegheny. *The Courant*, the University newspaper, would run many editorials in the early years of the century. Starry-eyed, most all heartily supported the City of Pittsburgh's talk of the times. "Cultural development that should surpass material achievements.... They call this the 'Greater Pittsburgh.'"

The Greater Pittsburgh, as Pittsburgh city government would then call it, and *The Greater University* were inextricably tied together. To recognize and support the fact that the University, on its little hilltop campus in Allegheny needed to look for more ground, was to also support Pittsburgh's enlighten-ment and thus a corresponding consolidation. Needless to say, Alleghenians harbored resentment as they realized that they might get swallowed up, certainly against their will, due to this kind of crazy rationale.

The inappropriate linkage occurring between these causes may have soured some Alleghenians toward the University. But the great bulk of ill feelings went toward Pittsburgh, a city that could not be trusted to respect Allegheny's decision to remain separate, and that was attempting to manipulate the populace of the entire region, including younger Alleghenians.

In 1903, when the great need for an endowment for the University became apparent, the Carnegie Technical Schools were being constructed on a campus adjacent to the Carnegie Institute in Oakland. Those in a position to help supported the idea that the University needed to move to a better location, perhaps nearer Pittsburgh's "City Beautiful" development in the East End. Oakland was fast becoming the place where educational and cultural institutions were locating.

The people of Allegheny were intelligent; they would have graciously accepted news of a move anywhere, including Oakland, a locale which certainly had an aura of excitement about it. But to present the idea that Allegheny wasn't cultured or intellectual enough to sustain a University fostered renewed resentment of Pittsburgh. It would be little forgotten by Alleghenians and their children for years and years to come.

Even though they knew that their society harbored and exhibited, for some time, the very characteristics that Pittsburgh was here claiming, Alleghenians were not not openly mad. Even though Pittsburgh was co-opting Allegheny by proclaiming itself savior of the University, it was against the grain of Alleghenians to protest. Instead the ugly subtleties, surely not lost on them, only simmered, as they continued to better their dear city and nary a one would talk of these matters too much in public. Indeed, though, plans for the University's leaving, foretold of the "clos[ing] of the bright chapter of Allegheny days, whose memories are still cherished by many older men and women in the community."

A 'Betterment Committee' for the Western University of Pennsylvania was formed in early 1903, and its secretary, Mr. W. Lucien Scaife, persuaded alumni and faculty committees "that steps be taken to change the name of the University to the 'University of Pittsburgh.'" And the committee working on the endowment would make a bold analogy, involving the great Allegheny

River, now, in the inappropriate paralleling of both University and
Pittsburgh, need and cause.

> Our Alma Mater needs a Moses. He may be an experienced educator
> and be called a chancellor. He may be wholly a business executive
> and be called president of the Board of Trustees, or by any other title.
> He must, however, above all else, be the right man to lead us to the
> promised land of a new site and building and enlarged faculties... a
> greater University, which the greater Pittsburgh needs and will have.

When John Brashear was made acting chancellor in 1901, it soon
became evident that he would not be able to devote the time and attention
needed in his lab, and behind lectern. Though he never complained, the
school realized they needed to find a replacement. It would take until 1904
for Dr. Carhart, dean of the Engineering School, to take over responsibilities
temporarily.

In May of that year, the Trustee Board, which included Felix Reville
Brunot, knew they had to soon move on a permanent replacement,

> the Moses to gather all the Schools and departments of the University
> together and set them up across the river in a new 'promised land.'

As remarked about this amazing retort back then, "Perhaps, to some
people, the details of the quarter century in Allegheny... seem of themselves
trivial and even unimportant."   (WILHELM)

After the Trustees remarks in 1904, Allegheny's accommodating and
nurturing the University would come to an end.

Samuel Black McCormick would be inaugurated the ninth Chancellor
of the University in a ceremony at one of the grandest halls in the region—
Carnegie Music Hall in Allegheny. McCormick had made clear to the
University that he would come on board only upon condition of its being
moved. The trustees knew they had found their man.

McCormick would formally champion this as soon as inaugurated.
His first report, a year later, had with it

> an attractive booklet... printed and sent throughout the city and the
> state to everyone who might have any interest in the University. This

booklet told briefly the story of the University's more than one hundred years; it gave the names of the men who had helped to make the
University what it was at that time; it said the historical location of the
University had always been Pittsburgh, except for its short enforced
term in Allegheny; and it said now that Pittsburgh and Allegheny were
about to be united in a greater Pittsburgh....   (STARRETT)

Allegheny City, which had to ward off unwelcome advance onto their
Commons in earlier years, but then had granted the University space, and
whose wealthy citizens donated a campus, not to mention world-class status
in an Observatory, was not mentioned.

A deeper insult could not have been passed to Allegheny City, yet it
seems that the callousness and ignorance of the University was not pointed
out in papers of the time. Allegheny, itself, gulped and swallowed hard the
comments of the University, delivered by a man being commemorated in one
of their great Halls.

McCormick would also state, "No great community can realize a high
destiny without a great university. He appealed to Pittsburghers to share in
helping make "a greater University for a greater Pittsburgh." To the city of
Allegheny, McCormick offered no words, not even gratefulness.

On February 2, 1903, J. Linwood Brown was paid $600 by Allegheny
City. He had transferred to the city legislature the "exclusive and perpetual
right, title and interest of J. L. Brown in and to a certain [outdoor hardware]
device called the 'Iron Stop Gate Box,' with the sole and exclusive right to
manufacture the same for use in all that territory over which Allegheny City
extends or over which it may be at any time made to extend by annexations
of other territory to the city of Allegheny."

Allegheny citizens and legislators, by 1903, were definitely apprehensive
regarding the fate of their fair city. But though talked about surely behind-
the-scenes of Council chambers, official records remarkably did not reveal
the cataclysm to come.

Only the tremendous civic energy spent on projects of infrastructure and other Allegheny City advancements, for the most part, made it on record. Perhaps the projects even took on a sense of urgency, during this time where so much talk of the future was indeed coming out of the University and the sister city across the way.

In Allegheny City's Annual Report of 1906, Controller James Brown reports a $221,000 balance in the Treasury. The population of that year was 145,000 (with Pittsburgh still three-times that due to its larger land area). Citizens were using 238 per capita gallons of water per day. There were two police stations and sixteen fire companies. James Wyman would be the mayor until May of 1906, when Charles P. Kirschler would take over.

Something else was to happen in 1906, however. A special election, requested by the City of Pittsburgh and granted by the Commonwealth of Pennsylvania, would take place. Allegheny citizens were forced to vocalize their sentiment over something that had been slowly but surely choking them up.

If they wanted to make their voice heard in opposition, or support, for proposed annexation by Pittsburgh, or "Consolidation," they had to vote for or against a Referendum on special ballot, entitled *The Greater Pittsburgh Act*.

Both Alleghenians and Pittsburghers would be voting. The state set that *the majority number of combined votes* would determine the outcome.

On June 12, 1906, the majority number of combined votes cast were for Consolidation. Since Pittsburgh's population was three times that of Allegheny's, Allegheny City did not have a chance.

Pittsburghers, all for extending their boundaries, despite how the campaign was cloaked, voted almost unanimously in favor of the referendum. Alleghenians voted two to one against it. But all that was required, as determined by the way the state set up the election, was that it was essentially wanted by the larger party, not that it should sensibly sustain a majority vote by citizens of the lesser party to prove its true viability.

Even though Allegheny was the state's third most powerful city, it was not given the opportunity to decide its own fate. The election should have been set to be determined by the *majority number of Alleghenians' votes*. (Or at very least by *two separate majorities* desiring the consolidation.)

But the Commonwealth had decided differently. Such a decision never would be allowed to happen in present modern-day politics for any American city.

Stunned, Allegheny City thus challenged the legality of the Referendum. Allegheny City first appealed to the county and state courts, to little avail. The case was then sent, late in 1906, to be heard by the U.S. Supreme Court.

While Allegheny City waited, she appeared to proceed as normal. There would be suggestions in councils to increase the Howard Street pump, because "the householder is paying for the large users of water—carpentries, factories, mills, brewers, steam users, etc." There was talk of a modern development, adding water meters to everyone's home, but the general public did not seem to like the thought of the water company having access to their personal property. So the thought was shot down, and a recommendation instead put forth, that a general re-inspection of every house and structure, by the city, was needed.

The contract for laying cast iron water pipes was signed in 1906, and an arrangement was finalized that had been in planning for many years—for Allegheny to make use of some sand filtration, and other general water treatment, from the facilities near Brilliant, up the Allegheny River.

Though Allegheny awaited a verdict by the U.S. Supreme Court, they feared the worst, and it appears that the Councils did everything they could to take care of any straggling business that might cause future problems. Relating to the Federal Street Extension project, many damage claims were resolved at this time, such that property holders "therefore will make no claims." Citizens acted in a similar fashion. On October 15, 1907, Catherine Ventor gave her damages from the city, for the Perrysville Avenue improvement, to the heirs of James Gray, for a $1 fee.

The gravity of the voting outcome, with the knowledge that Pennsylvania's Governor Pennypacker wanted to see the Consolidation happen, was very present in the air. Thus infrastructure projects were especially pushed through to completion in 1906, with November seeing a great number of these reported upon in Councils.

The annexation, "Consolidation," had to have been talked about in the outside chambers of council especially at this time, but the official record still shows Allegheny legislators, proud, not giving it their attention, but rather attending to their city. All the matters necessary to keep her in good order were addressed, but discussions also seemed to carry the undercurrent of

Figure 41. Greater Pittsburgh postcard

preparation, for imminent undesired union.

The *Pittsburgh Post-Gazette* made the argument at this time that the removal of tolls and establishment of free bridges would help to provide feelings of political unity. Far from it, however. Allegheny had already called for freedom of movement between the two cities, as well as the sharing of resources when necessary, humane, or sensible. Good feelings of any kind toward Pittsburgh would be hard to come by, let alone feelings of unity.

Henry Phipps, resident of New York for some time by 1906, tried to appease his old Allegheny by building very decent accommodations there for people of somewhat modest means—apartments called the Allegheny Dwellings. But very few people clamored to rent, despite its having the latest of water accommodations to be found at the time. Mary Schenley, too, gave $10,000 to Riverview Park, after her massive land donation to the East End.

The power brokers of Pittsburgh at the time (and ironically throughout almost all of its history, save for its recent history) came from the East End. Rarely was the annexed, poorer South Side (old Birmingham) represented in city government. Included back in 1906 was one of many men who helped orchestrate the *Greater Pittsburgh Act*—Albert Logan, from Pittsburgh's early East Liberty section. "Logan chaired the committee, that conducted the campaign, that paved the way for the creation of a single major city in Allegheny County." (He would also "serve on a court appointed committee that determined the new wards for the unified city.")

In later November, 1907, the validity of the already infamous vote, and the process that led to it, was subsequently upheld by the U.S. Supreme Court. What Allegheny had feared came to be realized, and a great disappointment hovered over Allegheny City.

On November 20, 1907, Allegheny City Mayor Charles Kirschler began an address to Councils:

> After a conference with Mayor Guthrie of Pittsburgh and the Presidents of the Select and Common Councils of the City of Pittsburgh... it was deemed advisable, in view of the decision of the Supreme Court of the State of Pennsylvania, declaring the so-called Greater Pittsburgh Act constitutional, and in view of the urgent necessity of having the appropriation and tax levying ordinance of the enlarged city prepared as soon as possible....

What followed on Council floor, then, was first a "motion to test the constitutionality of [the upheld merger]." It is not discernible what exactly was proposed with that statement, but essentially Councils dismissed any thought of dissent, as was Allegheny's noble style, and instead, intense fiscal legislation ensued. There were a lot of final payments made to businesses, etc.

A Special Meeting for Select Council was called on Friday, November 29th, one day after Thanksgiving. More settlements were pushed through and finalized, on infrastructure and general fiscal matters. Then, a final entry for the evening, the Minutes book, and the City:

> Mr. Keane moved that a committee of two be appointed to confer with a similar committee from Common Council to perfect arrangements for the removal of Council to the City of Pittsburgh.

[The motion was Agreed to, with Keane and Saver appointed. It was followed by one last item of business, relating to infrastructure on Troy Hill.]

An Ordinance Changing the Grade of Fleck Street, 13th Ward, from Lowrie Street to a point 200 ft. southwardly. Approved.

RESOLVED by the Select Council of the City of Allegheny that we hereby tender our President, Francis J. Terrance, our thanks for his courtesy, efficiency and faithfulness in the performance of his duties while he has been the presiding officer of Select Council.

ON MOTION ADJOURNED.
LAFAYETTE WILLS
CITY CLERK

It is anyone's guess what the following week, Allegheny City's last, would have been like for its residents. For its civil servants, it must have been especially difficult. On the date of December 9, 1907, Allegheny City, formally, was no more.

... One Hundred Plus Years as Part of Pittsburgh

chapter thirteen:
AFTER THE ANNEXATION

Though Alleghenians had reason to feel that the election was a 'setup,' backed by the Commonwealth, and their city had been treated shabbily at best, the transition afterward, come that fateful day of Dec. 9, 1907, was typical of the noble city, "quietly done." This according to Mary Wohleber, who despite being born after the Consolidation, is perhaps one of the last true Alleghenians living. Her parents, and others, like most living in Allegheny City, dealt with what was a devastating blow in a dignified manner. They shared with her that there was no rioting, no looting.

Instead, it seems among most of the citizens, there was only a steadfast, unspoken, and individually-decided upon pledge to continue to identify oneself as being from Allegheny City. Though they officially now had to play by the rules of Pittsburgh, Allegheny felt itself separate, and would for a long time to come.

Certainly, there was resentment, directed toward any legislative leaders who were behind the annexation and to power brokers who backed it. One of the first orders of business, as directed from the City of Pittsburgh, was the changing of names of streets in Allegheny that had a duplicate in Pittsburgh. Based only upon the initial which began the name of the old street, entirely new names would be given. Thus Second Street east of the Commons became Suismon Street, for example, and Harrison became Holyoke. The only exception granted was Federal Street. Residents were adamant about retaining that name (so the Federal Street in Pittsburgh's Hill District was instead renamed Fernando).

The first mayor of the combined cities would be Pittsburgh's Guthrie. The police and fire personnel of the City of Allegheny were immediately put under the jurisdiction of Pittsburgh. Motor cars for police and fire were introduced around this time, as was an innovative red light and bell mechanism, to alert beat cops to trouble. In Allegheny, there had been a rash of robberies in 1907, the only 'acting-out' perhaps had in the city, so the device was welcome. In short time, the Allegheny police departments would be celebrated with two awards, for best of all in Pittsburgh.

The City of Pittsburgh would immediately call Allegheny the *North Side*, but most Alleghenians resisted that name. For well over half a century, even other Pittsburghers would reference the land and its people as "Allegheny" and "Alleghenians."

The Allegheny City Society was formed in 1957, in order to promote the memory of Allegheny City. The volunteer group sponsors tours, holds lectures, spearheads movements to get historical markers and plaques erected, renovated the Soldiers Monument (which was moved off Monument Hill when Community College of Allegheny County bought the land in the 1960s), and conducts numerous other advocacy activities.

The Pittsburgh History & Landmarks Foundation was founded in 1964, due to the interest of James D. Van Trump and Arthur P. Ziegler, Jr., in the historic homes in Manchester, scheduled for demolition in the 1960s. Pittsburgh's preservation movement began on the North Side, and has taken root in many city neighborhoods. After saving the Allegheny Post Office from demolition in 1968, the Pittsburgh History & Landmarks Foundation located its offices there and opened the Old Post Office Museum. Pieces of demolished buildings and bridges were used to create a sculpture garden outside of the museum.

After the Consolidation, the Victorian park created in the 1860s flourished until the 1930s, when an effort was underway to redevelop some of the land areas. Lake Elizabeth stayed, but a popular Boathouse, built in the early part of the century, was torn down, and the shape and structure of the lake changed. No longer would there be ice skating in the park, and the building adjacent to the lake area would no longer be a floral conservatory.

An Aviary, designated the National Aviary in 1993, would occupy the conservatory (and once Penitentiary) site, and the Band Stand would be torn down. The Humboldt statue would be moved, and the fountains about all of the Commons would lose their luster and fall to decay before three-quarters of the century was up.

The Allegheny Commons Restoration Committee was yet another organization, coming together with the intent to revitalize the Commons once again. It was formed in 2004 to raise funds and oversee the rehabilitation of the park, according to a 2002 master plan completed by Pressley Associates of Cambridge, MA. The original park plans have been studied and actions set in motion to restore some of the Victorian qualities and renew some of the facets of the park that were created in the 1930s. With a special emphasis on replanting original trees that were found in the park plan of the 1860s, the steering committee has also been moving forward with benches and lighting that was found in the Commons park of the 1890s.

So much does not survive from Allegheny City, after a century has passed since its becoming the North Side. So much went by the wayside with civic structures, as the decades rolled on—even as the land itself couldn't seem to shake loose its mark and memory of times past, and though residential houses still bear the age-old Allegheny in their very bones. The people, save for rare individuals like Mary Wohleber, are also no longer, but there is a remnant left of this player in Allegheny's story, as well.

Civic groups were created in the 1960s and 70s, inspired by the work of Pittsburgh History & Landmarks Foundation, and appalled by one particular redevelopment effort—the Allegheny Center Mall.

The sacred central square (and then Diamond) of Allegheny Town was tremendously tampered with in the 1960s. To the credit of previous generations, it had survived until this point essentially unscathed, for about 180 years. But modern redevelopers talked Pittsburgh officials into creating what would end up being a concrete wasteland on that very town center of what was Allegheny. A one-way traffic circle around one of the nation's early mall designs sat now on top of the original 36 blocks.

Though the mall had its short day in the sun, it became apparent that the decision was a bad one, and citizens realized that their community's future would have a voice only if they organized to communicate their stake in their homeland. So people—some quite old who were once Allegheny citizens, others whose parents were, and still others, transplanted to the area from other sections of Pittsburgh or outside the region entirely—took up the cause of a land that had long been whispering of its original beauty and point of view.

And there were other reasons these citizens, of the neighborhoods north of the rivers, spoke up sharply. There had been a proposal to bring a highway running east to west right across the Mexican War Streets, to then cut sharply north above what was Pasture Lane (later Irwin and then Brighton Road), at the bend where once had been O'Hern's *Mount Relief Plan*. It would have wiped out most of the War Streets.

It failed, but another highway plan succeeded, also devastating, though in the name of progress, as an expressway was needed for travel from the downtown of Pittsburgh to areas far north of the city. After years of debate and conflict, tears and pleas, a plan was approved that attempted to listen to the citizen groups, but still move the city forward. Called the Madison Avenue Expressway at the point carved from North Side land (with lasting reference being simply the lower end of the Parkway North), a huge swath was cut through what was once Allegheny's East Street Valley. Displaced families, many of whom indeed had been on Allegheny's eastern side for generations, left the area completely or relocated to public housing. Essentially the whole neighborhood was demolished, with some houses hanging on sides of hills and St. Boniface Church being spared because it was listed on the National Register of Historic Places through citizen efforts. While Pittsburgh city council tossed the plans around for years, citizens living in that valley sensed far in advance that it would indeed happen in some gross form eventually, despite their uproar.

By the late 1970s the residential destruction and highway construction was under way. And any remaining inability to identify as a Northsider likely lost its grip on the elders from old Allegheny. It was clear "Allegheny" had been losing its meaning, but "North Side" was taking on great meaning, for it was pertinent to now strongly speak for this section of Pittsburgh that was undergoing such devastating residential loss.

There was little to grasp as being physically left of Allegheny in the public sphere, except for the Old Post Office building, the Carnegie Library complex, and in-between the two, the Buhl Planetarium (built after the Consolidation). These were the lone vestiges of the city, visible from afar. But in the private sphere, real gems had survived.

The houses of the North Side are some of the oldest in all of the city of Pittsburgh. (Some still stand in the Mexican War Streets from the 1840s; the district is akin to Philadelphia, Boston, or New York's residential brownstone districts.) These structures with sandstone foundations, held up by locust posts rooted in the ground, became the 'reveal,' the winning card that the people of the modern North Side realized they still held.

These homes tell stories, made of the finest materials by great artisans, sitting on land once sold at a Philadelphia auction, with inhabitants that surely could have written their own books about a time when their fair Allegheny City was swallowed up by their sister city across the river.

Come the arrival of the millennium, it would have seemed that the North Side of Pittsburgh was left with very little from Allegheny City, save for the century-old homes. Though much of its earlier identity had been torn down, however, the spirit of people living there had begun to be awakened by what had defined Allegheny.

Since tethered to Pittsburgh, the area had its share of ups and downs and collaborative accomplishments and disgruntlements with the metropolis, perhaps more intensely so than other neighborhoods. Unfortunately, urban decay had been showing for decades in and around the edges of the original town center, with a little-used shopping center leading a blight that had taken over many North Side neighborhoods. Right by that mall, only the still-beautiful Carnegie Library and Old Post Office building, now housing the Pittsburgh Children's Museum, defied the changes.

The evident decline was very difficult for citizens to accept and combat, even as they worked hard at organizing within their community. Grand house tours would take place even as the drug and gang wars of the 1990s ravaged community youth, and whole communities. Many citizens felt at times like prisoners in their own homes and on their very streets, and it felt as if the land itself had turned away in shame.

Future Glance:
Resurrection & Transformation
POSTSCRIPT

There are approximately sixteen neighborhoods of the North Side in this new century—the Central North Side, East Allegheny or Deutschtown, Spring Garden, Spring Hill, Troy Hill, Summer Hill and the Ivory Avenue district, Fineview, Perry Hilltop (the original Observatory Hill), Allegheny West, Chateau, Manchester, Observatory Hill, the Charles Street Valley area, Brightwood, Marshall-Shadeland, Brighton Heights, and the new North Shore. Though the North Side knows a bit of its past, it has been struggling too much with its present in the last several decades to do anything about the identity of Allegheny City, which still pervades the area much as the mist from the Ohio hangs over Manchester in early morning.

But with the development of the the North Shore, renewed community efforts, and the centennial marking of the North Side's one-hundred changed years, Allegheny City is poised to resurface.

The North Side has survived until this time, even though it seemingly lost its way toward the end of the twentieth century. What sustained every citizen unwilling to let urban blight destroy their love of house, hill, neighborhood, neighbors, parks, and museums, however, was a scrappy attitude, a feistiness, equal in passion to the opposite *grace* of Allegheny City. It was almost as if things needed to be turned inside out in order to bring calm to the chaos that the land was experiencing.

It is a well-known fact that most who chose to live and stay in North Side neighborhoods, even during the darkest of times, were fiercely protective of their neighborhoods and what they represent. With every second house dilapidated and run-down (usually by absentee landlords), to stay and reside in neighborhoods like Manchester, the Mexican War Streets, Perry Hilltop, or East Allegheny has not been for the faint of heart. To drive through parts of those areas felt uncannily like New York, the bad with the good—and only the most adventurous, courageous, creative, and spirited homeowners would begin to turn these neighborhoods around.

But indeed they are, one by one, civic group by civic group, house by house, and street by street. Leading the way, inspiring others to find sense of home and neighborhood are the great neighborhood and park developments, such as the Allegheny Commons Restoration Committee, properly addressing that unique community area that so set apart Allegheny from other regional urban centers. Allegheny's land, itself, turned back toward the North Side in pride with the recent study of the Commons—and the sensible decision to return it to the best from the Victorian park era while still ensuring its modernity. As well, the neighborhood groups-backed Federal North project can finally move forward. It will transform what is in current-day the central intersection of the North Side (the equivalent of the old town center) and the true gateway to the northern neighborhoods. The best in man is evident in both these recent projects, with a choice to honor historic land and structure while still being progressive.

To some Pittsburghers, still, the North Side is simple-mindedly summed up as a place of notorious crime and degradation, with a few optimistic afterthoughts thrown in about the area's cultural organizations (including the Andy Warhol Museum, the Mattress Factory installation art museum and the Carnegie Science Center).

And then there are the stadiums. What had been the place of Exposition Park, for baseball, at the time of the Consolidation—and prior to that the Exposition Building grounds, the place of the traveling circuses and the site of sunken Killbuck and other islands—had never lost its showmanship and exhibitionism, or it would seem, the last say in what would sit on that locale and how that would define the northern bank.

But Pittsburgh, for some reason, never really considered the stadiums and other novelties on the North Side as truly *being* the North Side.

Not unlike the days before the Consolidation, when those outside Allegheny tried to define its identity—or denounce its attributes while at the same time partaking of them—what is now being called the North Shore area has been indeed viewed as separate from the North Side neighborhoods. That is, until Northsiders began to feel an original voice inside them rising up once again, to proclaim that the development *must* link clearly and positively, economically, socially and logistically with the rest of the North Side. And that what was once Allegheny, in general, must stop taking an inaccurate rap once and for all.

Parts of the North Side had shared with Pittsburgh's East Liberty, Homewood and Hill District sections the distinction of being a place of notable drug and firearm activity. This would have been from about the 1970s on. This distinction occurred while the entire city of Pittsburgh echoed nationwide trends toward increased illegal gun violence and drug use. The North Side's Allegheny General Hospital was instrumental, for the region as a whole, in curbing both, with the *Goods for Guns* program and outreach drug forums, the latter often in conjuction with the Community College of Allegheny County.

At the same time, neighborhood groups were having successful *Safe Streets* programs initiated. Crime and poverty and neglect of structures were evident, but the North Side received more scorn than was measured— whether against its attributes or even happenings in the rest of the city. Crime percentages are on the books as lower here now, in the new millennium, than even the chic east-end Pittsburgh neighborhoods of Squirrel Hill and Shadyside. Recently-retired and revered Commander Kelly of Zone One police, who served on the North Side force for years, has publicly attested to this fact, numerous times. But the flock to buy houses that were once Allegheny's is less than in most areas of Pittsburgh. (Yet North Side homes, with the oldest and finest of attributes, as well as the treasured land expanses and views that oft go with them, can be gotten for a fraction of what they go for in posh neighborhoods.)

Neighborhood groups, of which there are also about sixteen in number, have also stressed for years that *all* of the North Side has felt scorn actually, when in reality the crime has ebbed and flowed even within individual sections of neighborhoods—the dire poverty and criminal activity occurring right around the corner or two doors down from affluent homes, condos and apartments that do fetch higher moneys (but not as high as in the rest of Pittsburgh).

The people of Pittsburgh's North Side have grown weary, of course, in vigilantly (and often quite successfully) fighting these neighborhood street-by-street and house-by-house battles. And they have grown sick of employees of North Side corporations who come there daily to work, only to leave in the evening with the misconception that the area doesn't have a lot to offer. These people of what was once Allegheny know differently, that all of its neighborhoods are full of gorgeous, affordable houses (either ready-to-live-in or easily rehab-able), with million-dollar views, diversity of neighbors, and truly the oldest park of the entire southwestern Pennsylvania region.

Nothing has made North Side citizens more wary, however, in the first years of the newest century, than the constant portrayal in the media of the North Side, as a whole, being the big bad wolf, and the North Shore being a separate glorious entity that the city of Pittsburgh should regale in.

There is a to-be-expected, usual skepticism about the new North Shore development from Northsiders. There is concern that the hotels and clubs will overtake or overshadow, infringe upon or inhibit the historic neighbor-hoods, and crowd out age-old business. The most recent concern is over the casino that the State Gaming Commission has slated for the bank of the Ohio, and bewilderment about the need for new mass transit planned to connect Pittsburgh's downtown with the North Side via underwater tunnel. But not too unlike the unspoken, determined identification with "Allegheny" after the Consolidation, there is indeed an unspoken hope that the glimmer and gleam about the North Shore activity will also reflect the bounty of the structures, people and land of the whole of the North Side.

The North Shore is essentially the north bank of the rivers, stretching from about where the Hopeville development used to be on the east, down across the area where Robinson had his ferry, to below the hump-shaped hill and along the western bank to the Chateau neighborhood (where Elliott had his ferry). In modern times of the North Side, this is the land running from the beginning of River Avenue just beyond the Warhol Museum, past PNC Park, Heinz Field, and to the Carnegie Science Center. The full area, of course, also lies south of the Allegheny Center Mall and highway underpasses, where the canal once ran and railroad still does, but elevated roadways now take Pittsburghers above and across the bank, and then to the Parkway North as it cuts through the East Street Valley.

Never to have a period in its history that was dull or unmarked by spectacle and show for the masses, what was Killbuck and other islands continued, after the Consolidation, in drawing crowds. Once Exposition Park would no longer be the place for baseball in Pittsburgh (as the sport, like so much else, had moved to Oakland, to Forbes Field), the land served again as place for recreation and transitory entertainments, with a lot of further industrial development scattered oddly all around it.

By the 1970s, the area would be marked by the nation's new love in sport—football. Three Rivers Stadium was erected for the Pittsburgh Steelers football franchise, south of Monument Hill—whose monument had been moved to the West Commons and now atop was buildings of the Community College of Allegheny County. Owned by Art Rooney, once-businessman in that industrial-commercial medley around the previous Exposition Grounds, the Steelers would take to their new home, and win four Super Bowl championships throughout that first decade at Three Rivers, and in 1980. And again, here, Northsiders began to make further use of their Pittsburgh neighborhood reference, proudly in connection with the Steelers' home.

Thirty years later, targeted for renewal was 'the area around Three Rivers Stadium' (the most-popular reference for the north bank at the turn of the century). First Three Rivers had to be imploded, with two new stadiums going up in its wake— PNC Park for the Pittsburgh Pirates baseball team (they, too, played ball at Three Rivers, coming back to their northside origin after so many years), and Heinz Field for the Steelers. The rest of the land, small-business commercial and industrial wasteland, was slated to have a rebirth. This was, and still is, becoming 'the North Shore,' a name decried by Northsiders as a fancy way to distance the land area from the rest of the troubled North Side, and also because, amusingly, most feel that "shore" can not apply to the bank of a river. (But indeed it is not the first time in its history to be called that.)

What helped to distance the northern bank from the neighborhoods surrounding it was something unfortunately put in place long ago. The Canal, in its cut through the Borough of Allegheny, oddly cut a swath through the land below the town center. Despite the boon to Allegheny's economy, it scarred Redick's survey and original land plots of the *Reserved*

Figure 42. Three Rivers Stadium & the Northern Bank with overlay of land circa 1795

Tract opposite Pittsburg, and indeed led to the wealthy of Second Bank (later Stockton Avenue) to flee the too-close industry sprung-up in its wake.

Partially to blame was the low-lying land, itself, on Butler's property, as it was conducive for the Canal's basin there. Of course the troublesome railroad occupied the Canal swath after that, and its corporation was the one that erected the underpasses for Allegheny City street traffic to move below their right-of-way. Either way, the cut of the Canal (despite its fit with the swampy land), and the railroad, both, sliced the northern bank into a somewhat separate stretch from the rest of the land.

One of the biggest issues concerning community groups (especially East Allegheny/Deutschtown), since about 2000, has been both the danger and economic barrier posed by the three underpasses of Federal, Sandusky and Anderson Streets. The first was decoratively painted in the 1990s, for commemoration and in decor of an earlier time, but all three lack proper and adequate lighting for pedestrians, and have posed safety risks.

As well, homelessness in Pittsburgh increased dramatically from the 1980s on, and the North Side's great amount of railroad and highway underpasses have invited encampment. (Sadly, the stretch between Federal and Sandusky, where the grand railroad depot once sat in Allegheny, is especially popular, for the holes left cut out near the underpass when the building was demolished.)

Physically, the underpasses prohibit the tremendous pedestrian traffic—present for Steeler and Pirate games, as well as for upcoming North Shore activities—from connecting with businesses and restaurants trying to take a stake in the community beyond. Ugly eyesores themselves (save for Federal Street's decorated example), the concrete structures literally prevent North Shore visitors from even *seeing* the shape of the hills and the neighborhoods beyond, including the little village lining the East Commons and on North Avenue. (The Mall, in the forefront, is worthy only of being seen *through*, or better yet, past, as its demolition is certainly called for, if there is to be any positive hearkening back to Allegheny City and looking forward to modern transformation of the North Side.)

A proliferation of social service organizations on the North Side have added to the encampment problem, which also has been evident, at times more than others, in the Commons. The North Side of Pittsburgh has been plagued with an inordinate amount of homeless and low-income population, and at least the former can be linked to the equally inordinate amount of charities catering to the needy, be it alcohol and drug rehabilitation, soup kitchens or literal homeless shelters. There are more social service agencies per capita on the North Side (and much of them are on the original first four wards of Allegheny) than in any other part of Pittsburgh.

Though these agencies are needed elements to be within any society, the North Side took on far too many of them for years, where other sections of the city would never have allowed the sheer number to multiply. Equally disturbing, of course, and pervading all of the nation, let alone any section of a city, is that mental health and substance abuse medical coverage is nonexistent, save for the wealthy and the lucky (who can buy or whose employers offer the best plans). Thus, what is essentially more significant for all people than *regular* medical coverage can not be gotten affordably in a

Figure 43. North Shore of Pittsburgh under development circa 2000

doctor's office, but instead only by community clinics and the like, of which the North Side has a plethora.

Those behind the North Shore advancement, in both private enterprise and City government, have pledged to tie in its development with the rest of the North Side. It has been heartily spoken on the public record that the effort will realize a new, vibrant section of the city that will offer premier entertainment, retail space and corporate office space that will bring people to the North Side, but community groups have pushed for ways to have the extension of that into their neighborhoods. Indeed some of the casino profits, once built on the North Shore, are pledged earmarked for the neighborhoods, in particular Allegheny West, who may be most adversely affected with traffic and parking.

Equitable Gas and Del Monte moved their headquarters to new buildings on the North Shore, alongside a new Marriott by Continental

Development. Other corporations, hotels and restaurants continue to now develop this land area. The Carnegie Science Center and River Quest are doing their part to balance and revitalize the riverfront stretch, as well as the Steelers organization doing what it can to see the development aspire to the ideal of benefitting the North Side. Current owner Dan Rooney lives in Allegheny West, not far from Heinz Field, and he and his wife have been very involved supporters of the Allegheny Commons Restoration Committee.

The Steelers have been also proposing to spearhead an amphitheater, to sit between North Shore corporate office space and Heinz Field. In recent years, on the blacktop where it is proposed, next to the beautiful new riverfront walk and water-steps, traveling show *Cirque de Soleil* has set up tents, wowing Pittsburgh audience. An amphitheater on the northern bank would symbolically bring full-circle the activity that once occupied the site, originally known as Smokey Island, set in the stage of the three rivers, graced on its sides by the great hills, and looked upon by all of Pittsburgh.

From the earliest of time, this spot of the North Shore was used for display and sport. Despite its relegation to exhibition, showmanship and entertainment, it always made recurring entrances on the broader stage that would be Allegheny's full story. With the comic relief of a Puck, this infamous spot that so resisted outside attempts to shape it has surfaced time and again to remind Alleghenians and Northsiders to take pause over their land. Rather than needing a boost itself, it yet again might serve, here in the new millennium, to actually pull up the rest of the North Side.

The North Shore, with its cornucopia of colorful acts through the ages, indeed has its own legacy, but one intrinsically connected to the happenings on the rest of the land north of the rivers. In the same manner, a resurrection of Allegheny City would not be possible without acceptance of this exotic parcel rich in heritage and fame. Inextricably tied with the success or failure of the North Side is the success or failure of this spot, the North Shore development. As citizens through the ages have seen, as control lies not necessarily in their hands, their response to what befalls them as a community will be everything.

Would the greater North Side turn its back on its linkages with the North Shore, or allow outside forces to disconnect it for them, all would be lost for good. Acceptance, making the best of what seems almost predetermined by the land itself, but also *accountability* of those developments will identify success for North Side citizens.

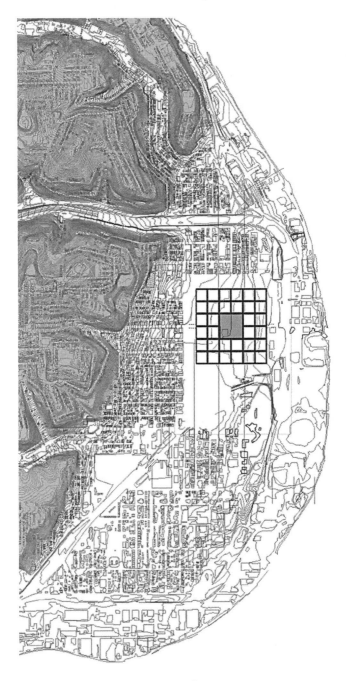

Never should that particular spot be disengaged from its historical, social and economic connectedness to the rest of the North Side. The collected knowledge about Allegheny City should be celebrated but also pragmatically used. The renewed community efforts from the whole of the North Side in the last couple years have begun to address this. The Children's Museum has sponsored a design competition to merge creativity with the challenge of renewing the neighborhoods. Proposals simply abound with new ideas, from international design firms, have been showcased. Doug Suisman Urban Design of Los Angeles is one of several emphasizing linking old Allegheny's gems and specifically champions resurrecting the literal core of the old town. Such commendable efforts point out that the history of a place can be explored and brought to practical usage within the mind and creative spirit, beyond the mere remnants left on land, within structure or even in the most mortal of the three, a people.

With such creative efforts, none of the North Side should ever be left disengaged from its historical components and current treasures. A very recent challenge that will need to employ fusing the practical with the historic is the future usage of the Carnegie Library building. With tower tragically struck by lightning at the very time when current renewal of the adjoining Music Hall was beginning, in 2006, the Carnegie Library of Pittsburgh's North Side branch was forced to vacate. (Its new home will be constructed on Federal Street beginning in the fall of 2007.) The clock tower of the old building literally stands for the last years of Allegheny City. Finding a purpose for the structure that will be intrinsically linked to the community will likely be as difficult as has been the fixing of the finial atop the tower. Contractors have finally succeeded with the latter; the former will surely get the same needed attention by North Side citizens and leaders, artists and designers, and historians.

Though the outward affectation has been different (perhaps even reactionary), Northsiders and Alleghenians indeed are one and the same due to the connection with their houses and land-plots. *Home* really meant

Figure 44 (opposite). North Side Topographical, 2007 with Allegheny Town center

something to Alleghenians; they put down roots and the roots became them. Many modern Northsiders, some quite young, feel similarly.

Since the 1960s, and on, they were forced to fight for their homes, in varied respects, prompted by being horribly ashamed at what their 'town' had become. Both societies of people, Alleghenian and Northsiders, found blessing in their larger home—in the acquaintance of neighbors with similar ideals yet uniquely original character, with the diversity of city life represented better than in all of the region, and in the glorious spots to look out from and be harbored within. Though the essence of Allegheny is at times ambiguous, it is palpably different, somehow, than what had been early garrison Pittsburg, and then brash young-city, across the river. In the same manner, Pittsburgh's North Side has always been oddly different, out-of-torque with the rest of the city.

The heritage of Allegheny City lives on in more than century-old structures. It survives within Northside citizens, mysteriously linked with the past society that occupied its land and its homes. Allegheny has hung around, never completely leaving. A resurrection simply but significantly involves *a bringing back into notice* what is very evident of its history, its story, its spirit—knowing what shaped its citizens and how Northsiders have been similarly shaped, and a true attention, mindfulness and *usage* of this history as the broad neighborhood moves forward.

It is very possible to be progressive with the past in mind. The past can, in fact, be as present, indeed as palpable as Allegheny has been to anyone looking with awe at some find, some remnant of the city: a child's ceramic marble long buried in their backyard, a billfold filled with photos from Germany tucked away in a basement crevice, a street sign in a neglected neighborhood naming a *Riffle* that had to do with long-ago glass, or the width of North Avenue that suddenly shrinks down in size past Allegheny General Hospital to its original dimension when first surveyed earlier in the nineteenth century—a Shannopin Lane never adjusted to modern traffic.

The past lives for those who see and feel it. And if it can be seen and felt, it should be known and celebrated by children, by visitors and newcomers, by those working in the area, and as inspiration to all residents of other historic neighborhoods. What no longer exists can be transformed—remade, redone, re-created in all manners that honor the original. Not faked, in such a way to discredit the genuine, but like the fine faux-work of 1880 artisans, exist alongside all other things of modern beauty, with a tip of the hat to the best of the old. New buildings can be built that honor the element of the age-old. Even old buildings, in need of repair or renovation, can infuse the new when necessary or desirable within reasonable respect of the surrounding old.

East Ohio Street, Western Avenue, as well as the intersection of Federal and North and others could all look again similar to what they did in the time of Allegheny City. Most and many of the old structures are literally still there in the first and second examples, in the form of a Victorian main street. The Priory and old Eberhardt & Ober Brewery building near East Ohio Street, and Emmanuel Episcopal Church and Calvary Church's Tiffany windows near Western Avenue, are all fine historic examples of Allegheny remnants still living and breathing. On the vacant lots that once held buildings near these and other historic structures, new ones could be built which blend with the old yet provoke the new.

Schoolchildren could go along paths, even using GPS finders, tracking the mulberry bush, or its site, where old Chief Killbuck is buried. John Brashear's lovely house, still standing on a too-neglected Perrysville Avenue could be sold and cared for, or open to tours. His factory, still standing behind, with patches of wood over window eyes, could be refurbished.

With creativity, possessed by the ordinary citizen but little recognized, civic pain and anguish, bad circumstance and even neighborhoods simply gone bad can be changed. Catalysts come in all forms, and if citizens are open to it, they can see both the past and the path to the future, linked. Transformation of the most painful civic and social scars can occur when the choice has been made to definitively move on and move forward. Though losing Allegheny City, municipally, was extremely ill-done and unfortunate, it can not be undone. But it can be transformed, in that the essence of the city has remained *available* to present-day citizens, to be made into something new that minimizes the pain of the past and creates something hopeful for the future.

Most important is that the old, when applicable and due, be revered. Where one lives, what one calls home should mean something to people: the land, what stood there, what kind of people owned and rented and worked the land, the factories and businesses and civic structures nearby, the stories of lives woven and that could be told, and even what *home* evokes in one's memory, character, and very essence.

By the same token, familiar and *known* historic landmarks give meaning to any place. The North Side should show the way for other communities to

respect, treasure and celebrate their own land, people, and the physical
mementoes of an earlier time.

Especially with the occasion of the centennial marking of Allegheny,
the current people of the North Side are called upon to transform their
identity yet again, rising from what Allegheny City has remarkably defined
and illuminated for them. The North Side of Pittsburgh has an opportunity
to commemorate Allegheny City at its Centennial and beyond. To truly
honor it, citizens must realize that the very essence of Allegheny is still
around, certainly sensed, able to be touched and talked about, and definitely
built upon. By resurrecting its identity founded in Allegheny City, with great
respect, devotion and strength, the North Side will move successfully forward
into its future.

Permissions & Credits

"Paleoindian Sites in Pennsylvania" provided by the Pennsylvania Historical and Museum Commission from the book *Ice Age Peoples of Pennsylvania*.

"Western Pennsylvania Indian Paths" provided by the Pennsylvania Historical and Museum Commission from the book *Indian Paths of Pennsylvania*.

"Pennsylvania in 1784" (Last Purchase) courtesy of Pennsylvania Historical and Museum Commission, Pennsylvania State Archives. MG-11 Map Collection, #495 Commonwealth of Pennsylvania, Dept. of Internal Affairs, Genealogical Map of the Counties.

"Depreciation & Donation Lands" from 1792 map variant of Reading Howell. Pennsylvania Archives, Second Series, Vol. IV. Reprinted 1890 under direction of Charles Warren Stone, Secretary of the Commonwealth. Edited by John B. Linn and Wm. H. Egle, M. D.

"Reserved Tract, 1785." Warrantee Atlas of Allegheny County, Plate 3. Digital Research Library, University of Pittsburgh.

"Depreciation Territory above the Reserved Tract." Warrantee Atlas of Allegheny County, Plate 7. Digital Research Library, University of Pittsburgh.

"Plan of the Reserved Tract opposite Pittsburg, circa 1789." Warrantee Atlas of Allegheny County, Plate 8.

"Allegheny Town Auction Record" taken from *Allegheny Town and Out Lots & Island; Town Lots*; and *In and Out Lots Reserved Tract Opposite Pittsburg 1791*. Microfiche 25.36; 11.1–4, 11.6; Bound Volume. Commonwealth Land Records of the Pennsylvania State Archives, Pennsylvania Historical and Museum Commission.

"Pittsburgh 1795" taken from *The Geological History of Pittsburgh* site by Mark A. Evans, **www.geology.pitt.edu/GeoSites/1795.jpg**

"Hump-Shaped Hill, Church & Barlow House" taken from records of the Allegheny City Society, including material from the *Allegheny City Society Reporter-Dispatch*.

"1815 'Darby' Map" taken from *The Geological History of Pittsburgh* site by Mark A. Evans, **www.geology.pitt.edu/GeoSites/1815.jpg** Original source "Plan of Pittsburg and Adjacent Country circa 1815," Geography & Map division, Library of Congress, Washington, D.C.

"Riverbeds & Islands." Warrantee Atlas of Allegheny County, Plate 51. Digital Research Library, University of Pittsburgh.

"1828 Map" source unknown.

"Allegheny City Seal & Currency" taken from Allegheny City Archives, Pennsylvania State Archives of the Pennsylvania Historical and Museum Commission.

"First Ward by the River, circa 1850" taken from *I-279/I-579 Expressway Project Records*, Series on Historical and Archaeological Investigations, Penn DOT & GAI Consultants. Original source unknown, etching in ownership of The Duquesne Club of Pittsburgh.

"Circa-1852 Map" source unknown.

"North Commons" taken from Records of the Allegheny City Society, including material from the *Allegheny City Society Reporter-Dispatch*.

"Allegheny Observatory, 1872." G. M. Hopkins Plat Map Collection, 1872 Atlas, Plate 77. Digital Research Library, University of Pittsburgh.

"Northern Wards, 1876." G. M. Hopkins Plat Map Collection, 1876 Atlas, Plate 52. Digital Research Library, University of Pittsburgh.

"Views of West Commons & Lake Elizabeth" courtesy of Suisman Urban Design (G. M. Hopkins Plat Map Collection, Atlas of the Cities of Pittsburgh, Allegheny, and the Adjoining Boroughs, 1872) and second, source unknown.

"1870s Sign Painting & Transom Business" taken from Allegheny City Archives, Pennsylvania State Archives of the Pennsylvania Historical and Museum Commission.

"John Brashear's house" taken from Records of the Allegheny City Society, including material from the *Allegheny City Society Reporter-Dispatch*.

"Change of Grade notice" taken from Allegheny City Archives, Pennsylvania State Archives of the Pennsylvania Historical and Museum Commission.

"Center of Allegheny City, 1890" courtesy of Suisman Urban Design (G. M. Hopkins Plat Map Collection, 1890 Atlas of Allegheny City).

"Western University of Pennsylvania." G. M. Hopkins Collection, 1901 Vol. 1, Plate 9. Digital Research Library, University of Pittsburgh.

"Center of Allegheny City, 1900" courtesy of Suisman Urban Design (original source unknown).

"1899 Map of the City of Allegheny" & "Greater Pittsburgh postcard" taken from Records of the Allegheny City Society.

"Three Rivers Stadium & Northern Bank with 1795 overlay" taken from *The Geological History of Pittsburgh* site by Mark A. Evans, **www.geology.pitt.edu/GeoSites/Point.jpg**

"North Shore under development" taken from *The Geological History of Pittsburgh* site by Mark A. Evans, **www.geology.pitt.edu/GeoSites/grandview%.jpg**

"North Side Topographical, 2007" courtesy Suisman Urban Design (Suisman Urban Design over 2007 Topographical Info.)

BIBLIOGRAPHY

Agnew, Daniel. *A History of the region of Pennsylvania north of the Ohio and west of the Allegheny River....* Philadelphia: Kay & Brother, 1887.

Allegheny City Archives. Pennsylvania Historical and Museum Commission. Harrisburg, PA. Quote passages **not** referenced in the text as coming from elsewhere come from this broad source, which contained Public Works and Public Safety records, Housing Surveys, Common and Select Councils notes, and Mayor, Comptroller and Treasurer Office records.

Records of the Allegheny City Society, including material from the *Allegheny City Society Reporter-Dispatch*. Pittsburgh, PA.

Allegheny Observatory. *Miscellaneous Scientific Papers of the Allegheny Observatory of the University of Pittsburgh.* Lancaster, PA: New Era Printing Co., 1913.

Allegheny Town and Out Lots & Island; Town Lots; and *In and Out Lots Reserved Tract Opposite Pittsburg 1791.* Microfiche 25.36; 11.1–4, 11.6; Bound Volume. Commonwealth Land Records of the Pennsylvania State Archives, Pennsylvania Historical and Museum Commission. Harrisburg, PA.

Baldwin, Leland D. *Pittsburgh: The Story of a City, 1750–1865.* Pittsburgh, PA: University of Pittsburgh Press, 1937.

Bothwell, Margaret Pearson. "Killbuck and Killbuck Island." *Western Pennsylvania Historical Magazine,* Vol. 44. 1961.

Canning, John. *Davisville to Brighton Heights: A Trip Through Time....* Pittsburgh, PA: Allegheny City Society & The Brighton Heights Citizens' Federation, 1998.

Ibid. *Troy Hill: Homeland In Allegheny.* Pittsburgh, PA: Allegheny City Society & Troy Hill Citizens, 1999.

Ibid. *Along the Towpath and the River Road: A Historical Sketch of Duquesne Borough, The Eighth Ward of Allegheny City.* Pittsburgh, PA: Allegheny City Society, 2000.

Ibid. *Osterling in Brighton Heights.* Pittsburgh, PA: Allegheny City Society, 2002.

Ibid. *The Czech Community of Allegheny City.* Pittsburgh, PA: Allegheny City Society, 2002.

Carr, Kurt and James Adovasio. *Ice Age Peoples of Pennsylvania.* Harrisburg: Pennsylvania Historical and Museum Commission, 2002.

"The Contrecoeur Papers," circa 1752–1755. Compiled for *La Belle-Riviere,* by Fernand Grenier. Papers translated by Donald Kent. Found within the archives of the

Historical Society of Western Pennsylvania, Senator John Heinz Pittsburgh Regional History Center, and as provided by the Pennsylvania State Archives.

Cumberland County Land Records (including Bedford County records, transferred upon creation of new county). Historical Society of Cumberland County.

Dahlinger, Charles W. *Old Allegheny*. Pittsburgh: Historical Society of Western Pennsylvania, 1918.

Dixon, David. *Fort Pitt Museum, Pennsylvania Trail of History Guide*. Mechanicsburg, PA: Stackpole Books, 2004.

"The Geological History of Pittsburgh." *www.geology.pitt.edu/GeoSites*

Library & Archives Division, Historical Society of Western Pennsylvania, Senator John Heinz Pittsburgh Regional History Center, Pittsburgh, PA.

I-279/I-579 Expressway Project Records. Series on Historical and Archaeological Investigations. Harrisburg: Penn DOT & GAI Consultants, August 2005.

G. M. Hopkins Plat Maps Collection, Historic Pittsburgh. *www.digital.library.pitt.edu/p/pitttext/*

Historic Pittsburgh site, operated jointly by the University of Pittsburgh and the Historical Society of Western Pennsylvania, Full Text collection, *www.digital.library.pitt.edu/p/pitttext*

Jordan, Frank C. "Allegheny Observatory, Riverview Park." *Pittsburgh First*, May 15, 1926.

Kelly, George E. *Allegheny County: A Sesqui-Centennial Review, 1788–1938*. Pittsburgh, PA: Allegheny County Sesqui-Centennial Committee, 1938.

Kidney, Walter. *Allegheny*. Pittsburgh, PA: Pittsburgh History & Landmarks Foundation, 1980.

"Killbuck, the Indian Chief." *The Alleghenian*, July 17, 1886.

Killikelly, Sarah H. *The History of Pittsburgh: Its Rise and Progress*. Pittsburgh, PA: B. C. Gordon Montgomery Co., 1906.

Landers, Diane Beynon. Voegtly Church Cemetery: *Transformation and Cultural Change in a Mid-19th Century Urban Society*. Harrisburg: Pennsylvania Historical and Museum Commission for the Pennsylvania Department of Transportation, 2006.

Legislature of Pennsylvania. *Files of the House of Representatives*. Various Nos. Found within the Allegheny City Archives. Pennsylvania Historical and Museum Commission. Harrisburg, PA.

McCrea, Kenneth. Consultation with this scholar/author on the Pennsylvania Depreciation Lands region. August, 2006.

"Metrovisions." *Pittsburgh Post-Gazette*, August 8, 2004. Describing townships and historical figures.

"A New Incline Railway" & "The Nobel Red Men." *The Alleghenian*, June 26, 1886.

Parke, John E. *Recollections of Seventy Years and Historical Gleanings of Allegheny, Pennsylvania*. Boston: Rand, Avery & Company, 1886.

Pittsburgh History & Landmarks Foundation. James D. Van Trump Library, and newsclipping archives. Pittsburgh, PA.

The Pittsburgh Record. Volume 1. Alumni Magazine of the University of Pittsburgh. Pittsburgh, PA.

"PNC Park/General Robinson Site." Christine Davis Consultants. Project Database.

Pressley Associates, Inc. *Allegheny Commons Master Plan*. Pittsburgh, PA: Allegheny Commons Restoration Committee, 2002.

Presutti, Donald H. *McKees Rocks Centennial History, 1892–1992*. McKees Rocks Centennial Celebration Committee, 1992.

Rimmel, William M. *The Allegheny Story*. Pittsburgh, PA: The Guttendorf Press, 1981.

Roberts, Robert. *Encyclopedia of Historic Forts*. New York: MacMillan.

Sipe, C. Hale. *The Indian Chiefs of Pennsylvania*. Lewisburg, PA: Wennawoods Publishing, 1997.

Smithsonian Institution Archives. *Pittsburgh Locomotive and Car Works Collection, 1874–1910*. Smithsonian Institution. Washington, D.C.

Starrett, Agnes Lynch. *Through One Hundred and Fifty Years: The University of Pittsburgh*. Pittsburgh: University of Pittsburgh Press, 1937

Story of Old Allegheny City. Workers of the Writers' Program of the Works Projects Administration in the Commonwealth of Pennsylvania. Pittsburgh, PA: Allegheny Centennial Committee, 1941.

Tannler, Albert M. *Allegheny Observatory: An Overview 1858–1912*. Prepared for the College of Arts and Sciences, the University of Pittsburgh. 2005.

Ibid. " 'Temple of the Skies': Observatory Hill Renaissance of Art and Science." *Pittsburgh Tribune-Review* Focus, Feb. 13, 2005.

Traveler's Guide to Historic Western Pennsylvania. "Indian Cemetery" and other stories. 1954.

Wallace, Paul A. W. *Indian Paths of Pennsylvania*. Harrisburg: Pennsylvania Historical and Museum Commission, 1998.

Wallace, Paul A. W. *Indians in Pennsylvania*. Harrisburg: Pennsylvania Historical and Museum Commission, 1999.

Warrantee Atlases, Historic Pittsburgh, Maps Collection. *www.digital.library.pitt.edu/p/pitttext/*

Wilbur, C. Keith. *The Woodland Indians*. Old Saybrook, Connecticut: The Globe Pequot Press, 1995.

Wilhelm, Carl. *Complete History of the City of Allegheny, Pennsylvania*. Pittsburgh: Allegheny Centennial Committee, 1890.

William Penn Association. *Tales of Frontier Pittsburgh*. American Guide Series. Pittsburgh: William Penn Association, as sponsored by the Western Pennsylvania Committee on Folklore, 1937.

INDEX

Burr, Aaron 93

Burying Ground 34, 57, 61, 74, 77, 88, 93, 102, 111, 130, 137

Bushy Run 15

Butchers Run 77

Butler County 59

Butler, PA 143, 195

Butz, Edward 157

C. Kingland Engine Works 82

C. Reel and Company 92

Caecelia Maennerchor 130

California Avenue, *see also* Island Lane 149, 166, 204

Callow, Mayor 150

Calvary Church 251

Campbell, Henry 103

Campbell, Reverend 98, 110

Campbell, Robert 59, 72

Canal turn basin 72, 73, 111, 244

Canal, the (Pennsylvania) 72, 129

Carnegie Library 186, 188, 216, 237, 249

Carnegie Music Hall 188, 189, 216, 225, 249

Carnegie, Andrew 102, 183, 186, 188, 194, 219

Carnegie Institute 220, 221, 224

Carnegie Science Center 240, 242, 247

Carnegie Steel 209

Carnegie Technical Schools 224

Carroll, D.W.C. & Company 169

Cassatt, Mary 127

Castle Lane, *see also* Water Lane and Western Avenue 41, 71

Catherine Street 179

Cayuga indians 6

Celoron 13, 222

Central North Side (neighborhood) 239

Central Park of New York City 135

Charles Street Valley 239

Chartiers Creek 1, 19

Chartiers, Peter 10

Chateau 117, 167, 239, 242

Cherry Street 157

Chestnut Lane and Street 36, 43, 45, 85, 95, 166, 214, 216

Chisslet Alley 84

Cirque de Soleil 247

City Beautiful, Pittsburgh's 224

City Farm and Poor House or Work House 68, 94

City Hall, 124, 128, 140

Civil War 121, 123–127, 130, 133, 140, 147, 158

Civil War Fair 158

Clayton Avenue 145, 207, 217

Clayton, William 140, 145

Clifton Park 180, 181

Clyde Street 177

Coal Hill 19, 55, 150

Colonnade Row 81

Columbia Avenue 77

Columbus, Ohio 123

Commercial Gazette 195

Commodore Perry 63, 70, 103

Commonwealth Colonial Records 51

Community College of Allegheny County 234, 241, 243

Confederates 124

West View 186

Western Avenue, *see also* Castle Lane and Water Lane 167, 170, 175, 176, 195, 209, 251

Western University of Pennsylvania, *see also* University of Pittsburgh 64, 68, 69, 132, 163, 174, 181, 189, 190, 193, 198, 209, 220, 221, 224, 254

Westinghouse Air Brake Company 129

Westinghouse Electric 195

Westmoreland County 17, 25, 28

Wheeler, Henry Company 127

Wheeler, Joseph 174

White Horse Tavern 59, 60, 72

White Mingo Chiefs 16

White Oak Alley 84

Whiteside, Peter 65, 67

Wicklines Lane 178

Wightman, D.A. 129

Wilkins, Charles 49, 63

Williams, Eli 55, 172

Wills, Lafayette 231

Wilson, William 56

Wilson Avenue 182

Wohleber, Mary 233, 235

Woods Run 112, 113, 189, 210, 211, 212

Woods, John 36, 37, 48, 56, 91, 112

Woodville 139

Workingman's Bank 128

Wyman, Mayor James 219, 227

Yale Street 178

Yohogania County 17

Zanibec, John 170

Ziegler, Jr., Arthur P. 234

Zoller, (Henry) Meat Packing Company 77